This book
was donated by

Robert L. Nugent, Ph.D.
1920-2012

Professor Emeritus
of Modern Languages

Director of the
James F. Lincoln Library

THE POEMS OF THE TROUBADOUR PEIRE ROGIER

To my parents

DEREK E. T. NICHOLSON

THE POEMS
OF THE TROUBADOUR PEIRE ROGIER

MANCHESTER UNIVERSITY PRESS
BARNES & NOBLE BOOKS . NEW YORK

© 1976 DEREK E. T. NICHOLSON

Published by

MANCHESTER UNIVERSITY PRESS

Oxford Road, Manchester M13 9PL

ISBN 0 7190 0614 7

USA

Harper & Row Publishers Inc
Barnes & Noble Import Division

ISBN 0 06 495960 0

Library of Congress catalog No. 76 15797

Text set in 10/12 pt. Monotype Bembo, printed by letterpress,
and bound in Great Britain at The Pitman Press, Bath

Contents

Preface		*page* vi
List of abbreviations		ix
Introduction		
I.	Life of Peire Rogier	1
II.	The place of Peire Rogier's work in the poetry of the troubadours	20
III.	Metric tables	26
IV.	Order of the poems	28
V.	The manuscripts	30
VI.	Choice of base manuscript; establishment of text; explanatory notes and variants	32
Vida		34
Poems		
I.	Al pareyssen de las flors	43
II.	Tan no plou ni venta	50
III.	Per far esbaudir mos vezis	59
IV.	No sai don chant e chantars plagra'm fort	68
V.	Tant ai mon cor en joy assis	79
VI.	Ges non puesc en bon vers fallir	84
VII.	Entr'ir'e joy m'an si devis	97
VIII.	Seign'en Raymbaut, per vezer	104
VIIIa.	Raimbaut d'Orange's reply—Peire Rotgier, a trassaillir	114
IX.	Dous'amiga, no'n puesc mais	122
Glossary		128
Index of proper names		158
Appendices		
I.	Extract from *Les Vies des plus célèbres et anciens Poètes provensaux, qui ont floury du Temps des Comtes de Provence* by Jehan de Nostre Dame	159
II.	Ermengarda, Viscountess of Narbonne, and her relations with other troubadours	160
Bibliography		165

Preface

The only previous complete edition of Peire Rogier's poetry is that of Carl Appel, *Das Leben und die Lieder des Trobadors Peire Rogier* (Berlin, 1882). Reference should also be made to the duc de la Salle de Rochemaure's *Les Troubadours cantaliens* (Aurillac, 1910), in the second volume of which R. Lavaud offers a full collection of Peire's poems, based generally on Appel's text and supplemented by notes and a translation.

The preparation of a second edition of the twelfth-century troubadour was originally suggested to me by my postgraduate supervisor, Mr John Hathaway, of the Department of French Language and Literature at the University of Birmingham. The present volume is a modified form of my thesis, which was accepted for the award of the degree of M.A. of that university in 1969. Carl Appel's edition has been a valuable guide and of considerable assistance to me; of particular interest is its excellent introduction, which contains an important section on the versification of Peire Rogier's work in relation to that of the work of other troubadours. I have benefited, in the preparation of the present edition, in having available not only Appel's work but also numerous editions, articles and commentaries on the poetry of the troubadours which have appeared since the end of the last century.

My introduction includes an extensive section on Peire Rogier's life and his relations with others which, it is hoped, will form a useful supplement to the observations originally made by Appel in his introduction. I have decided to provide for the poems and the *Vida* a more detailed critical apparatus than Appel does, offering in each case a detailed classification of manuscripts and an exhaustive list of variants. The base manuscript has been followed as far as possible in the establishment of the text and the opportunity taken to include in the notes to each poem and the *Vida* comments on the choice of particular readings. I have been fortunate in having at my disposal all the manuscripts which are known to contain Peire Rogier's work, including those which were not available to Appel as well as those containing the relevant extracts from Matfré Ermengaud's *Breviari d'Amor*. Although Lavaud offers a translation of the poems, neither his edition nor Appel's contains a glossary. I have therefore chosen to provide a comprehensive glossary containing every word appearing in the text, parsed and with line references.

I have followed Appel in including in this edition *Peire Rotgier a trassaillir*, Raimbaut d'Orange's reply to Peire Rogier's *sirventes*. In editing the poem I have chosen the same base manuscript (A) as W. T. Pattison in his edition of Raimbaut;* the resulting text therefore differs very little from his. It has also seemed appropriate

* W. T. Pattison, *Life and Works of the Troubadour Raimbaut d'Orange*, Minneapolis, 1952.

to provide as appendices Jehan de Nostre Dame's version of Peire Rogier's life and some notes on the connections which Peire's patron, the Viscountess Ermengarda of Narbonne, may have had with other troubadours.

I am grateful to the following libraries which have provided me with books, manuscripts and other facilities: the library of the University of Birmingham; the Biblioteca Laurenziana, Florence; the reference division of the British Library; the Biblioteca Estense, Modena; the library of the University of Newcastle upon Tyne; the Pierpont Morgan Library of New York; the Bodleian Library, Oxford; the Bibliothèque Nationale, Paris; the Biblioteca Vaticana, Rome.

I am particularly grateful to my postgraduate supervisor, Mr John Hathaway, who has helped me considerably with his continued interest and knowledgeable advice. My deep gratitude is further expressed to my family for their constant support and encouragement. I wish also to thank Dr D. J. Shirt for his helpful advice in the final preparation of the manuscript.

Finally, my sincere thanks are offered to the Sponsorship Committee for Publications of the University of Newcastle upon Tyne for the generous financial assistance which has made the publication of this work possible.

Newcastle upon Tyne   D.E.T.N.

List of abbreviations

(other than references to works listed in the bibliography)

acc.	accusative	lit.	literally
adj.	adjective	m.	masculine
adv.	adverb	neut.	neuter
art.	article	nom.	nominative
comp.	comparative	obj.	object(ive)
cond.	conditional	ord.	ordinal
conj.	conjunction	part.	participle
dat.	dative	partit.	partitive
def.	definite	perf.	perfect
dem.	demonstrative	pers.	personal
emphat.	emphatic	pl.	plural
eth. dat.	ethic dative	pluperf.	pluperfect
f.	feminine	poss.	possessive
fut.	future	prep.	preposition
imp.	imperative	pres.	present
imper.	impersonal	pret.	preterite
imperf.	imperfect	pron.	pronoun
indef.	indefinite	reflex.	reflexive
indic.	indicative	s.	substantive
inf.	infinitive	sing.	singular
inter.	interjection	subj.	subjunctive
interrog.	interrogative	superl.	superlative
intr.	intransitive	tr.	transitive
invar.	invariable	v.	verb

Introduction

I LIFE OF PEIRE ROGIER

Peire Rogier's poetic activity is generally placed in the third quarter of the twelfth century, part of the Golden Age of Provençal poetry.[1] Of his work there remain eight *cansos*, including one of doubtful authenticity, and a *sirventes* addressed to Raimbaut d'Orange. Not a great deal is known about the poet's life; the only sources of information at our disposal are the Provençal *Vida*, the poems themselves and possible references to Peire in the works of other troubadours. The imprecise and inconclusive nature of some of the information, combined with the absence of other independent sources, leaves a number of questions unresolved and makes a certain amount of speculation inevitable.

1 *The Provençal Vida*. B. Panvini has attempted to show that the Provençal *Vidas* of the troubadours, including that of Peire Rogier, were based on an independent source. He concludes that all the information contained in Peire's *Vida* is, without exception, entirely reliable.[2] However, we prefer, like Appel,[3] to be much more cautious. While for some details, involving persons of the time, the biographer could have had available an independent authority, other parts of the *Vida* may well be merely an elaboration of assumptions based on the contents of certain of the poems. It is therefore appropriate to examine in detail the *Vida*'s account of Peire Rogier's life, given below, in the light of what little biographical information is provided by the poems.

Peire Rogier, a native of the Auvergne, was a canon at Clermont. He was a man of noble character, handsome and affable, and was wise through learning as well as natural intelligence. He was a good singer and composer of songs. He left the canonry, became a *joglar* and wandered from court to court; his songs were well received. He came to Narbonne, to the court of the lady Ermengarda, a lady of great worth and merit. She received him cordially and granted him considerable benefits. He fell in love with her and celebrated her in his *vers* and *cansos*. She gladly accepted the poems and he called her *Tort-n'avetz*. He stayed with her at the court for a long time and it was thought that he received joy of love from her. She was reproached on this account by the people of that area. Through fear of what people were saying, she dismissed him and sent him away. He went away, doleful and pensive, full of care and grief, and came to Raimbaut d'Orange, as he stated in the *sirventes* which he composed about this man:

> Lord Raimbaut, it is to see the comfort and fellowship you offer rather than on account of your wealth that, promptly and with all speed, I have come here; for when I depart I wish to know whether the praise you are given is justified and whether the reports one hears about you exceed or fall short of reality.
>
> I possess so much intelligence and knowledge and am so wise and shrewd that when I have viewed your behaviour I shall know, on my departure, the truth: whether the praise, as it is recounted, is well founded; for people at home are asking me about this.

> He remained a long time with Raimbaut. He was next in Spain, where he stayed with the good King Alfonso of Castille and with the good King Alfonso of Aragon; he then stayed with the good Count Raimond of Toulouse. He was held in high esteem all the time he was in the world, but then he retired into the order of Grandmont, and it was there that he died.

Although no documentary evidence has been found to confirm that Peire was born in the Auvergne and was a canon of Clermont cathedral,[4] we should perhaps bear in mind the view of certain scholars that the authors of the *Vidas* attempted, as a rule, to be accurate and well informed about such details as a troubadour's place of birth and death, his family background and his social class.[5] At the same time, we should not ignore the possibility, discussed later in this section, that the biographer based his statement about Peire Rogier's beginnings on the conclusions he had drawn from the reference to the troubadour in Peire d'Alvernhe's *sirventes*, *Cantarai d'aqestz trobadors*.

The *Vida* describes Peire as a *gentils hom*, which a number of scholars have taken to mean 'gentilhomme'. However, we agree with Appel[6] that *gentils* tells us nothing about Peire's extraction and prefer to interpret the word as meaning 'of noble character' rather than 'of noble birth'.[7] Only very rarely does the title of nobility *En* appear with Peire's name, and it is significant that neither of his contemporaries, Raimbaut d'Orange and Peire d'Alvernhe, uses the title in referring to him in their respective *sirventes*, *Peire Rotgier a trassaillir* and *Cantarai d'aqestz trobadors*.[8] The appearance of the title in the MSS CDRf, in Raimon Vidal's *Abrils issi' e mais intrava* and in the *Breviari d'Amor*[9] may well be explained by the confusion in the scribe's mind between the troubadour and Peire Rogier de Mirepoix, a lord prominent in the early part of the thirteenth century.[10] It is also suggested that posthumous admirers of a celebrated troubadour would be quite likely to honour him with the title.[11]

It is appropriate, at this point, to mention the attempt by the duc de la Salle de Rochemaure in *Les Troubadours cantaliens*[12] to trace Peire Rogier's ancestry. The conclusions which he reaches should be viewed with a good deal of scepticism. His theory, received with inevitable willingness by fellow *Cantaliens*[13] but rejected by other scholars,[14] is that Peire Rogier came from the family of the Lords of Rogiers, the present-day Rouziers (canton of Maurs, Cantal).[15] His arguments are accompanied by a number of detailed references to genealogies, but are based on the assumption, which we have shown to be doubtful, that Peire belonged to a family of noble class.[16]

The *Vida* recounts that, after leaving the canonry and becoming a *joglar*, Peire visited a number of courts and came to settle at the flourishing court of Ermengarda of Narbonne. The viscountess appears to have been an enthusiastic patron of the troubadours and was renowned for the wisdom and skill with which, for the greater part of half a century, she governed her lands.[17]

According to the *Vida*, Peire fell in love with Ermengarda and called her *Tort-n'avetz*. Panvini[18] considers that the biographer could not have deduced from the poems that Ermengarda was designated by this *senhal*, since nowhere in Peire's work is her name mentioned. He concludes, therefore, that the biographer probably obtained this information from an independent source. However, the reference in III, l. 64 to *n'Aimeric lo tos* (*cf.* the note to this line on p. 67) and the association of *Tort-n'avetz* with *Narbones* in V, l. 43 would seem to point fairly clearly to the viscountess.

It is quite possible, though not certain, that the biographer resorted to Peire's work as the basis not only for his information about the *senhal* but also for his entire reference to the troubadour's visit to Narbonne. No independent evidence has been found to verify the *Vida*'s account of the suspicion of a familiar relationship between Ermengarda and Peire or of the troubadour's enforced departure from Narbonne. We suggest later [19] that the biographer may possibly have based the account, at least in part, on sections of poems VII and IX. If this is the case, and the details have not derived from an independent source, then some doubt should be attached to them. For any allusions to actual events or situations found in these poems are too vague for Ermengarda to be identified firmly with the lady concerned or for any other definite conclusions to be drawn. It is also worth remembering, in any consideration of IX, that the poem is of doubtful authenticity.[20] None of the references to *Tort-n'avetz* found in other songs lends any support to the *Vida*'s account of the circumstances of Peire's departure, although each of the poems concerned appears to have been composed while the troubadour was absent from Narbonne.[21]

The *Vida* states that after leaving Narbonne Peire proceeded, full of grief, to Raimbaut d'Orange's court, where he composed the *sirventes*, *Seign'en Raymbaut*. We might reasonably have expected that this poem, from which the biographer quotes an extract, would make reference to Peire's distress on being dismissed from Ermengarda's court. It contains, however, no hint of such a misfortune. In fact Peire explains, in the first stanza, that his reason for visiting Raimbaut is to learn what the situation is at his court and to see whether Raimbaut's high reputation is merited for, he says, *enqeront m'en lai entre nos* (l. 7).[22] It is unlikely that anyone dismissed from an eminent court for the reason indicated in the *Vida* would be asked by members of that court to visit a court elsewhere and to report back on the conditions there. The contents of the first stanza and the absence in the poem of any allusion to Peire's misfortune thus lead us to one of the following conclusions:

(*a*) The circumstances of Peire's departure from Narbonne, as recounted by the *Vida*, are incorrect.

(*b*) Peire's visit to Raimbaut's court took place *before* any dismissal from Narbonne.

(*c*) Peire had not come to Raimbaut's court direct from Narbonne but from another place not mentioned in the *Vida*.

The contents and tone of the *sirventes* and of the host's reply would suggest that it is a question of a youthful Raimbaut receiving the older and more established Peire Rogier. Raimbaut's youth is indicated by l. 33 of *Seign'en Raymbaut* (*pel saur e bai*)[23] and is further borne out by the modest and polite way in which he replies to the older troubadour, his senior.[24] His attitude forms, in fact, a sharp contrast with his usual boastful and haughty manner.[25] Peire, for his part, assumes the role of counsellor and for much of the *sirventes* adopts the familiar didactic tone found elsewhere in his poetry.[26] The advice which he offers to the younger man possibly contains a hint of disillusionment as he perhaps does not find the brilliant welcome which rumours had led him to expect.[27]

Seign'en Raymbaut is one of the few poems to which it is possible to give an approximate date.[28] W. T. Pattison produces sound arguments for allocating Raimbaut's reply to the period 1165-67,[29] and it is therefore in this period that we place *Seign'en Raymbaut*, on the reasonable assumption that the two poems were composed within a very short space of time.

Panvini considers that for the visit to Orange the biographer must have had available an independent contemporary source, as, in his view, all that could have been deduced from the poem *Seign'en Raymbaut* on the identity of the person Peire was visiting is that it was a certain Raimbaut, with no other designation.[30] He states that it would have been difficult for the biographer, on the basis of so little information, to identify this Raimbaut with the troubadour in question. There would appear, however, to be adequate evidence in the poem, despite the absence of a surname, to bring the name of Raimbaut d'Orange to the biographer's mind. Raimbaut's noble family, indicated by the use of the title *Seign'en*, the reference to his youth, his growing reputation as a poet and hospitable patron, considered together, help to confirm Raimbaut's identity. It is also quite possible that the biographer was aware of the troubadours' common link with Puivert.[31]

If the poem was in fact the only source for the biographer's reference to Peire's visit, then some doubt should be attached to the statement in the *Vida* that Peire remained at Raimbaut's court for a long time. The poem mentions only one particular occasion and contains no suggestion that the stay was a long one.[32] Peire indicates that he intends to report elsewhere on the conditions he finds at the court and repeats at the end of the poem that he will depart but not before receiving Raimbaut's reply.[33] On the other hand, the possibility that the two troubadours spent a period of time together at some stage or other following the exchange of *sirventes* is perhaps suggested by subsequent traces of a connection between their work.[34]

There seems to be little reason to question the visits which, according to the *Vida*, Peire subsequently made to the courts of King Alfonso VIII of Castille, King Alfonso II of Aragon and Count Raimond V of Toulouse.[35] All three persons were well known for their hospitality towards the troubadours, for whom their courts were an obvious attraction.[36] The close friendship which existed between Alfonso II and Ermengarda[37] renders a visit by Peire to Aragon all the more likely. A connection with the court of Aragon may, in fact, be suggested by a possible reference, in poem No. IV, to Sancho, Alfonso II's brother.[38]

The *Vida* recounts that Peire finally entered the religious order of Grandmont. Noted for the austerity of its rule, in the twelfth century the order was among the most flourishing in the Midi.[39] Of the other troubadours who are reputed to have spent the latter part of their life in a cloister, Guilhem Adémar is the only one who, according to his *Vida*, entered this particular order.[40] No reference to Peire Rogier has come to light in documents and other works concerning Grandmont to confirm the biographer's information which, in so far as it concerns the troubadour's place of death, would otherwise normally be considered as reliable.[41]

Jehan de Nostredame included in his *Vies des plus célèbres et anciens Poètes provensaux* a completely worthless biography of Peire Rogier (see appendix 1 of this edition). The references to Peire's position of canon at Clermont and to Ermengarda indicate that the author knew the Provençal *Vida*. This did not prevent him, however, from attaching the troubadour to Provence and from placing him in the fourteenth century.[42] The *Histoire générale de Languedoc* singles out the biography as an example of the extent to which Jehan de Nostredame and the authors he used as sources added fables to the Provençal *Vidas*, introduced anachronisms and attributed to Provence, in order to honour the region, several poets who had been born in other areas.[43]

2 *References to Peire Rogier in the works of other troubadours*. Peire Rogier is called to witness in the *tornada* of the poem *Lanqan chanton li auzeil en primier*, which most of the MSS concerned attribute to Aimeric de Peguilhan:

> Salamos, ten lo vers per dreiturier!
> A garentis en trac Peire Rotgier,
> Q'el conois ben si li mot son cabau.
> Si'l sos es bons, midonz ador e lau.[44]

There would appear to be no reason to doubt the authenticity of the *tornada*, since it appears in all the MSS. The tone of the poem tends to confirm the identification of our troubadour with the Peire Rogier in question; it is appropriate that a *canso* which criticises false lovers and lays great emphasis on the poet's discretion and his submissive devotion to his lady should call to witness a troubadour who, throughout his work, is an ardent advocate of such courtly virtues.

W. P. Shepard and F. M. Chambers consider that the author of the poem is more likely to have been Guillem Rainol d'At than Aimeric de Peguilhan. They admit that this attribution poses certain problems, especially relating to the period of Guillem's activity as a poet, but they regard them as being less serious than the difficulties raised by Aimeric's authorship, which they produce very sound reasons for questioning.[45] A. Jeanroy places Guillem in the first third of the thirteenth century[46] but Shepard and Chambers find no grounds for assuming that he lived long after 1216.[47] They consider the limit of 1180, normally attached to Peire Rogier's activity,[48] to be far from definitely fixed and conclude that it would not have been impossible for Guillem to have known Peire towards the end of Peire's life. They even suggest that, geographically, it would have been very easy for Guillem, born at Apt (Vaucluse), to meet Peire, whose visit to nearby Orange was, in their view, probably made towards the end of his career. We have, however, no firm evidence to suppose that Peire lived much beyond 1180.[49] It should also be remembered that his *sirventes* to Raimbaut d'Orange was probably written as early as 1165–67 (see p. 4 above) and that even if he had stayed on at Raimbaut's court it would have been only until 1173, the year of Raimbaut's death.[50] Guillem Rainol might well have been too young at that time to meet him. Only with strong reservations, therefore, should the poem be attributed to Guillem, particularly in view of the general uncertainty about dates.

Of the few references to Peire Rogier found in the works of other troubadours perhaps the most interesting is the one in Peire d'Alvernhe's *sirventes*, *Cantarai d'aqestz trobadors*.[51] Peire Rogier is the first of the twelve poets to be passed under review, appearing immediately before Giraut de Bornelh and Bernart de Ventadour. The following comments are made about him:

> D'aisso mer mal Peire Rotgiers,
> per qe n'er encolpatz primiers,
> car chanta d'amor a presen;
> e valgra li mais us sautiers
> en la glieis'o us candeliers
> tener ab gran candel'arden. [ll. 7–12]

The *sirventes*, in which Raimbaut d'Orange is also named, has generally been placed in the period 1165–73.[52] It is possible that it was composed on an occasion when those named in it were actually present.[53] If this was the case, and Peire Rogier and Raimbaut were both in attendance at Puivert, then the satire is likely to have been composed *after* the troubadours' exchange of *sirventes* at Raimbaut's court placed in the period 1165–67; for it is fairly clear from the tone and contents of their *sirventes* that the meeting at Orange was their first.

The circumstances in which the satire was written and the location of Puivert are uncertain and have given rise to a considerable amount of discussion. Until fairly recently the tendency has been to identify the Puivert in question with the town in the western part of the Department of Aude on the road linking Foix with Carcassonne and Narbonne.[54] Pattison has suggested, in fact, that the troubadours from different regions named in the satire formed part of the wedding party which accompanied Eleanor, the daughter of Henry II of England and Eleanor of Aquitaine, from Bordeaux to Spain for her marriage with Alfonso VIII of Castille in 1170.[55] The party would have been particularly attractive to the troubadours in that it included the bride's mother, renowned for her interest in poetry, and Alfonso II of Aragon, a well known patron of the troubadours and a troubadour himself.[56] The bride was also to become a patron of the troubadours in her own right.

Geographical and historical objections to this theory are, however, raised by Rita Lejeune, who casts serious doubts upon the identification with Puivert (Aude).[57] She proposes, as an alternative possibility, a Puivert in Catalonia, *Puigverd de Agramunt*, situated on the road linking Foix, Puigcerda and Lérida.[58] She sees no reason for supposing that Eleanor's wedding party passed through either Puigverd or Puivert (Aude) and considers that if Puigverd was connected with Peire d'Alvernhe's satire it was under circumstances other than the Castilian wedding.

Either of the locations of Puivert proposed above would be consistent with what little information the *Vida* contains of Peire Rogier's travels. We have already noted that Peire's visit to Raimbaut d'Orange's court is likely to have taken place before the composition of Peire d'Alvernhe's satire but that his movements immediately before and after the visit are open to speculation. We cannot, therefore, be certain about the starting point of any journey Peire may have made to Puivert. One possibility is that Raimbaut and he travelled together to Puivert direct from Raimbaut's court. If this was the case, and if the gathering at Puivert took place in 1170, the year of the Castilian wedding, then Peire's stay at Raimbaut's court would have probably lasted at least three years.[59] Alternatively Peire might well have returned to Narbonne before proceeding to Puivert, in which case Puivert (Aude) would have been easily accessible to him, as it lies about 100 km or so from Narbonne on the road to Foix. A gathering at Puivert involving the Castilian wedding party would have given Peire the opportunity of meeting members of the Castilian court as well as Alfonso II of Aragon. He would thus have been able to strike up a relationship, at one and the same time, with the two Spanish courts which, according to the *Vida*, were to receive him in turn at a later stage in his life.[60] As far as the Catalonian Puigverd is concerned, it would not have been difficult for Peire to make the necessary journey if he was already in Spain at the time of the composition of the satire, as the courts of both Castille and Aragon were within fairly easy reach.

It is generally assumed that the remarks Peire d'Alvernhe makes about Peire in his *sirventes* refer indirectly to Peire's early life as a canon. A. Del Monte notes, however, that on the whole the stanzas devoted to the other troubadours are not of a biographical nature.[61] It therefore seems reasonable, before we examine the likelihood of a biographical reference in Peire's case, to consider alternative explanations which have been offered for Peire d'Alvernhe's remarks.

Del Monte considers that line 15 of III (*a dieu m'autrey*) is the only part of Peire Rogier's known work which could have formed the basis for the contents of the stanza.[62] It is unlikely, however, that a conventional line of this nature has any particular significance and throws any light on the troubadour's religious beliefs or practices.[63] The content and style of Peire's *sirventes*, *Seign'en Raymbaut, per vezer*, suggest to J. Storost[64] a clumsiness and awkward shyness on Peire's part. He mentions the possibility—in our view, fairly remote—that it is to these characteristics of the troubadour that Peire d'Alvernhe is alluding in his satire. Perhaps a more likely explanation of Peire d'Alvernhe's remarks is the didactic tone of much of Peire Rogier's work.[65] C. de Lollis is more specific on this point, recognising at the same time an ecclesiastical influence in certain aspects of Peire's style.[66] He suggests that Peire d'Alvernhe had in mind the 'intonazione generale, ch'étra il predicatorio e il coralo, del canzoniere di Pietro Rogier', and in particular the poem *No sai don chant*, in which a number of the lines are in interrogative form and reminiscent, he says, of certain biblical lines.

We prefer, however, on balance, to support the generally accepted view that the stanza is biographical in content. Perhaps Peire d'Alvernhe's reason for drawing attention to a canonship which had probably been renounced some years before was the close similarity between Peire Rogier's beginnings and his own. Both troubadours had originated from Clermont and had entered the Church. Peire d'Alvernhe's *Vida* states that he was Bishop of Clermont, while a *sirventes* by Bernart Martí[67] indicates that he was a canon before becoming a troubadour. He is also said to have been among the first Provençal poets to compose religious poems.[68]

The absence in the stanza of any reference to a canonship or to Clermont has led Panvini to suggest that Peire d'Alvernhe's remarks could not have formed the basis of the statement in the *Vida* that Peire Rogier had been a canon at Clermont before becoming a *joglar*.[69] In his view the remarks serve, rather, to confirm the biographer's information.[70] The biographer is, however, likely to have known the whole of Peire d'Alvernhe's satire; it is significant that the stanzas devoted to Bernart de Ventadour and Peire d'Alvernhe himself are quoted in full in the respective *Vidas*. Having therefore possibly deduced from the contents of the stanza concerned with Peire Rogier that Peire had belonged to the Church at one time, the biographer may have gone on to assume that the troubadour had a background similar to Peire d'Alvernhe's. This assumption would have been strengthened by Peire's special position in a list which also includes such celebrated poets as Bernart de Ventadour and Giraut de Bornelh and which is therefore unlikely to indicate an order of merit. The doubts attached to the independence of the *Vida*'s account of Peire Rogier's early life should, therefore, perhaps lead us to accept the account a little less readily than would normally be the case with biographical statements of this nature, which are generally assumed to be reliable.[71]

Given that Peire's appearance at the head of Peire d'Alvernhe's list is not arbitrary, then perhaps the most likely explanation is the similarity in the background of the two troubadours. Other explanations which have been offered should, however, also be mentioned. If the *sirventes* was composed at Puivert (Aude), Peire could have been named first by virtue of his position as the resident troubadour at Narbonne, which was a fairly short distance away.[72] We have noted above, however, the difficulty in determining whether Peire would have gone to Puivert direct from Narbonne. Appel considers that Peire Rogier's special position in the *sirventes* could be explained by the fact that one of his poems may have been heard by the gathering only a short time before. The possibility is suggested to Appel by the appearance in two of the MSS (CR) of the reading *chantet* (l. 3 of the stanza), which he tends to favour in preference to *chanta*. It is, however, the present tense which is offered by all the other MSS and which is generally adopted.[73] The suggestion, made by E. Hoepffner,[74] that Peire was perhaps the organiser of the gathering is presumably also based on the troubadour's position in the poem.

It is quite possible that Peire knew some of the troubadours, apart from Raimbaut d'Orange, who make an appearance in the poem. The close relationship between Peire's poetry and Bernart de Ventadour's is generally recognised;[75] we discuss later the similarity between certain aspects of Peire's work and Giraut de Bornelh's, observing the influence which the one may have had upon the other.[76] Furthermore Bernart, Giraut and Peire d'Alvernhe may well have all been at Ermengarda's court at one time or another[77] and could have had the opportunity of meeting Peire there.

Another possible reference to Peire Rogier found in the poetry of other troubadours is suggested by J. Mouzat in his edition of Gaucelm Faidit.[78] Gaucelm ends his *canso Una dolors esforciva*[79] with the following *tornada*:

> Dieus m'ajut!
> Que de mi dons no·m remut —
> Peironet, tu la·m saluda
> e Linhaure la·m salut!

Mouzat considers that *Linhaure*, mentioned here and in seven other poems by Gaucelm, is to be identified with Raimbaut d'Orange[80] and he assumes that the

Peironet named alongside him is Peire Rogier, whose stay at Raimbaut's court might have been known to Gaucelm.[81] If Mouzat's assumption is correct the poem might have been written at some stage during Peire's visit to Orange, which would place it in the early part of Gaucelm's career.[82]

It is worth noting that, far from playing a secondary role in the *tornada* and being named simply as an acquaintance of Raimbaut's, *Peironet* is mentioned first, and is in fact addressed in the second person, while the reference to Raimbaut is made in the third person. It would therefore be reasonable to assume that *Peironet* was known to Gaucelm personally, or at least in his own right, and not merely through an association with Raimbaut. There are, however, no positive grounds for suggesting that Peire Rogier and Gaucelm knew each other. The most that can be said is that, apart from having a common acquaintance in Raimbaut, the two poets reveal in their work a close link with Bernart de Ventadour and may well have both had personal contact with him.[83] The *senhal* appears in a number of other places in the poetry of the troubadours, where it is clear, in fact, that the person concerned is not Peire Rogier.[84] Furthermore, the request which Gaucelm makes would seem to imply that *Peironet* knew the lady in question or was near her at the time, but we have no evidence to indicate that Peire was acquainted with any of the ladies who are said to have played a part in Gaucelm's life.[85] Any connection between *Peironet* and Peire Rogier should therefore be regarded largely as a matter of conjecture.

3 *Peire Rogier's lady and the* senhal '*Tort-n' avetz*'. The origin of the *senhal Tort-n' avetz* by which Peire Rogier appears to have referred to Ermengarda, is uncertain. It may relate to a particular unknown incident or to Ermengarda's discouraging attitude to the poet's supplications.[86] Peire Rogier's references to his love are almost always made in conventional courtly terms, and we learn very little about it from any of the *cansos*, including those which allude in some way to *Tort-n' avetz*.

The only *cansos* which make no reference to the *senhal* are IX, which is discussed below, and I and II. The absence of the *senhal* in I and II is one of the factors which have led us to assume that the poems belong to the same period of composition.[87]

The *tornada* in I is linked with the main theme of the poem and consists of much more than a mere dedication or address.[88] Peire is clearly referring in the *tornada* to the lady (*midons*) mentioned throughout the rest of the poem. However, no indication of her identity is given. In the case of II we are again provided with no clue as to the identity of *sidons*, named in the *tornada* as the lady to whom Peire sends the poem. It is not clear whether this lady is the same person as the subject of the poem.

In the introductory stanza of III Peire states that it is *Tort-n' avetz* who gives him the encouragement to sing. It is to her, in fact, that the troubadour asks, in the second *tornada*, that the poem be sent. We have observed above that the reference to *n'Aimeric lo tos* in the following line serves to confirm that the *senhal* denotes Ermengarda and may have helped to form the basis of the *Vida*'s reference to the viscountess.[89] In the rest of the poem Peire sings the praises of his lady (*midons*), emphasising throughout the importance of secrecy and discretion where she is concerned, which leads Appel[90] to conclude that at that time Ermengarda could not yet have known to whom the *senhal* alluded. Appel must have based his conclusion upon the assumption that *midons* and *Tort-n'avetz* are one and the same, although the contents of the poem do not make clear whether there is a connection between these two persons. It is possible, as L. Cocito suggests,[91] that while *Tort-n'avetz* is the lady to whom Peire pays homage and dedicates his song, the beloved subject of the poem is *midons*, an unspecified lady belonging to the conventional world of courtly love. This suggestion is supported by the fact that the *tornada* addressed to *midons*, like the *tornada* in I, continues the motifs of the poem, while the second *tornada* involving *Tort-n'avetz* is unrelated to the rest of the poem and is of a formal dedicatory nature. *Midons* and *Tort-n'avetz* are both described as a source of *joy e pretz* (see ll. 9, 20, 31, etc.), which might suggest their common identity, were it not for the frequent appearance of these particular words elsewhere in Peire's work[92] and for their function as a refrain in this poem. However, the troubadour's use of the words *sai* and *lai* prevents us from ruling out the possibility of a direct connection between *midons* and *Tort-n'avetz*. The juxtaposition of the words in ll. 8 and 9 and the reappearance of *lai* in l. 62 would seem to indicate that at the time the poem was composed Peire was not in Ermengarda's company. It is possible that, in employing the words to the same effect in stanza III (ll. 29 and 33) with regard to *midons*, the troubadour was in fact thinking of one and the same lady in both instances.

The reference to *Tort-n'avetz* in the first *tornada* of IV takes the form of a dedication and homage to the defender of *bon pretz*. Both *tornadas* are independent of the rest of the poem, and there appear to be no positive grounds for associating *Tort-n'avetz* with the lady mentioned elsewhere in the poem.[93] The use of the word *tramet* (l. 50) suggests that Peire was not at Narbonne at the time.

V, in which the courtly virtues of *amor*, *pretz* and *joy* are extolled in general terms, contains only a very brief reference to a particular lady (l. 42: *midons*). Again, nothing suggests that the allusion is to *Tort-n'avetz*, to whom the troubadour sends greetings in the *tornadas*. It is appropriate, in view of the subject matter, that the poem should conclude by acknowledging *Tort-n'avetz*, the staunch upholder of true *pretz* and *joy*. The contents of the first *tornada* indicate that the song was among those composed when Peire was absent from Narbonne.

In the *tornada* of VI Peire requests that *Tort-n'avetz* learn the poem and that it be then sent to *Dreit-n'avetz*, whose identity is unknown. The words *lai en Saves* which follow *Dreit-n'avetz* lead Cocito[94] to suggest that the *senhal* probably denotes the distant lady, mentioned in the body of the poem, near whom the heart and mind of the poet remain (ll. 37-8). However, the *tornada* as a whole again appears to be divorced from the rest of the poem, and we have no reason to identify either *Dreit-n'avetz* or *Tort-n'avetz* with the beloved lady. The use of the word *mant* (l. 57) would imply that the troubadour was again away from Narbonne when the song was composed.

In VII, as well as in I, it is clear from the contents of the *tornada* that the lady to whom the poem is dedicated (*midons*) is also the subject of the poem[95] and that Peire is not merely paying formal homage to her. He refers in the sixth stanza to the separation from his lady and ends by sending the poem to her as a source of encouragement until they meet again. Although the *senhal Tort-n'avetz* is not mentioned specifically, an allusion to it may well be found in ll. 10-11:

> Oc, ben leu, mas sempre *n'a tort*. —
> Tort *n'a*? Qu'ai dig! Boca tu mens. [96]

If these lines were designed to be an indirect reference to *Tort-n'avetz* they would support the suggestion made earlier that the *senhal* may have had its origin in the lady's cool response to the poet's supplications. If Ermengarda was the lady in question, then the song would have been among those composed at a time when the troubadour was not at Narbonne. It is interesting to note that in this poem Peire departs to some extent from his characteristically discreet tone and implies that his love for his lady is returned. His remarks may be regarded as bearing out the *Vida*'s reference to the suspicion of a familiar relationship with Ermengarda[97] or may, in fact, have formed part of the basis for the biographer's statement.[98]

Any information which IX provides on the troubadour's relations with his lady must of necessity be accepted with reservations in view of the doubt about the poem's authenticity. While the poem makes no mention of the *senhal* or of Narbonne, it is the only one which appears to refer to a particular occasion on which the poet and his lady were separated; the references in other poems to Peire's absence from his lady are made only in general terms. Again, the allusion may be seen either as support for the *Vida*'s account of Peire's enforced departure from Narbonne or as a possible source from which the biographer obtained his material.[99] It is difficult, however, to identify Narbonne with *freidur'e montagna* (l. 16). It is perhaps more likely to be a question of the Auvergne which the poet was leaving,[100] in which case the lady mentioned in l. 19 and elsewhere in the poem would probably not be Ermengarda.

The nature of Peire Rogier's references to *Tort-n'avetz* would seem to indicate clearly that Ermengarda was the troubadour's patron. There is, however, inadequate evidence in his work to conclude with absolute certainty that the viscountess was ever the object of his courtly sentiments and combined the role of the beloved lady with that of protector. We should not discount the possibility that the beloved lady of whom Peire sings in the most general terms has no particular identity but is simply an abstract figure essential to the courtly themes of his poetry.

Notes

1 Cf. Appel, p. 12. Diez (*Leben und Werke*, p. 79) and Jeanroy (*Poésie Lyrique*, I, p. 409) indicate, in fact, the period 1160–80.
2 *Le biografie provenzali: valore e attendibilità*, Florence, 1952, pp. 113–15.
3 Page 2.
4 Appel (p. 4) states that he was unable to find any reference to Peire Rogier in records at Clermont. We have consulted, without success, a number of works on the history of the city, including the following: F. Renaud, *Histoire de la commune de Clermont-Ferrand*, Clermont-Ferrand, 1873; A. Imberdis, *Histoire générale de l'Auvergne depuis l'ère gallique jusqu'au XVIIIe siècle*, Clermont-Ferrand, 1868, vol. I; A. Tardieu, *Histoire de la ville de Clermont-Ferrand*, Moulins, 1870–71, vol. I; P. Audigier, *Histoire de la ville de Clermont*, Clermont-Ferrand, 1887, vol. I. The only references to Peire Rogier which we have discovered are based on Jehan de Nostredame's erroneous version of Peire's life (see appendix 1): Tardieu (*op. cit.*, p. 263) includes Peire in the list of canons of the old cathedral chapter but with the date 1330. Similarly, Audigier (*op. cit.*, p. 336) mentions him in a list of the houses of Clermont. He describes him as a canon of the cathedral around 1330 and adds that he was assassinated.
5 A. Jeanroy, *Archivum Romanicum*, I, (1917), 305, and *Poésie Lyrique*, I, pp. 127–32; Panvini, *op. cit.*, p. 113.
6 Page 4.
7 Boutière and Schutz (*Biographies*, p. 269) follow this interpretation in their translation of Peire Rogier's *Vida* and throughout their edition of the *Vidas* make a clear distinction between the two meanings of *gentils*. In other *Vidas* the word very often appears on its own with *hom*, without any other adjectives. The translation of 'gentilhomme' which is given in these cases is generally borne out by what is known of the particular troubadour's family; cf. the *Vidas* of the following troubadours as given in the edition of Boutière and Schutz: Blacasset (p. 515), Gausbert de Poicibot (p. 229), Guilhem Adémar (p. 349), Lanfranc Cigala (p. 569), Monk of de Montaudon (p. 307), Peire de Bussignac (p. 145).
8 Appel, *loc. cit*; V. Crescini, *Le caricature trobadoriche di Pietro d'Alvernia* in *Atti del Reale Istituto Veneto di scienza, lettere ed arti*, LXXXVI, (1926–27), 212.
9 We have not checked the appearance of *En* in f, which does not contain any of Peire's poems, but rely on Appel's information (p. 4). In C it appears with *Peire Rogier de Mirapeys* at the head of *No sai don chant*, and in R it appears at the head of the *Vida*. The scribe of D uses it in introducing Raimbaut d'Orange's *Peire Rotgier, a trassaillir*, in the same way as Raimon Vidal (*Abrils issi'e mais intrava*) in his preamble to the quotation from *Seign'en Raymbaut, per vezer*. The MSS of the *Breviari d'Amor* also employ it in the introductory line to the first quotation from the same poem (l. 32,616).
10 Peire Rogier de Mirepoix was prominent in the struggles against the crusaders in the first part of the thirteenth century. During this period Mirepoix, situated in the Department of Ariège, was an established centre of the Cathar heresy and Peire Rogier de Mirepoix one of the most prominent Cathars. The castle was, in fact, attacked and captured by Simon de Montfort in 1209 (cf. P. Belperron,

La Croisade contre les Albigeois, p. 193). Peire Rogier is said to have remained closely attached to the sect all his life. It is reported that after being mortally wounded in combat he was taken to Fanjeaux to receive the *consolamentum* from the eminent Cathar bishop Guillabert de Castres (*cf.* R. Nelli, *L'érotique des troubadours*, p. 233).

The Mirepoix family is mentioned quite often in the *Histoire générale de Languedoc*, the earliest date concerned being 1062 (III, p. 340). In 1242, a later Peire Rogier de Mirepoix, presumably the son of the above named, played a prominent role in the massacre of the inquisitors at Avignonet. He also took part in the defence of the castle of Montségur during the subsequent siege of 1243-44. For details of these events and of the lord of Mirepoix's part in them see *Hist. gen. Lang.*, VI, pp. 738 ff and p. 768, and Belperron's *Croisade contre les Albigeois*, pp. 427-33.

The MSS C and a[1] attribute, in fact, all the poems by Peire which they contain to Peire Rogier de Mirepoix.* It has been assumed from this that the lord of Mirepoix had himself written poetry (*cf.* Chabaneau, *Biographies*, p. 166; Nelli, *op. cit.*, p. 234). However, Appel's explanation (p. 4) of the appearance of his name in these MSS would seem to be more likely: the lord is mentioned in one of the *razos* of Raimon de Miraval together with the Count of Foix, Olivier de Saissac, Aimeric de Montréal and Peire Vidal, who are all reputed to have courted the *Loba* of Pennautier, Raimon's lady; this brief reference in the history of the troubadours may well have provided the scribes of C and a[1] with sufficient grounds for giving the lord of Mirepoix's name to the troubadour.

Raimon himself also mentions a Peire Rogier in the *sirventes*, *A Dieu me coman, Bajona*, which names a number of lords with whom Raimon is acquainted (see P. Andraud, *La Vie et l'oeuvre du troubadour Raimon de Miraval*, p. 52; L. T. Topsfield, *Les Poésies du troubadour Raimon de Miraval*, p. 317). The contents of the poem make it clear that the person concerned is at Carcassonne. As the poem is fixed in the period 1200-04, he is identified with Peire Rogier de Cabaret, who became viguier of Carcassonne in 1204 (*cf.* Appel, p. 4, note 1; Andraud, *op. cit.*, pp. 59-60 and p. 178; Topsfield, *op. cit.*, p. 26) and who, like Peire Rogier de Mirepoix, took an active part in the Albigensian Crusade. He defended Carcassonne during the siege of 1209 (*cf. Hist. gen. Lang.*, VI, p. 292). His attempt to defend the castle of Cabaret in 1210 against Simon de Montfort failed, and the surrender of the castle was followed by that of several others in the area (*cf. ibid.*, VI, p. 350).

11 See Crescini, *op. cit.*, LXXXVI, 212, note 4. He draws attention to the *Vida* of Bernart de Ventadour, in which the biographer begins by describing Bernart as a man *de paubra generation, fills d'un sirven qu'era forniers* and then proceeds to place *En* before his name (see Appel, *B. von Vent.*, pp. xi-xvi).

12 I, pp. 326-70.

13 R. Four, in the Aurillac journal *Croix du Cantal* (4 December 1910), accepts with enthusiasm the conclusions of the duc de la Salle, stating that he has made 'une découverte d'érudition'. Nelli and Lavaud retain the duc de la Salle's theory for their brief notes on Peire Rogier in their anthology (*Les Troubadours*, II, p. 84): 'Peire Rogiers appartenait très probablement à la famille des seigneurs de Rogiers, aujourd'hui Rouziers, . . .'

* According to Appel (p. 3, note 2), the same title appears in f in the only place in which reference is made to Peire.

14 Jeanroy (*Romania*, XLII (1913), 115) makes the following comments on the duc de la Salle's work: 'C'est l'ouvrage d'un amateur enthousiaste et fort érudit, mais non moins étranger aux procédés et aux scrupules ordinaires de la critique . . . Si la plupart des poètes énumérés plus haut sont authentiquement auvergnats, plusieurs, en revanche, ne deviennent "cantaliens" que par la grâce du duc de la Salle, qui rattache, par exemple, Peire Rogier à la famille seigneuriale de Rogiers (aujourd'hui Rouziers, canton de Maurs, arr. d'Aurillac) . . .' Later, in his *Bibliographie sommaire des chansonniers provençaux* (p. 41), Jeanroy describes the same section of *Les Troubadours cantaliens* as 'sans valeur'.

15 *Cf. Annuaire du département du Cantal*, Aurillac, 1830, p. 219; J. B. Bouillet, *Nobiliaire d'Auvergne*, Clermont-Ferrand, 1852, V, pp. 418-19.

16 As support for his assumption that Peire was of noble origin the duc de la Salle cites the reference to *gentils hom* in the *Vida* (*op. cit.*, I, p. 336). He considers that the troubadour must have belonged to the old family of the lords of Rogiers, since there existed no other of noble status by that name in the whole of the Auvergne (*op. cit.*, I, pp. 335-7). He assumes that Peire was a younger brother and was therefore destined as a child for the Church (*op. cit.*, I, p. 337 and pp. 341-2). A canonry at Clermont Cathedral, he suggests, could have been a mark of appreciation on the part of the Bishop of the Auvergne for the family's past generosity to the Church of Saint-Julien de Brioude (*op. cit.*, I, p. 342). A number of the family of Rogiers are in fact included in lists of admissions to the chapter of Brioude (*cf.* M. Laîné, *Archives généalogiques et historiques de la noblesse de France*, Paris, 1834, IV, p. 29; Bouillet, *op. cit.*, V, p. 418). Tardieu (*op. cit.*, p. 255) states that in the early days of Clermont Cathedral, particularly in the twelfth, thirteenth and fourteenth centuries, almost all its canons belonged to the oldest and most illustrious houses in the Auvergne.

17 *Cf.* pp. 37-8 below.

18 *Op. cit.*, p. 114.

19 See p. 12 below.

20 See the introduction to IX and p. 12 below.

21 See pp. 10-12 below. In V (ll. 45-46) Peire states that he will see *Tort-n'avetz* shortly *si trop grans afars no·m rete*, which would seem to suggest that, at that particular time at least, reasons other than those reported by the *Vida* were keeping the troubadour away from Narbonne.

22 Appel (*Raimbaut von Orange*, p. 19) suggests that Raimbaut's reputation had perhaps spread as far as Narbonne.

23 Raimbaut was still fairly young, probably in his late twenties, when he died in 1173 (*cf.* Pattison, *R. d'Orange*, pp. 12, 25 and 36).

24 *Cf.* Appel, *op. cit.*, p. 20; Pattison, *op. cit.*, p. 90, note 1.

25 *Cf.* Appel, *Peire Rogier*, p. 18; Pattison, *loc. cit.* See also Peire d'Alvernhe's remarks on Raimbaut in the satire *Cantarai d'aqestz trobadors* (stanza x).

26 Appel (*op. cit.*, p. 17) quotes other examples of didacticism in Peire's work: I, ll. 8-28; II, ll. 37-45, 50-4, 59-63; IV, ll. 4-7, 10-14; V, ll. 8-35; VII, ll. 32-3.

27 *Cf.* note to VIII, ll. 15 ff., and Jeanroy, *Poésie Lyrique*, I, p. 169.

28 The other poems which may be dated approximately are III (see note to l. 64: *n'Aimeric lo tos*) and possibly IV (see note to l. 54: *dons Sanz*).

29 *Cf. op. cit.*, p. 37 and p. 90, note 1. Among the reasons Pattison puts forward is that since Peire speaks of Raimbaut as of one who is only in the early stages of his career the reply must fall fairly near the beginning of Raimbaut's career but

late enough for him to have already achieved some fame. Pattison dates Raimbaut's first poem around 1162 and therefore fixes the reply some three to five years later.

Pietsch (*Modern Language Notes*, x, col. 401) places the reply around 1170.

30 *Op. cit.*, p. 114.
31 See the discussion on Puivert below.
32 *Cf.* Diez, *op. cit.*, p. 95. J. Ajalbert (*Les Troubadours d'Auvergne*, p. 73) assumes, on the other hand, that Peire stayed at the court of Orange until Raimbaut's death.
33 J. Storost (*Ursprung und Entwicklung des altprovenzalischen sirventes bis auf Bertran de Born*, Halle, 1931, p. 103) considers that Peire uses Raimbaut's reputation and the uncertainty about his marital status merely as an excuse for the visit. In his view Peire's repeated references to his proposed departure imply, in fact, a desire to be retained by Raimbaut. He suggests that the author of the *Vida* has interpreted the poem in the same way in stating that Peire was at Raimbaut's court a long time.
34 Pattison considers that one of Raimbaut's *gaps* may be meant to parody the theme of Peire's *Al pareyssen de las flors* (see the notes to this poem) and also mentions Raimbaut's likely imitation of Peire's dialogue form (*cf. op. cit.*, p. 23 and p. 54). A. Kolsen even suggests that Raimbaut may possibly have shared in the composition of part of Peire's *Ges non puesc en bon vers fallir* (see pp. 24–5 below).
35 Appel (*op. cit.*, p. 9) has reservations about the reported visit to Castille. He considers that insufficient evidence is available to confirm the visit and claims that only one MS (R) makes reference to it. It should be noted, however, that the visit is also mentioned in E, which we have generally adopted as base for the latter part of the *Vida*. R. Menéndez Pidal (*Poesía juglaresca y juglares*, Madrid, 1924, p. 163, note 2) suggests that the omission of the reference in the other MSS (AB) may have been caused by an error on the part of the scribe, whose eye was probably attracted by the second *Anfos* appearing a few words after the first.
36 See notes to the *Vida*.
37 See notes to the *Vida*.
38 See note to l. 54 of IV (*No sai don chant*).
39 See notes to the *Vida*.
40 It is interesting to note the similarity between the end of Peire's *Vida* and that of Guilhem Adémar's

Peire Rogier	Guilhem Adémar
Gran honor ac e·l mon tan com el hi estet, mais pueis se rendet a l'orde de Granmon e lai el definet.	. . . e fo fort honratz per tota la bona gen. E pois el se rendet e l'ordre de Granmon. [*Biographies* p. 349]

41 See note 5 above.

We have consulted the following works, which are among those cited by K. Almqvist in connection with his thorough but unproductive search for a record of Guilhem Adémar (see G. *Adémar*, pp. 14–15): Dom Beaunier, *Recueil historique, chronologique, et topographique des archevêchez, évêchez, abbayes et prieurez de France* . . . two vols., Paris, 1726; Dom Beaunier, *Recueil historique des archevêchés, évêchés, abbayes et prieurés de France* (*Abbayes et prieurés de l'ancienne France*) . . . (new edition, introduction), 1906, pp. 185-8; C. U. J. Chevalier, *Répertoire des sources historiques du moyen-âge, Topobibliographie*, two vols., Montbéliard, 1903; C. Couderc, *Les Manuscrits de l'abbaye de Grandmont* (*Bibliothèque de l'Ecole des Chartes*, vol. 62, 1901); D. de Sainte-Marthe, *Gallia Christiana*, vol. 2, Paris, 1720; L. Guibert, *Les Manuscrits du séminaire de Limoges* (*Bulletin de la Société archéologique et historique du Limousin*, Limoges, 1892, pp. 493-509, Nos. 68-84); A. Lecler, *Histoire de l'abbaye de Grandmont* (*Bulletin de la Société archéologique . . . du Limousin*, vols 57-60, Limoges, 1907-10; J. Levesque, *Annales ordinis grandimontis*, Troyes, 1662; M. Prou, *Additions et corrections au Gallia Christiana* (*Mélanges d'archéologie et d'histoire de l'Ecole française de Rome*, Rome, v, (1885), pp. 254-5).

42 For an explanation of references contained in the biography by Jehan de Nostredame and other comments on it see the edition of Chabaneau-Anglade, Paris, 1913, pp. 30, 139, 163, 343.

43 *Hist. gen. Lang.*, III, p. 870.

44 Lines 50-3 of the critical edition of the poem by W. P. Shepard and F. M. Chambers in *Romance Philology*, II (1948), 86.

45 For the discussion by Shepard and Chambers on the authorship of the poem, see *op. cit.*, II, 83-90, and their edition, *The Poems of Aimeric de Peguilhan*, Evanston (Illinois), 1950, p. 28. Pillet and Carstens had earlier expressed doubts about the poem's authenticity (*cf. Bibliographie der Troubadours*, p. 13).

Shepard and Chambers point out that important aspects of the poem's content and style are foreign to Aimeric's poetry. They mention the picture of spring which introduces the poem and the other references to nature as well as the vocabulary and rhyme forms. Moreover they fix Aimeric's birth not later than 1175 (see *The Poems of Aimeric de Peguilhan*, p. 4) and make the point that Peire Rogier is likely to have died while Aimeric was still a child. This is consistent with the approximate period of 1195-1230 in which Jeanroy places Aimeric's poetic activity (*op. cit.*, I, p. 331).

One MS (D) attributes the poem to Guillem Rainol d'At. None of the five extant poems by Guillem is a *canso*, but the vocabulary and picturesque references to nature in a number of passages which Shepard and Chambers quote from the poems are reminiscent of *Lanqan chanton*.

46 *Op. cit.*, I, p. 381.

47 They refer to a *sirventes* written to Simon de Montfort, which has been dated around 1216-18, and to a *tenso* composed with Guillem Magret, who was a protégé of Peter II of Aragon (1196-1213) and Alfonso IX of Léon (1188-1230) and to whom Jeanroy gives the approximate dates 1200-15 (*op. cit.*, I, p. 379).

48 See note 1 above.

49 See note to l. 54 of IV (*dons Sanz*), however, about the possibility of a slight extension of Peire's career beyond 1180.

50 See note 23 above.

51 A. Del Monte, *P. d'Alvernha*, No. XII (pp. 119-27).

52 *Cf.* references quoted by Del Monte in his edition (p. 129); P. Rajna, *Romania*, XLIX, 81; Appel, *B. von Vent.*, p. liv. Appel (*P. Rogier*, p. 10) was the first to establish the *terminus ad quem* of Peire d'Alvernhe's *sirventes* by identifying the *Raembautz* mentioned in the tenth stanza as Raimbaut d'Orange, who died in

1173 (see note 23 above). The earlier limit was proposed by Zenker in his edition of Peire d'Alvernhe.

53 Among the reasons for supposing that the persons mentioned in the satire were in fact present at its reading is the inclusion of little known and foreign troubadours alongside well known, established ones, together with a certain emphasis, in the descriptions, on the troubadours' visual and audible features (*cf.* Appel, *B. von Vent.*, p. xxi; Rajna, *op. cit.*, XLIX, 89 ff; Crescini, *op. cit.*, LXXXVI, 1229 ff; Pattison, *Mod. Phil.*, XXXI, 20; R. Lejeune, ' "La Galerie littéraire" du troubadour Peire d'Alvernhe' (*Actes et mémoires du IIIe Congrès international de langue et littérature d'oc*, Bordeaux, 1964, II, p. 36)). The intended tone of the poem is open to discussion (*cf.* N. Zingarelli, *Ricerche sulla vita e le rime di Bernart de Ventadorn* (*Studi medievali*, I, (1904–05), 319 ff); Appel, *op. cit.*, pp. xix–xx; Rajna, *op. cit.*, XLIX, 91 ff; Crescini, *op. cit.*, LXXXVI, 203 ff; Pattison, *op. cit.*, XXXI, 19; Riquer, *Lírica*, p. 208). Pattison (*loc. cit.*) considers that it is a light-hearted poem and suggests that for the playful humour to be fully developed the troubadours in question must have been present in person.

54 It is on this site that one still finds the imposing ruins of a former castle a brief description of which is given by Rita Lejeune (*op. cit.*, pp. 43–4).

Another possibility would be the Puivert in the Department of Vaucluse, but it has been rejected on the grounds that the place in question has preserved no mediaeval ruins and has no mention in mediaeval history (*cf.* Appel, *op. cit.*, pp. xxi–xxii; Pattison, *loc. cit.*; R. Lejeune, *op. cit.*, pp. 49–51).

55 See Pattison, *op. cit.*, XXXI, 23–32, for full details of this theory. Pattison identifies the subject of Peire's twelfth stanza, Gonzalgo Roitz, as Gonzalo Ruiz de la Burueba, who was among the party of dignitaries charged with accompanying Eleanor to Spain. Pattison explains why, in his view, the party would have been likely to decide against the more normal routes to Tarrazona in order to follow the less direct one through Puivert, situated in the territory of Count Raimond V of Toulouse. Since the journey to Spain lasted from July to September 1170 it is in this period that Pattison places the satire.

56 *Cf.* Pattison, *op. cit.*, XXXI, 30–1, and *PMLA*, L, 22–3.

57 *Cf. op. cit.*, pp. 39–40, 43–9. Mme Lejeune proposes a much more straightforward route from Bordeaux to Spain, not mentioned by Pattison, which would have taken the party along the road joining Pau and Saragossa via the Somport pass and Jaca. She also observes that in August 1170 Count Raimond V of Toulouse was still an enemy of Henry II of England. A journey through the count's territory was therefore unlikely.

Well documented evidence is provided by Mme Lejeune to show that the castle mentioned by Pattison (see note 54 above) did not in fact exist in 1170. Official records contain no reference to Puivert, the place, before about 1175. The castle is not mentioned until 1210, when it was attacked by Simon de Montfort.

58 *Cf. op. cit.*, pp. 51–3. Mme Lejeune suggests that Puigverd de Agramunt may have been the forerunner of Puivert (Aude). She considers that it is possible for the Catalonian name to have been transferred to the Aude in the second half of the twelfth century through a family migration, particularly as the lords of this region had paid homage to the King of Aragon, Count of Barcelona.

Pattison (*Mod. Phil.*, XXXI, 20) makes reference to three places named Puivert in Catalonia but observes that, like Puivert (Vaucluse), none of them shows any trace of mediaeval ruins or is mentioned in official documents.

59 We have placed the exchange of *sirventes* between Peire and Raimbaut in the period 1165–67 (see p. 4 above).
60 Pattison (*op. cit.*, XXXI, 30–1, and *PMLA*, L, 22–3) considers that a number of those troubadours present at Puivert probably followed the wedding party into Tarrazona, since large numbers of troubadours were often found at the lavish Spanish weddings.
61 *Op. cit.*, p. 129.
62 *Ibid.*
63 The same may be said of the reference to God in VI, l. 61. The reference in IX, l. 11, is perhaps less conventional in that it is supplemented, in the following line, by the description of God as *espirital seinhor*. Attention has, however, already been drawn to the doubtful authenticity of this poem (see also the introduction to IX).
64 *Op. cit.*, pp. 102–4.
65 See note 26 above.
66 *Su e giù per le biografie provenzali*, in *Mélanges Chabaneau*, Rome, 1907, pp. 387–8. De Lollis considers two of the lines (8–9) to be paraphrases of passages from the book of Ecclesiastes.
67 *D'entier vers far eu no pes* (Pillet-Carstens, 63, 6).
68 *Cf.* Jeanroy, *op. cit.*, II, p. 307.
69 *Op. cit.*, p. 114.
70 The same view is held by Jeanroy (*op. cit.*, II, p. 137, note 2).
71 See note 5 above.
72 *Cf.* Appel, *B. von Vent.*, p. xx.
73 *Cf.* Appel, *P. Rogier*, pp. 10–11 (note), and *B. von Vent.*, p. xxi. The version of CR (*chantet*) is later strongly supported by Rajna (*op. cit.*, XLIX, 90) while it is rejected by Crescini (*op. cit.*, LXXXVI, 221 ff and 1229 ff).
74 *Les Troubadours dans leur vie et dans leurs oeuvres*, Paris, 1955, p. 65.
75 *Cf.* Appel, *B. von Vent.*, p. lii; Jeanroy, *op. cit.*, II, pp. 136–7. The approximate period in which Jeanroy (*op. cit.*, I, p. 347) places Bernart's poetic activity (1150–80) is also very similar to that given for Peire's (1160–80).
76 See pp. 23–5 below.
77 See pp. 160–3 below.
78 *Les Poèmes de Gaucelm Faidit*, Paris, 1965, p. 151.
79 *Op. cit.*, No. 15 (pp. 149–50).
80 *Op. cit.*, p. 151 and pp. 31–2.
81 *Op. cit.*, p. 151.
82 The poem must have been written before 1173, the year of Raimbaut's death. Gaucelm's poetic activity is placed approximately in the period 1170–1205 (*cf.* Mouzat, *op. cit.*, p. 31, note 17).
83 *Cf.* note 75 above and Mouzat, *op. cit.*, p. 31.
84 *Cf. Onomastique*, p. 223.
85 Mouzat mentions the ladies concerned in his section on Gaucelm's life (*op. cit.*, pp. 25–41).
86 Appel, *P. Rogier*, p. 6; Diez, *Leben und Werke*, p. 81. Jeanroy (*op. cit.*, I, p. 318) cites the *senhal* as a rare example of one used to describe feelings 'de dépit ou d'humeur'. Millot's view (*Histoire littéraire des troubadours*, I, p. 105) that the *senhal* is used to express praise of Ermengarda's conduct would seem to be based on a misinterpretation whereby he has read *n'* as a negative. Ginguené (*Histoire littéraire de la France*, XV, p. 460) appears to have copied the mistake in regarding

the *senhal* as an expression of 'la haute opinion qu'elle [Ermengarda] avait donnée d'elle par sa manière de gouverner'. Balaguer (*Los trovadores*, III, p. 355) has done the same. He writes *Tort no avetz* and translates *sin tacha, no tenéis tacha*. The duc de la Salle's interpretation of the *senhal* indicates that he also has treated the *n'* as a negative: '. . . une expression de la langue romane qui ne contient pas seulement une approbation du passé et du présent, mais est encore une sorte de confiante affirmation que l'être adoré ne peut se tromper, prendra en toutes circonstances la décision la plus sage et la plus opportune'. (*Troub. Cant.*, I, p. 353.)

87 See section on the order of the poems (p. 29).
88 *Cf.* L. Cocito, *Romania: scritti offerti a F. Piccolo nel suo LXX compleanno*, Naples, 1962, p. 234.
89 See p. 3 above and note to III, l. 64.
90 *Op. cit.*, pp. 7–8.
91 *Op. cit.*, pp. 234–5.
92 *Cf.* Cocito, *op. cit.*, p. 235 (note).
93 The second *tornada* deals with an entirely different matter concerning *dons Sanz* (*cf.* note to l. 54 of the poem and Cocito, *op. cit.*, pp. 235–6). There appear to be no strong grounds for supporting Bergert's suggestion (*op. cit.*, pp. 7–8, note 6) that l. 29 (*Tost venra temps que conostra son tort*) may allude to the *senhal*.
94 *Op. cit.*, pp. 236–7.
95 *Cf.* Cocito, *op. cit.*, p. 237.
96 *Cf.* Appel, *op. cit.*, p. 7. On the other hand, Cocito (*op. cit.*, pp. 233–4, note) considers *n'a tort/tort n'a* to be a common expression and doubts whether it is an allusion to the *senhal*. It should be noted, however, that the expression occurs twice in the two lines. It would not be unreasonable for a poet, reluctant to reveal openly his lady's identity, to employ this kind of device. *Cf.* notes to ll. 49 and 50 of VIIIa.
97 *Cf.* Appel, *op. cit.*, p. 9; Bergert, *op. cit.*, p. 8. On the other hand, Diez (*op. cit.*, p. 80) finds in the poem no grounds for such a suspicion.
98 *Cf.* Bergert, *loc. cit.* See also p. 3 above.
99 *Cf.* Cocito, *op. cit.*, p. 233. See also p. 3 above and the introduction to IX.
100 See IX, note to l. 17.

II THE PLACE OF PEIRE ROGIER'S WORK IN THE POETRY OF THE TROUBADOURS

The conventional themes of troubadour lyrical poetry form the subject matter of Peire Rogier's love poems. The attitude of the poet towards his lady and the advice he offers to others in this respect are strictly in line with the standard doctrines of courtly love. He strongly advocates adherence to the courtly virtues of humility, discretion, patience, moderation, and complete loyalty and devotion to the lady who is the source of *joy* and *pretz* and from whom the submissive and faithful lover may hope to receive, as his reward, a long-desired favour (*merce*). The conventional expressions of discouragement or despair found in Peire's songs usually give way to an appeal for hope and patience, and none of the poems is allowed to end on a pessimistic note.

With the exception of IX, which is of doubtful authorship, the poems do not, on the whole, seem to be concerned with particular events or situations personal to the troubadour; rather, the sentiments they express tend to be couched in objective and general terms. Peire's work quite often appears to be less a means of voicing the poet's individual feelings than a vehicle for instruction in courtly behaviour, an impression which is strengthened by the frequent adoption of a didactic tone.[1]

While the subject matter of Peire Rogier's songs may be conventional and lack originality, his style is generally free from the artificial novelties and contrived obscurities found in the work of many of those troubadours who strove after originality of one kind or another. It is perhaps in the clarity, simplicity and naturalness of his style that Peire's chief merit as a poet lies. These are the qualities which have led him to be described as a forerunner, with Bernart de Ventadour, of the *trobar leu*.[2]

Jeanroy observes that, in his versification, Peire adheres closely to the conventions of his day, making frequent use of word refrains and isolated rhymes and showing a clear preference for the octosyllabic line. At the same time, the troubadour differs from his contemporaries in his avoidance of rare rhymes and over-complicated stanza constructions.[3]

Dialogue form. A distinctive feature of Peire Rogier's poetry and one to which particular attention is usually drawn in references to the troubadour is his skilful use of the dialogue form.[4] It introduces a lively, dramatic element into his poetry, varying the pace of a poem and breaking the uniformity of the lines. In IV, for example, the use of dialogue prevents any heaviness which might have resulted from the monotonous repetition of the long decasyllabic line.[5] In none of the songs does Peire continue the dialogue through all the stanzas; it is his economic and measured use of the device which makes it all the more effective.[6]

In the three poems chiefly concerned (IV, VI and VII), the dialogue may be seen as conveying, in dramatic form, the struggle of the various conflicting emotions between which the poet appears to waver,[7] a struggle which ultimately serves only to emphasise his strength of mind.[8] In IV the dialogue enables the poet to advocate the discreet and patient conduct of the courtly lover by providing the opportunity of replying point by point to the practical objections raised by the interlocutor.[9] The same is true of VI, except that here the poet is not on the defensive but, rather, offers positive advice to combat the discouragement of the interlocutor. It has been observed that the dialogue has the effect of reinforcing the motifs expressed in the first half of the poem.[10] The device is employed differently in VII but the poem, like IV and VI, still ends on a note of encouragement. A series of apparently involuntary complaints and expressions of doubt and despair, interjected in dialogue form, occupy the first half of the song but eventually give way to an uninterrupted reassertion by the poet of his devotion to his lady and of his general optimism.

Peire appears to have been among the first troubadours to use dialogue. A few of his contemporaries include it in some of their work but the difficulty in dating the poems concerned prevents us from determining whether any of them employed the device before Peire.[11]

Notes

1 *Cf.* pp. 4, 8 and 15 (note 26) above. Jeanroy (*Poésie Lyrique*, II, p. 138) makes the following observation: 'Peire Rogier ne manquait, on le voit, ni de finesse ni d'esprit; mais la poésie n'est pour lui qu'un jeu, et dans ces agréables badinages il serait vain de chercher l'écho d'un sentiment sincère.'
2 *Cf.* Jeanroy, *op. cit.*, II, pp. 136–8.
3 *Cf.* Jeanroy, *op. cit.*, II, p. 138. See our section on metrics (pp. 26–8) for an analysis of the metrical schemes and rhymes employed by Peire.
   Appel (*P. Rogier*, pp. 21–33) examines various aspects of the versification of Peire's work with reference to that of the work of other troubadours.
4 Reference is made to this particular stylistic device in the *Leys d'Amors* under the heading *cobla tensonada o tensonans, en autra maniera dicha enterrogativa o enterrogans o razonans* (J. Anglade, *Las Leys d'Amors*, II, pp. 165–6). As both Appel and Selbach observe, however, only the fifth example quoted may be suitably placed in this category (see Appel, *op. cit.*, p. 16, and L. Selbach, *Das Streitgedicht in der altprovenzalischen Lyrik und sein Verhältnis zu ähnlichen Dichtungen anderer Litteraturen*, Marburg, 1886, p. 36). It clearly corresponds to the dialogue form found in Peire Rogier's work:

> Halas! ques has? Greu mal. E qual?
> Fervor d'amor? O yeu. Coral?
> O be. De me? De te. Per que?
> . . .

Cf. VI in this edition.
5 *Cf.* Cocito, *op. cit.*, p. 231.
6 This view is supported by Appel (*op. cit.*, p. 14), Cocito (*op. cit.*, p. 229) and Jeanroy (*op. cit.*, II, p. 138). The latter considers that, in contrast, Giraut de Bornelh is too persistent in his use of dialogue. Nelli and Lavaud are of the same view (*Les Troubadours*, I, p. 625, note 2). It is interesting to note, however, that M. de Riquer (*Resumen de literatura provenzal trovadoresca*, Barcelona, 1948, p. 47) is of the opposite opinion and that it is Peire whom he regards as using dialogue excessively.
7 *Cf.* Appel, *loc. cit.*, and Selbach, *loc. cit.* As for the identity of the person with whom the poet is conversing in each of the poems, it is clear that, whenever the first person of the verb is used for the interlocutor as well as for the poet, the poet is addressing himself (see VII, ll. 7–22) (*cf.* Appel, *loc. cit.*). The two cases found in III of the use of the first person may well be regarded as rhetorical questions

rather than examples of the dialogue form (see ll. 16-17 and 40-2). (Rhetorical questions or statements also appear in V, ll. 20, 34, and VI, l. 3.)

In the case of IV, V and VI it is evidently a question of two different interlocutors. We agree with Appel (*op. cit.*, pp. 14-16) in ruling out the presence of a second person and in assuming that the poet has in fact *imagined* a second person in order to provide himself with an adversary. Jeanroy (*loc. cit.*) implies his support of this view ('. . . en engageant, avec lui - même *ou un interlocuteur supposé*, . . .').

This interpretation seems to us preferable to that offered by Cocito, who considers the dialogue in each of the three poems, as in VII, to be between the poet and his heart (*op. cit.*, pp. 225 and 230-2). The heart would become, as a result, clearly inconsistent in its attitude and, as Cocito himself indicates, would in fact assume two contradictory roles. In IV it would be the opponent, and in VI the advocate, of the conduct of the courtly lover. It is interesting to note that, in the case of IV, Suchier (*Goett. gel. Anzeigen* (1883), 1343) identifies the interlocutor with the reader.

8 *Cf.* Cocito, *op. cit.*, p. 228.
9 Appel (*op. cit.*, p. 14, note 2) describes the part played by the dialogue in the development of the mood of IV. The dialogue consists initially of long sentences but the exchanges become shorter as the struggle between hope and doubt becomes more intense. The state of uncertainty conveyed by the dialogue finally gives way, in the last stanza, to a mood of confidence and joy.
10 *Cf.* Cocito, *op. cit.*, p. 224.
11 Appel refers to this difficulty (*op. cit.*, p. 16) and names a number of other troubadours who used the dialogue form (pp. 12-13).

A comparison of the last two stanzas of Peire Rogier's *Ges non puesc en bon vers fallir* with parts of Giraut de Bornelh's *Ailas, com mor!* (Kolsen, *G. de Born*, No. 2 (I, pp. 6-10)) suggests a close connection between the two poems. Kolsen (*op. cit.*, II, p. 17) refers to the similarity between the first lines in each case and goes on to compare ll. 54 and 55-6 of the first poem with ll. 33-4 and 38, 40 respectively of the second. There are, however, other parallels between the two poems both in content and in style. The following comparison provides a fuller indication of the similarities:

Ges non puesc en bon vers fallir

Lines 41-3: Ailas! — Que plangz? — Ia tem murir. —
Que as? — Am. — E trop? — Ieu hoc, tan
que·n muer. — Mors? — Oc. — Non potz guerir?

Ailas, com mor!

Lines 1-3: Ailas, com mor! — Quez as, amis? —
Eu sui traïs! —
Per cal razo? —

Lines 8-12: As enaissi to cor en lai? —
Oc eu, plus fort. —
Est donc aissi pres de la mort? —
Oc eu, plus fort que no·us sai dir. —
. Per que 't laissas aissi morir? —

Ges non puesc en bon vers fallir

Lines 49–56: Cosselh n'ai. — Qual? — Vuelh m'en partir. —
No far! — Si faray. — Quers ton dan. —
Que·n puesc als? — Vols t'en ben jauzir? —
Oc, mout. — Crei mi. — Era diguatz. —
Sias humils, francs, larcx e pros. —
Si·m fai mal? — Sufr'en patz. — Suy pres? —
Tu oc, s'amar vols; mas si·m cres,
aissi·t poiras jauzir de liey.

Ailas, com mor!

Lines 25–34: Senher, e cals conselhs n'er pres? —
Bos e cortes. —
Er lo·m diatz! —
Tu venras denan leis viatz
Et enquerras la de s'amor. —
E si s'o ten a dezonor? —
No·t chal! —
E s'ela·m respon lach ni mal? —
Sias sofrens,
Que totztems bos sofrire vens! —

Lines 37–9: Nos? — Oc be. — Sol qu'ilh o volgues! —
Er. — Que? — Si·m cres. —
Crezutz siatz! —

Kolsen (*op. cit.*, II, pp. 16–17) considers that in *Ailas, com mor!* Giraut has not only imagined the presence of a second person, as Peire Rogier generally does, but has a particular friend in mind. He gives reasons for supposing that the friend is, in fact, Raimbaut d'Orange. This leads him to suggest that the poem could have been written jointly by Giraut and Raimbaut during the time of their first acquaintance before Giraut gave Raimbaut the name of *Linhaure*, and to propose the date 1166. He then makes reference to Peire's stay at Raimbaut's court and to the similarity between *Ailas, com mor!* and *Ges non puesc* and suggests that Peire and Raimbaut may possibly have been jointly responsible for the composition of the two stanzas of dialogue in *Ges non puesc*. The fact that the dialogue is introduced suddenly and without warning after five regular stanzas and continues uninterrupted for the whole of the last two stanzas could imply that these stanzas were composed separately from the rest of the poem. It is worth noting that in the case of Peire Rogier's other songs, IV, V and VII, the dialogue is introduced less obtrusively and fits more naturally into the body of the poem.

If we accept the possibility of collaboration on the part of the two troubadours an approximate date may be suggested for *Ges non puesc*. A good deal of speculation is inevitable, however, in view of the imprecise nature of the other dates we have available. In order to co-operate in any joint project of this kind Peire and Raimbaut would probably have needed to be on more intimate terms than their exchange of *sirventes* suggests. The long stay which the *Vida* claims Peire enjoyed at Raimbaut's court would have given them the opportunity of getting to know each other better. The poem is therefore unlikely to have been composed before the period 1165–67 (if Pattison is correct in placing Raimbaut's *sirventes*, *Peire Rotgier, a trassaillir*, in this period (*cf. R. d'Orange*, p. 37 and p. 90, note 1)). This assumption is consistent with the stage at which the use of dialogue appears in Raimbaut's poetic development; it occurs, for the first time, in a poem composed about 1165 (Pattison, *op. cit.*, p. 39) but is common in poems dating from the middle of his career, i.e. about 1167-69 (*cf.* Pattison, *loc. cit.*). On p. 45 of his edition Pattison gives a table showing a suggested chronology of Raimbaut's works. Kolsen (*op. cit.*, II, p. 17) refers to the unexpected way in which the dialogue is introduced in *Ges non puesc* and sees a close similarity with the *gap* genre of Raimbaut, particularly with his poem *Escotatz, mas no say que s'es* (R. d'Orange, XXIV), in which lines of prose alternate with the poetry. Pattison places the *gap* series of poems between the years 1168 and 1171 (*op. cit.*, p. 43) and, within this period, fixes *Escotatz, mas no say que s'es* about 1169 (*op. cit.*, p. 42 and p. 154, note 1). If Raimbaut did contribute to *Ges non puesc* these dates would lend support to the suggestion that the poem was written after the exchange of *sirventes* with Peire.

If Raimbaut was partly responsible for the composition of *Ges non puesc* in the period suggested above and if Kolsen's approximate date of 1166 for *Ailas, com mor!* was correct, then we could conclude that Giraut de Bornelh's poem had been the forerunner of Peire's. However, the strong case for placing *Ailas, com mor!* later than 1166 leaves unresolved the question as to which of the two poems was the earlier. Kolsen himself (*op. cit.*, II, p. 16) remarks that it seems surprising that, at this early stage in a career which dated only from about 1165 (*cf.* Jeanroy, *op. cit.*, II, p. 51, note 2), Giraut should address his interlocutor, Raimbaut, in the familiar second person in contrast with his much more formal manner a few years later in the *tenson* on *trobar clus*, placed by Pattison shortly before Christmas, 1170 (*op. cit.*, p. 23). One may wonder why Giraut should write his part of the *tenson* with such deference to Raimbaut if they had met and written together as early as 1166. Kolsen (*loc. cit.*) considers that the apparent discrepancy may be explained by the difference, in nature and content, between the dialogue form and the *tenson*. Pattison (*op. cit.*, p. 176, note to l. 58) regards Giraut's constant deference to Raimbaut in the *tenson* as support for his theory that the troubadours were at Raimbaut's court at the time of the composition. It is quite possible, of course, that Giraut's confident attitude at such an early stage in his career was a reflection of Raimbaut's youth. If Pattison's conclusions about the year of Raimbaut's birth are correct (*op. cit.*, p. 12 and p. 36) the troubadour would, in fact, have been only about twenty years old in 1166.

There are, however, other possible reasons for placing *Ailas, com mor!* later than 1166. Firstly, Raimbaut had probably produced by that time only one poem containing dialogue and, according to Pattison, did not begin to employ the device to any great extent until about 1167. Secondly, if Giraut's career dated from about 1165 (see above) there is the question as to whether his art would have developed sufficiently by 1166, after only one year of writing, for him to produce a work such as *Ailas, com mor!* Even if it had, one wonders whether he would have been ambitious enough to attempt a work of this kind with Raimbaut who, although still young and with perhaps not more than four years' experience of writing, was clearly the more established poet (Pattison regards Raimbaut's career as dating from 1162 (*op. cit.*, p. 36)).

It is perhaps appropriate here to observe the similarity between the two stanzas of dialogue in *Ges non puesc* and parts of the narrative romance *Flamenca* written in the following century. (*Cf.* Appel, *op. cit.*, pp. 15-16.) There are several instances of dialogue in the romance, but it is the conversation which Guillaume and his lady succeed in holding in church, at the rate of two or three words every Sunday and Feast day, which is especially reminiscent of Peire Rogier's two stanzas. (*Cf.* S. Debenedetti, 'Flamenca', in *Oposculi di filologia romanza*, Turin, 1921; Nelli and Lavaud, *op. cit.*, I, p. 625.) In the course of more than 1,500 lines of poetry the following words are exchanged:

> Ailas! — Que plans? — Mur mi. — De que? — D'amor. —
> Per cui? — Per vos. — Qu'en puesc? — Garir. — Conssi? — Per gein. —
> Pren l'i! — Pres l'ai. — E cal? — Iretz. — Es on? — Als banz. —
> Cora? — Jorn breu e gent. — Plas mi.

The beginning of stanza six of *Ges non puesc* particularly springs to mind when, at one stage in the dialogue, Flamenca and her companions review the individual words exchanged so far in order to find the next suitable word with which to reply to Guillaume. The words are repeated as one line to see if they fit together satisfactorily:

> Ailas! — Que plans? — Muer mi. — De que?

(P. Meyer's edition: l. 4,577; Nelli and Lavaud edition: l. 4,574.) (*Cf.* Appel, *op. cit.*, p. 14, note 3; Nelli and Lavaud, *op. cit.*, I, p. 625.)

III METRIC TABLES

We have adopted the system of tables employed by Kurt Almqvist in *Les Poésies du troubadour Guilhem Adémar* (Uppsala, 1951), pp. 76 ff, and by Peter T. Ricketts in *Les Poésies de Guilhem de Montanhagol* (Toronto, 1964), pp. 33 ff. The first series of tables are also similar to those employed by Appel (pp. 30–1). Short horizontal lines indicate where the *tornadas* begin. The number of such lines denotes the number of *tornadas*. Feminine rhymes are indicated by the sign '.

(a) *Metrical scheme and rhymes of each poem*

I seven stanzas		II seven stanzas		III five stanzas	
7a	ors	5a′	enta	8a	is
7b	uelh	6b′	ire	8b	an
7c′	ura	5a′	enta	8b	an
7d	ais	6b′	ire	8c	ei
7a	ors	7c	e	4c	ei
7c′	ura	8d	al	8d	ètz
7e′	uelha	7c	e	4e	ai
		8d	al	4e	ai
		6e′	vivre	8d	ètz
				8f	os
				8f	os

| IV | V | VI |
| seven stanzas | six stanzas | seven stanzas |

IV		V		VI	
10a	*ort*	8a	*is*	8a	*ir*
10b	*e*	8b	*an*	8b	*au*
10b	*e*	8b	*an*	8a	*ir*
=		=		–	
10c	*en*	8c	*es*	8c	*atz*
10d	*ir*	8d	*ai*	8d	*os*
10d	*ir*	8d	*ai*	8e	*es*
10e	*er*	8e	*e*	8e	*es*
				8f	*èis(liey)*

| VII | VIII | IX |
| seven stanzas | seven stanzas | six stanzas (+ three missing) |

VII		VIII		IX	
8a	*is*	8a	*er*	7a	*ais, an, anha', itz, itz, ura'.*
8b	*ir*	8b	*atz*	7a	,,
8b	*ir*	8b	*atz*	7a	,,
–		8a	*er*	7a	,,
8c	*ort*	–		7a	,,
8d	*ens*	8c	*ai*	7b	*or*
8e	*uelh*	8c	*ai*		
		8d	*os*		

(b) *Detailed features of Peire Rogier's metrics*

Number of stanzas per poem	Number of poems	Number of tornadas per poem	Number of poems
Five: No. III.	1	One: I, VI, VII, VIII.	4
Six: No. V.	1	Two: II, III, IV, V.	4
Seven: Nos. I, II, IV, VI, VII, VIII.	6		
Nine: No. IX. (Three stanzas are missing.)	1		

Number of lines per stanza	Number of poems	Number of lines per tornada	Number of poems
Six: VII, IX.	2	Three: I, II, VII, VIII.	4
Seven: I, IV, V, VIII.	4	Four: IV, V.	2
Eight: VI.	1	Five: III, VI.	2
Nine: II.	1		
Eleven: III.	1		

Number of syllables per line	Number of poems	Number of rhymes per stanza	Number of poems
Five, six, seven and eight: II.	1	Two: IX.	1
Seven: I, IX.	2	Four: VII.	1
Eight: V, VI, VII, VIII.	4	Five: I, II, IV, V, VII.	5
Eight and Four: III.	1	Six: III, VI.	2
Ten: IV.	1		

Proportion of masculine and feminine rhymes	Number of poems
Masculine rhymes only: III, IV, V, VI, VII, VIII.	6
Feminine rhymes only: none.	–
Mixed rhymes: I (two rhymes out of five), II (three rhymes out of five), IX (one rhyme out of two in two of the stanzas).	3

IV ORDER OF THE POEMS

It is impossible to establish the chronology of the poems, as only three of them (III, VIII and possibly IV[1]) contain any evidence which enables us to give them an approximate date. We have therefore placed them in the order adopted by Appel, according to the stage in Peire Rogier's career to which he suggests they might belong. It is in fact the order in which the poems appear in the MSS I and K.[2] Appel[3] observes the following peculiar features shared by poems I and II which suggest that they belong to the same period of composition: they are the only *cansos*, apart from IX, to make no allusion, direct or indirect, to the *senhal Tort n'avetz* and, with III, are the only ones in which the dialogue form is not used; they are also alone in including Peire's name in the *tornada* and in opening with a reference to the season.[4] IX is placed last in view of its independent nature and the doubt attached to its authenticity,[5] while the position of VIII is governed by its link with VIIIa.

The attempt at a systematic order which Appel sees in I and K[6] may also be found in D; here the order is the same except that III, IV, V appear last after VIIIa. We may thus assume, with Appel,[7] that these poems were originally omitted only to be added later in a different place. An examination of the order of poems in the MSS A and C also reveals a certain similarity to that in IK:

A: VI, I, VII, VIII, VIIIa, II, III.
C: IV, III, VI, V, I, II, VII, VIII, VIIIa.

In the case of C it is worth noting that, apart from following the sequence of IK for I, II, VII, VIII, VIIIa, it groups together III, IV, V, VI, but in a different order. Of the other MSS, which on the whole offer an independent order, E links VIII with VIIIa and M VI with VII.

Further justification for choosing the order of IK may be provided by the metre and rhyme schemes employed in the poems (see the metric tables): (*a*) IV and V have a common rhyme scheme which is fairly similar to that of III and that of VII; (*b*) I, VI, VII, VIII each have one *tornada*, while II, III, IV, V each have two; (*c*) the octosyllabic line is the most common in Peire Rogier's work; the four poems in which the line is adopted throughout are V, VI, VII, VIII; (*d*) in most of the poems masculine rhymes only are employed; the only exceptions are I, II, IX, in which the rhymes are mixed.

With the title of each poem we give the number in this edition followed, in brackets, by the number in Pillet and Carstens, *Bibliographie der Troubadours*.

Notes

1 See note to III, 1. 64, and IV, 1. 54, and p. 4 above.
2 *Cf.* Appel, *P. Rogier*, pp. ii–iii and p. 8, note. Like Appel, we prefer a less arbitrary basis for grouping the poems than their alphabetical order, which Bartsch (*Grundriss*) and Pillet and Carstens (*Bibliographie der Troubadours*) employ. It should be noted that Bartsch later considers Appel's order to be justified (*Literaturblatt*, IV, 66).

3 *Op. cit.*, p. 7.
4 Jeanroy (*Poésie Lyrique*, II, p. 128, note 3) observes that Peire Rogier differs from his contemporaries in departing from the troubadours' well established tradition of beginning many of their poems with a description of the season. In fact the second of the only two examples found in Peire's work occupies no more than one line.
5 *Cf.* introduction to IX.
6 *Op. cit.*, p. 8, note.
7 *Ibid.*

V THE MANUSCRIPTS

In most cases we have obtained microfilms or have consulted the MSS themselves. However, as we have been unable to locate ω, which is no longer at Bergamo, we have resorted to the diplomatic edition of the MS. The only other cases in which use has been made of the diplomatic edition are G in VIII, N^2 in the *Vida*, D^c in VIIIa, and β^2 in VIII.

By means of the following abbreviations we indicate at the end of the description of each MS below the kind of document consulted: (M) microfilm, (MS) where the MS itself has been consulted, (ED) diplomatic edition.

The poems of Peire Rogier are found in the following MSS:

A   Rome, Biblioteca Vaticana, 5232, Diplom. ed.: Pakscher and De Lollis, *Studi di filologia romanza*, III, 1–670. (M) Six poems: I, II, III, VI, VII, VIII. *Vida*.
B   Paris, Bibliothèque Nationale, fr. 1592. Collation with A in Pakscher and De Lollis, *op. cit.*, 671 ff. (MS) Two poems: I, III. *Vida*.
C   Paris, Bibliothèque Nationale, fr. 856. (MS) Eight poems: I, II, III, IV, V, VI, VII, VIII.
D   Modena, Biblioteca Estense, α, R, 4, 4, ff. 1–151. (M) Five poems: I, II, VI, VII, VIII.
D^a *Ibid.*, ff. 153–211. (M) Three poems: III, IV, V.
D^c *Ibid.*, ff. 243–60. Diplom. ed.: Teulié and Rossi, *L'Anthologie provençale de maître Ferrari de Ferrare* in *AdM*, XIII, 60 ff., 199 ff., 371 ff.; XIV, 197 ff., 523 ff. (M) Three poems (all fragmentary): IV (stanzas I and VI), V (stanzas II and IV), VIII (stanzas III, IV and VI).
E   Paris, Bibliothèque Nationale, fr. 1749. (MS) Four poems: I, V, VII, VIII. *Vida*.
G   Milan, Biblioteca Ambrosiana, R71. Diplom. ed.: Bertoni, *Il canzoniere provenzale della Biblioteca Ambrosiana R71*, Dresden, 1912 (in *Gesellschaft für romanische Literatur*, XXVIII). (ED) One poem: VIII.

I   Paris, Bibliothèque Nationale, fr. 854. (MS) Eight poems: I, II, III, IV, V, VI, VII, VIII. *Vida*.
K   Paris, Bibliothèque Nationale, fr. 12473. (MS) Eight poems: I, II, III, IV, V, VI, VII, VIII. *Vida*.
M   Paris, Bibliothèque Nationale, fr. 12474. (MS) Six poems: I, II, IV, V, VI, VII.
N   New York, Pierpont Morgan Library, MS 819 (formerly Cheltenham Library of Mr T. Fitz-Roy Fenwick, 8335). (M) Two poems: II, III.
N^2 Berlin, Königliche Bibliothek, cod. Phillips 1910. Diplom. ed.: Pillet, *Archiv.*, 101, 365 ff.; 102, 179 ff. (ED) *Vida*.
O   Rome, Biblioteca Vaticana, 3208. Diplom. ed.: De Lollis, 'Il canzoniere provenzale O (Cod. Vat. 3208)' in *Atti della R. Accademia dei Lincei. Anno CCLXXXIII*, 1886. (M) One poem: VI.
R   Paris, Bibliothèque Nationale, fr. 22543. (MS) Seven poems: I, II, III, IV, VI, VII, VIII. *Vida*.
S   Oxford, Bodleian Library, Douce 269. Diplom. ed.: Shepard, *The Oxford Provençal Chansonnier*, Princeton and Paris, 1927. (MS) One poem: VI.
T   Paris, Bibliothèque Nationale, fr. 15211. (MS) Four poems: IV, VI, VII, VIII.
U   Florence, Biblioteca Laurenziana, Plut. XLI, cod. 43. Diplom. ed.: Grützmacher, *Archiv.*, 35, 363 ff. (M) One poem: VIII.
a^1 Modena, Biblioteca Estense, Càmpori γ. N. 8. 4; 11, 12, 13. Diplom. ed.: Bertoni, *Il canzoniere provenzale di Bernart Amoros (Complemento Càmpori)*, Friburg, 1911. (M) Three poems: III, VII, VIII.
c   Florence, Biblioteca Laurenziana, Plut. XC inf. 26. Diplom. ed.: Mario Pelaez, 'Il canzoniere provenzale c' in *Studi di filologia romanza*, VII, 244 ff.; E. Stengel, *Die apr. Liedersammlung c der Laurenziana in Florenz nach einer in seinem Besitz befindlichen alten Abschrift*, Leipzig, 1899. (M) Three poems: I, VI, IX.
ω   Bergamo, Biblioteca di Paolo Gaffuri. Diplom. ed.: De Lollis, 'Un frammento di canzoniere provenzale' in *Studi medievali*, I, 561 ff. (ED) Five poems (fragmentary): I (p. 577), II (pp. 577–8), III (pp. 578–9), IV (p. 579), V (pp. 576–7).
$β^2$ Folio 137v of R, constituting the text of Raimon Vidal's *Abrils issi'e mais intrava*. Diplom. ed.: Bartsch, *Denkmäler*, pp. 144 ff.; W. Bohs, ' "Abrils issi'e mays intrava," Lehrgedicht von Raimon Vidal von Bezaudun' in *Romanische Forschungen*, XV (1904), 204 ff. (ED) One poem: VIII (extract: stanza VI).

Quotations from Peire Rogier's work (Nos. VI and VIII) are included in the *Breviari d'Amor* of Matfré Ermengaud de Béziers (ed. G. Azaïs, Béziers and Paris, 1862–81). We have been able to employ all the MSS of this work[1] and denote them by the letters used by Brunel (*Bibliographie des Mss littéraires en ancien provençal*, Paris, 1935). In order to distinguish them from the other MSS we have placed the letters in brackets.

(A) Paris, Bibliothèque Nationale, fr. 857. Diplom. ed.: Azaïs, *op. cit.*
(B) Paris, Bibliothèque Nationale, fr. 9219.
(C) Paris, Bibliothèque Nationale, fr. 858.
(D) Paris, Bibliothèque Nationale, fr. 1601.
(F) Vienna, K. K. Hof. Bibliotek, 2563.
(G) Vienna, National Library, 2583.
(H) Lyons, Bibliothèque Municipale, 1351.
(I) Carpentras, Bibliothèque Inguimbertine, 380.
(K) London, British Museum, Harleian, 4940.
(L) London, British Museum, Royal 19. C. I.
(M) Escurial, Biblioteca de San Lorenzo, S, I, No. 3.
(N) Leningrad, Public Library, Ms. Prov., F. v. XIV, I.

We list at the head of each poem the MSS concerned, indicating the exact location of the poem in each MS. The references follow Pillet and Carstens, *Bibliographie der Troubadours*, except in the case of N, where the new foliation is adopted,[2] the old reference being given in brackets. Where appropriate, the page, or number of the poem, in the diplomatic edition follows in brackets immediately afterwards. The other previous editions of the poem are also listed.

Notes

1 Dr P. T. Ricketts, Senior Lecturer in Romance Philology at the University of Birmingham, is engaged in preparing a critical edition of the *Breviari* and kindly consulted all the MSS for us.
2 *Cf.* C. F. Buhler, 'The Phillips manuscript of Provençal poetry now MS 819 of the Pierpont Morgan Library', in *Speculum*, XXII (1947), 68–74.

VI CHOICE OF BASE MANUSCRIPT, ESTABLISHMENT OF TEXT, EXPLANATORY NOTES AND VARIANTS

We have employed C as the base MS for all the poems except VIII, for which A has been preferred, and IX, which is offered only by c. Our reasons for choosing A in the case of VIII are given in the classification of the MSS. In our edition of Raimbaut d'Orange's reply to Peire Rogier (VIIIa) we have followed Pattison in adopting A as the base MS. For the choice of the base MS in the case of the *Vida* see the classification of the MSS.

The choice of C as base MS is justified by the quality and general clarity of its readings, which contain few individualisms. In a number of cases it offers a sensible and comprehensible text where other MSS are unintelligible. Another factor in its favour is the general coherence and uniformity of its spelling. However, reference should be made at the same time to the reservations which have been expressed about the chansonnier of C generally[1] and which apply equally to the section containing the work of Peire Rogier. The scribe of C, with a large number of sources at his disposal, tends to offer eclectic texts, establishing the text of the poem on the basis of several traditions. A comparison with other MSS leads us to suspect that the scribe has also, at times, introduced his own version in order to improve upon the reading of his model or where his model appears to him to be either obscure or corrupt. As a result the text offered by C is sometimes rendered suspect by its very quality.

In each poem we have adhered to the base MS as far as possible. The reading of another MS has been chosen only (*a*) where the metre or meaning requires it and (*b*) in *most* of the instances where the base MS is clearly independent and opposed to all the other traditions. In those cases where none of the MSS offers an acceptable reading we have corrected the base MS. The letters and words added are placed in brackets, while replacements and corrections are italicised.

In the notes accompanying the *Vida* and each poem account has been taken of important textual points, historical and personal references, and problems of interpretation. The notes have also been used, to a great extent, (*a*) to explain, in each case, the reasons for departing from the base MS, (*b*) to justify a number of the instances in which it is retained despite its independence, (*c*) to comment wherever our text differs from Appel's and, in the case of VIIIa, from Pattison's.

The text of the *Vida* and that of each poem is followed by a list of *all* the variants, essential, secondary and orthographical. Semicolons are used to indicate which variants pertain to a particular word, or group of words, appearing in the text. Where it is not obvious which is the word or group of words concerned we have placed it in front of a single bracket (]) and then listed the variants.

Note

1 *Cf*. G. *Adémar*, p. 92, in which Almqvist quotes from Gröber, *Romanische Studien herausgeg. von E. Boehmer*, II, pp. 574–6, and from Bertoni, *I trovatori d'Italia*, p. 188, note 2. *Cf*. also Bartsch, *Literaturblatt*, IV, 66 (review of Appel's edition).

Vida

Seven MSS. A 107 (p. 332); B 107 (p. 695; Mahn, *Biogr.*, p. 9); E 189; I 12; K 2; N² 23 (XIV, *Archiv.*, 102, 204); R 3a.

Editions. Parn. Occ., p. 24; Raynouard, *Choix*, v, 330; *MW*, I, 116; Appel, p. 34; Chabaneau, *Biographies*, p. 261; Piccolo, *Primavera*, p. 96; Riquer, *Lírica*, p. 219; Panvini, *Biografie*, p. 113; Favati, *Biografie*, p. 214; Boutière-Schutz, *Biographies*, p. 267.

Classification. The MSS may be clearly divided into three groups: AB, ER, IKN². This classification is borne out particularly by the following instances.*

AB: omission of *e trobava* (1) and *N'Anfos de Castela* (11); independence of B where the text is omitted in A: (6) *receup els*, (7) *et apellava*, (9) *e partit lo de si*; together with the sections in the latter part of the *Vida* which are omitted in all the other MSS.

ER: contain only the first two lines of the quotation from *Seign'en Raymbaut*; inclusion of *N'Anfos de Castela* (11).

IKN²: inclusion of *d'aqella encontrada e per temor del dit (dir) de la gen s'il* (8) and (9), and of *dolenz e pensius e consiros e marritz* (10); inclusion of the second stanza of the quotation; absence of the part of the *Vida* following the quotation.

R, followed by AB, is the most individualistic of the MSS.

I is chosen as base for most of the *Vida*.† E is employed for the latter part, omitted in I, as it is the most consistently reliable of the other MSS, apart from being quite closely linked with IKN², *cf.* (1) *e trobava* (with R); (4) *fort* (with R); (5) *e f.*;

---

* See G. Favati, *Biografie* (pp. 415–16), for further examples of the relationship between the MSS.

† Favati (*op. cit.*) chooses AB as base while Boutière and Schutz (*Biographies*) prefer I both for this *Vida* and for the other *Vidas* as a whole. The reasons for their general preference of IK to AB are outlined in *op. cit.*, p. xlv.

Boutière (*op. cit.*, p. xxxiv and 'Quelques Observations sur le texte des *Vidas* et des *Razos* dans les chansonniers provençaux AB et IK' in *French and Provençal Lexicography*, Ohio, 1964, pp. 133–7) cites the respective readings of A(E) and B of the *Vida* from *lonc temps estet* to *gran honor al mon ac* as an example of the numerous occasions on which A and B separate, one of them joining the MSS of a different group and the other being independent. The MS offering the longest text is generally the independent one. He thus attempts to demonstrate that the two MSS which Favati has generally followed were far from being 'vrais jumeaux' in the same way as IK and that a number of intermediate versions must have existed between them and the archetype.

(6) *receup e·ls* omitted (with R); (8) *cum, elan f.*; (10) *que f.*; (10) 1 *senher*.

(1) Peire Rogiers si fo d'Alverne e fo canorgues de Clarmon. E fo gentils hom e bels et avinenz, e savis de letras e de sen natural; e cantava e trobava ben. (2) E laisset la canorga e fetz se joglars et anet per cortz, e foron grasit li sieu cantar. (3) E venc s'en a Narbona, en la cort de ma domna Ermengarda, qu'era adoncs de gran valor e de gran pretz. (4) Et ella l'acuilli fort e ill fetz grans bens. (5) E s'enamoret d'ella e fetz sos vers e sas cansos d'ella. (6) Et ella los pres en grat. (7) E la clamava Tort-n'avez. (8) Lonc temps estet ab ela en cort e si fo crezut qu'el agues joi d'amor d'ella; don ella·n fo blasmada per la gen d'aqella encontrada. (9) E per temor del dit de la gen si·l det comjat e·l parti de se. (10) Et el s'en anet dolenz e pensius e consiros e marritz a·n Rambaut d'Aurenga, si cum el dis e·l sirventes que fetz de lui:

> Seingner Raimbaut, per vezer
> de vos lo conort e·l solatz
> son sai vengutz tost e viatz,
> mas que non sui per vostr'aver;
> que saber voill, quant m'en partrai,   5
> s'es tals lo caps com hom lo fai,
> E se n'es plus o meinz o mai
> Qu'om aug dir ni comtar de vos.
>
> Tant ai de sen e de saber
> e tant sui savis e membratz,   10
> Quant aurai vostres faiz gardatz,
> Qu'al partir eu sabrai lo ver,
> S'es tals lo caps com hom retrai,
> Qu'enqueron m'en lai entre nos.

(11) lonc tems estet ab En Raimbaut. Et estet en Espanha ab lo bon rei N'Anfos de Castela et ab lo bon rei N'Anfos d'Arago, et ab lo bon comte Raimon de Toloza. (12) Gran honor ac e·l mon tan com el hi estet, mas pueis se rendet a l'orde de Granmon e lai el definet.

Variants. (1) Rotgier *ER*, Rotgiers *AB*; si *lacking R*; Alvergne *N²*, Alvernge *AB*, Alvernhe *ER*; d'A. de la ciutat de Clarmon e f. c. *N²*; e fo *lacking R*; canorges *ABKN²*; e fo *lacking R*; gentils] bels *R*; homs *R*, om *K*; e bels *lacking E*; bel *E*; avinen *E*, avinens *ABR*; e savis hom de letras *A*; e cantava be *E*, e chantava ben *N²*, e quantava ben *K*; e trobava *lacking AB*; be *ER*. (2) e laisset la canorga *lacking R*; laiset *E*; canorgua *E*; fes *ER*, fez *KN²*; joglar *IKN²R*, jotglar *E*; e a. p. c. *R*; e. f. g.] e fō mot grazitz *R*; foror *N²*; grazit *ABE*; li sieu cantar *lacking R*; sei *E*, seu *N²*; chantar *ABEN²*. (3) Nerbona *A*; dompna *ABN²*, dona *ER*; eimeniarda *E*, na esmēiartz *R*, n'Esmergarda *AB*; qera *AN²R*, qe era *B*; adoncs *lacking AR*, adonx *E*; e de gran pretz *lacking R*; *between* valor *and* e s'e.: qeil fetz gran ben e gran honor *A*. (4) *Cf.* (3) *A*; ela *R*; lacoillic *B*, lacuillit *E*, laculhi *R*; fort ben *B*; *between* fort (ben) *and* e ill f.: el honret *B*, el onret *ER*; e ill] el *R*; fes *ER*, fez *KN*², gran *R*; ben *R*, bes *E*. (5) et el s'e. *ABEN*²*R*; dela *ER*; e] en *ABR*; fazia *A*, fes *ER*, fez *K*; sos vers e *lacking A*; ses *I*; cansons *K*, chansos *EN*²*R*, chanssons *B*, chanssos *A*; d'ella *lacking AR*, dela *E*. (6) et ella *up to* Tort n'avez *lacking A*; ella los] elal *R*; *between* los *and* pres: receup els *B*. (7) *Cf.* (6) *A*; et *K*; e l. c.] et apellava la *B*, et el la clama *N*², et el la clamava *ER*; t. mavetz *B*, t. naves *E*, t. navetz *KR*. (8) loncs *KN*²; tems *ER*; a. e. e. c.] en cort ab ella *A*; ab] com *EK*, cum *IN*²; ella *BEKN*²; e si] don *A*, e *R*; fon *ABR*; creut *KN*², crezutz *I*; qel *BN*²*R*, q̄ el *A*; j. d'a. d'e.] dela joi damor *R*; dela *E*; ella·n] ela *R*, elan *E*, ella *A*, ella en *B*; fon *A*; per la gen *lacking A*, de la gens *ER*, per la gens *K*, per las gens *BN*²; d'aqella encontrada *lacking ABER*. (9) et *A*; dir *N*²; e. p. t. d. d. d. l. g. *lacking ABER*; s'i. d. c.] e det li comjat *AB*, el det comjat *R*, esill det comjat *E*; e·l parti de se *lacking A*, e partit lo de si *B*; partit *E*; si *R*. (10) s'en] si sen *ER*; d. e p. e c. e m. *lacking ABER*; conssiros *KN*²; Raembaut *AB*, Raimbaut *E*, Rambautz *N*², Raymbaut *R*; d'Aurenca *R*, d'Aurengua *E*; com *ER*; e. s. q. f. d. l.] ē .i. loc *R*; qe *N*², qel *AB*; fes *E*, fotz *N*²; *after* lui: qe ditz *B*, que ditz *AE*. (10) 1, Seignen *AB*, Seinger *N*², Senhen *R*, Senher *E*; Raembaut *A*, Rambaut *BI*, Rambautz *N*², Raubaut *K*, Raymbaut *R*. (10) 2, vos] vetz *R*; solas *R*, saber *IKN*². *Quotation ends with this line in* R. (10) 3, soi *EKN*², sui *AB*. *Quotation ends with* vengutz *in* E. (10) 4, mai *B*, mais *AKN*²; qe *BKN*²; soi *KN*². (10) 5, qe *AN*²; vuoill *A*; qan *ABN*²; p.] irai *AB*. (10) 6, gabs *B*, gaps *A*; con *N*², cum *AB*; om *K*. (10) 7, e s. n'e. p.] si n'e. p. *A*, si ni a tant *B*; meins *AB*. (10) 8, qu'om] com *N*², cum *AB*; cointar *N*². *Lines* (10) 9 *to* (10) 14 *lacking ABER*. (10) 10, soi *KN*²; menbratz *K*. (10) 11, faitz *N*². (10) 12, qal *N*²; eu] en *K*. (10) 13, cū *N*²; om *K*. (10) 14, *lacking N*²; quenqron *I*. *The Vida ends with this line in* I. *In KN*² *it ends with the following words:* e fez (fetz *N*²) aquestas (aqestas *N*²) cansons (chansos *N*²) que vos auzires (autzirez *N*²) scriptas sai desotz. (11) l. t. e.] el estet lonc temps *B*; temps *A*; estec *R*; Raembaut *AB*, el *R*; r. daurenga *B*; *before* et . . . : e puois sen partic de lui *B*; e *R*; e. e. e. *E*.] et anet sen en espaigna estar *B*; Espaigna *A*; ab lo bon rei n'Anfos de Castela et *lacking AB*; rey (1) *R*; bon (2) *lacking R*; rey (2) *R*; n'Anfos] Amfos *AB*; daragon *AB*; e *B*; *before* ab: pois estet *B*; Raimon] *R*. *R*; Tolosa *AB*; *after* Tolosa: tant qant li plac et el volc *B*. (12) g. h. a. e. m.] gran honor al mon ac *A*, mout ac gran honor el mon *B*; onor *R*; tant *AB*; cum *AB*; hi] i *BR*; estec *R*; mas] e *AB*; pois *AB*; p. el s. r. *A*; a] en *B*; orden *AB*; lay *R*; el *lacking R*; definet] fenic *AB*. *In* R *the Vida ends with the following words*: et aysi a de sa obra.

Errors contained in Appel's list of variants
  A: (11) It is falsely implied that *d'Aurenga* follows *Raembaut*.
  B: (11) *en espaigna* omitted from *et anet sen en espaigna estar*.
  E: (1) No reference to *be* after *cantava*. (3) should read *ma dona e*, not *na dona*

(8) should read *de las gens*, not *per las gens*. (9) should read *esill det comjat*, not *esill dit comjar*. (10) should read *que*, not *q'el*. (11) should read *raimbaut*, not *raembaut*; it is falsely implied that *d'Aurenga* follows *raimbaut* and that *ab lo bon rei n'Anfos de Castela et* is lacking.

I: (1) *be* erroneously included after *cantava*. (10) should read *que*, not *q'el*.

K: (5) should read *sos vers*, not *ses vers*. (8) should read *loncs*, not *lonc*; should read *per la gens*, not *per la gen*. (10) should read *que*, not *q'el*. (10) 1 should read *raubaut*, not *ranbaut*.

R: (1) Typographical error attributes *rotgier* to M instead of R; should read *homs*, not *hom*.

Notes

The reading of I is supported generally by at least K. Both MSS are joined almost always by N² and not infrequently by ER. Appel follows AB on the whole, and in almost all the cases where our text differs from his it is a question of IK or IKN² opposing ABER and, in particular, AB (either individually or jointly): (3) *Ermengarda;* (4) *el honret* omitted; (5) *el* omitted, *e f.*, *d'ella;* (8)–(9) *d'aqella encontrada e per temor . . .;* (10) *dolenz e pensius e consiros, Rambaut, que fetz, que ditz* omitted; (10) 5 *m'en partrai;* (10) 7 *e se n'es plus*. On the other hand, in the latter part of the *Vida* omitted in IKN² the difference in our choice of texts rests, to a large extent, on the division between AB, still favoured by Appel, and ER.

(1) *cantava e t*. Appel mistakenly states in his variants that *be* follows *cantava* in I. This is true of KN², however, as well as of E, which he does not mention. The retention of the reading of I is justified here in view of the support of R. AB omit *e trobava*.
(2) *joglars*. The accusative form of the word (*joglar*) is given by EIKN²R. We have chosen, however, the usual form of the nominative offered by AB and required after *se faire* and other similar expressions, e.g. *se tener per, aver nom*. See *Altprov. Elem.*, p. 120.
(3) *Ermengarda*. The Viscountess of Narbonne. The precise year of Ermengarda's birth is not known but it is likely to have been about 1120 or slightly later. (*Cf.* Bergert, *Damen*, p. 6; Appel, *P. Rogier*, p. 11; Anglade, 'Les troubadours à Narbonne' in *Mélanges Chabaneau*, p. 742.) Being older than her sister Ermessinde, she succeeded her father, Aimeric II, on his death in 1134 (*Hist. gen. Lang.*, III, pp. 691–2; VI, p. 151). However, apparently using Ermengarda's minority as a pretext, Alphonse-Jourdain, Count of Toulouse, is assumed to have taken possession of her lands from 1134 to 1143. After regaining control of them Ermengarda thenceforth preserved them from the endeavours both of Alphonse-Jourdain and of his son, Raimon V (*ibid.*). In 1142 she married Alfonso, a Spanish count whose family name is not known (*ibid.*, III, p. 725). Her second marriage, probably in 1145, was to Bernard d'Anduze (*ibid.*, III, p. 777). She exercised sole responsibility for the administration of her lands for over fifty years, and during this time profited from the protection afforded to her by Count Raimon Bérenguer IV of Barcelona and subsequently by King Alfonso II of Aragon. She remained on close terms with each of them and, we are told, acknowledged them as overlords out of friendship and gratitude rather than out of duty (*ibid.*, VI, p. 151).

She played an important part in political events in the Midi during the second half of the twelfth century and gained a reputation for her skilful and wise government (*ibid.*; Anglade, *op. cit.*, p. 738). Both King Louis VII (Le Jeune) and Pope Alexander III held her in special esteem (*ibid.*, III, pp. 821-2, 843, 844, and VI, p. 55). Apart from acting as arbiter in disputes between eminent lords and princes, she obtained from King Louis the prerogative of administering justice in her own name (*ibid.*, VI, p. 151) and placed herself at the head of her troops in various military expeditions (*ibid.*; *cf.*, in particular, III, pp. 737, 828, 847; VI, p. 102). Reference should also be made to the important services she rendered to Pope Alexander and to her generosity towards churches (*ibid.*, VI, p. 151; *cf.* also IV, p. 675).

As Ermengarda had no heirs she decided in 1168 to call to Narbonne Aimeric de Lara, the son of Ermessinde, her sister, in order to prepare him for government. As he died a few years later, Ermengarda's other nephew, Pierre de Lara, was brought to Narbonne for the same purpose. (For details of these and related events see note to III, l. 64 (*n'Aimeric lo tos*).) Although Pierre de Lara succeeded Ermengarda near the end of 1192 (*ibid.*, VI, p. 151; VII, p. 17), he had apparently had a share in the government of Narbonne as early as 1188 (*ibid.*, VI, p. 139). Ermengarda subsequently retired to Perpignan, a domain of Alfonso II's, where she remained for the rest of her life. She did not die until 1194 at the earliest (*ibid.*, VI, p. 151), and there is some evidence to suggest that it may even have been as late as 1197 (*ibid.*, VII, 18).

The extent to which Ermengarda may have been involved in the lives of troubadours other than Peire Rogier is discussed in appendix II.

(5) *sos.* The reading of all the MSS except I, which has a scribal error (*ses*).

(7) *e la c.* Appel follows EN²R in inserting *el* between *e* and *la*. It is notable, however, that B, despite its otherwise independent reading here, supports IK in the omission of *el*. This section of the *Vida* is missing in A.

(8) *ab.* We have preferred the reading of ABR to that of EIKN² (*cum*) for the same reason as Boutière, namely that the italianism *cum* is merely a product of the copyists.

Boutière (*op. cit.*, pp. xxviii–xxix) quotes the appearance of *cum* in IKN² to illustrate the close relationship of the three MSS and to attempt to disprove Panvini's thesis whereby N² occupies the top of his stemma and IK is placed as low as the fourth rank (Panvini, *Appunti*, p. 105).

crezut. The reading of all the MSS except I, which has the usual nominative form (*crezutz*). The impersonal construction employed here requires the invariable neuter form (see *Altprov. Elem.*, p. 71; Anglade, p. 231).

(10) IKN² contain two stanzas of the poem, AB the first stanza and ER the first two to three lines only. The stanzas ought to contain seven lines each, but instead the first has eight and the second six. The order of the lines is also disarranged: ll. 6–8 are in fact the last three of the second stanza in the actual poem and l. 14 should be the last line of the first stanza. Line 6 is almost identical to l. 13 and replaces the original l. 6 of the poem (*cum es de vos ni cum vos vai*). (Boutière, *op. cit.*, p. 270, note 6, indicates l. 7 in error.)

Both Boutière (*op. cit.*, p. xliv) and Favati (*op. cit.*, p. 415), observing that the confusion in the line order and the stanza structure, as well as the omission of an original line, applies to all the MSS (except ER, which do not contain a full stanza), consider that the quotation was originally missing in the archetype from which

(10), 1 *Raimbaut*. The trisyllabic version of the word, found in ER and in A (*Raembaut*), is chosen for reasons of metre. The other MSS all offer versions of two syllables. For the development of the three-syllabled form of the word from the original *Raginbald* see *Altprov. Elem.*, p. 33. *Cf.* VIII, l. 50.

(10), 2 *solatz*. The reading of ABER is adopted in preference to that of IKN² (*saber*). The rhyme scheme requires the ending *-atz*. It may well be that the version of IKN², which is not offered by any MS in the corresponding place in the poem itself, is the result of the influence of *saber* in the first line of the second stanza.

(10), 5 *que saber voill*. It should be noted that, for this half of the line, the reading of all five MSS (ABIKN²) closely resembles those of CT in the actual poem (C: *e vuelh saber;* T: *eu voigll saber*).

(10), 6 *lo fai*. This reading contained in all five MSS is, in fact, the one offered by ET in l. 12 of the actual poem. However, the version of the line repeated in the second stanza in IKN² (*retrai*) is that offered by the majority of the MSS for l. 12 of the poem.

(11) The latter part of the *Vida*, following the quotation from *Seign'en Raymbaut*, is lacking in IKN². Like Appel, Favati and Boutière-Schutz, we have followed ABER in including it. It is interesting to note, however, that Panvini (*op. cit.*, p. 113) rejects Favati's view (*Appunti*, pp. 88-9) that the omission in IKN² is erroneous. He refers to the earlier inclusion of *dolens e pensius e consiros* in IKN² and of *de la ciutat de Clarmon* in N² and, rather, is of the opinion that this part of the *Vida* was added at a later stage in ABER according to a common original, further evidence of which, he says, is found in the reading of ER, *N'Anfos de castela*. It is in fact not unusual for R to contain, at the end of certain *Vidas*, information which is not included in other MSS (*cf.* Boutière and Schutz, *op. cit.*, p. xxxix).

Panvini (*op. cit.*, p. 113) considers that the author of this common original was a biographer who not only wrote original biographies (Bertran de Born, Raimon Jordan, etc.) but also added information to biographies which had already been compiled. Panvini includes in this category the *Vidas* of Aimeric de Peguilhan and Perdigon and, slightly more tentatively, that of Peire Rogier.

Raimbaut. It seems reasonable to adhere to the spelling of E, to which that of AB (*raembaut*), favoured by Appel and Favati, is fairly close. R is independent here (*el*). The spelling preferred by Boutière and Schutz (*rambaut*) is not given by any of the MSS but is in fact the version offered by BIKN² in l. 1 of the quotation.

The additional words found only in B (*d'aurenga e puois s'en partic de lui*) must be regarded as suspect in view of their omission in all the other MSS (AER). Appel encloses them with brackets, as he does later in the case of the other independent versions of B: *pois estet* and *tant qant li plac et el volc*.

N'Anfos de Castela. The retention of the reading of E is justified by the support of R. AB, followed by Appel, omit the reference to Anfos de Castela (*cf.* p. 16, note 35). Favati's version is based on ER but also appears to be influenced by AB. He follows AB for *Amfos*, ER for *de Castela* and then omits the second *N'Anfos* before *d'Arago*.

The king concerned is Alfonso VIII of Castille (1158–1214). Son of King Alfonso VII, who died in 1157, he married in 1170 Eleanor, daughter of Henry II, the Plantagenet. He is described as a valiant warrior and clever politician as well as a champion of Christianity (*cf.* Jeanroy, *Poésie lyrique*, I, p. 208). His court was one where many troubadours of various kinds assembled, and his marriage with Eleanor probably attracted, in addition, some of the poetic following of the Plantagenets (*cf.* Jeanroy, *op. cit.*, I, p. 209). The other troubadours who, according to the *Vidas* and *Razos*, visited his court are Giraut de Bornelh, Aimeric de Peguilhan, Folquet de Marseille and Uc de Saint Circ (*cf.* Boutière and Schutz, *op. cit.*, and Favati, *Biografie*). (Boutière and Schutz (p. 243, note 11) consider the *Anfos* mentioned in Uc de Saint Circ's *Vida* to be Alfonso VIII of Castille while Favati (*op. cit.*, p. 313) omits the reference to him.) Jeanroy (*Les Troubadours en Espagne*, p. 165 and p. 170, note 2) also names the following troubadours who, he considers, visited Alfonso's court: At de Mons, Bernard Calvo, Guiraut Riquer, Pons Barba and Paulet de Marseille. (Milà (*De los trovadores en España*, p. 131) includes Savaric de Mauléon in the list, but there appears to be no supporting evidence (*cf.* H. J. Chaytor, *Savaric de Mauléon, Baron and Troubadour*, Cambridge, 1939).) Alfonso was well known for his hospitality and friendliness towards the troubadours (*cf.* Jeanroy, *Les troubadours en Espagne*, p. 172) and his high reputation among them is reflected in the praise with which a number of them sang of him: namely Peire Vidal, Perdigon, Guillem de Bergadan, Aimeric de Peguilhan, Guiraut de Calanson, Raimon Vidal (*cf.* Jeanroy, *Poésie lyrique*, I. pp. 209–10).

N'*Anfos d'Arago*. Born in 1152 or 1158, son of Raimon-Bérenger IV, this Alfonso was known initially as Alfonso I. He became Count of Barcelona in 1162, King of Aragon (under the name of Alfonso II) in 1164, Count of Provence in 1166, and died in 1196 (*cf.* Boutière and Schutz, *op. cit.*, p. 526, note 1). The references to Alfonso in the *Vidas*, *Razos* and poems of the troubadours are numerous. Jeanroy (*op. cit.*, I, p. 190) makes the point that the troubadours did not need to cross over into Spain to pay homage to him as he himself had many opportunities to visit their regions: we find him in Provence in 1167 and 1174, in Languedoc in 1179, around Carcassonne and Toulouse in 1181, 1186 and 1193, and at Perpignan (where he died) in 1196. The *Vidas* or *Razos* of the following troubadours, apart from Peire Rogier, allude to him: Arnaut de Mareuil, Bertran de Born, Folquet de Marseille, Guillem de Cabestaing, the Monk of Montaudon, Peire Raimon de Toulouse, Peire Vidal and Uc Brunet (*cf.* Irénée Cluzel, 'Princes et troubadours de la maison royale de Barcelone-Aragon' in *Boletín de la Real Academia de Buenas Letras de Barcelona*, xxvII (1957–58), 324). One must add the following troubadours who, according to their poems or other evidence, have also been connected with him: Aimeric de Sarlat, Arnaut Daniel, Guillem de Bergadan, Giraut de Bornelh, Guiraut (or Guerau) de Cabrera, Guiraut del Luc, Raimbaut de Vaqueiras, Raimon Vidal de Besalù and perhaps Pons de Capdeuil, Raimbaut d'Orange (*cf.* Irénée Cluzel, *op. cit.*, xxvII, 323) and the anonymous author(s) of *Jaufré* (*cf.* M. de Riquer, 'Los problemas del "Roman" provenzal de "Jaufré"' in *Recueil de travaux offert à M. Clovis Brunel*, Paris, 1955, pp. 444–7). Bertran de Born and Guillem de Bergadan show themselves hostile towards Alfonso, while the references of most of the other troubadours are favourable. Peire Vidal, regarded as Alfonso's favourite, is particularly generous in his praises (*cf.* Irénée Cluzel, *loc. cit.*).

Not content with merely encouraging the troubadours, Alfonso composed poetry himself and has handed down to us one *canso* and a *tenso* with Giraut de Bornelh (*cf.* Pillet and Carstens, 23, 1, and 23, 1[a]). For further reference to Alfonso's literary role *cf.* Boutière and Schutz, *op. cit.*, p. 526, note 2.

Throughout his reign Alfonso was closely involved in the affairs of southern France. For much of this period he was engaged in war with Count Raimon V of Toulouse (*cf. Hist. gen. Lang.*, VI, pp. 23–4) while remaining a very close friend and ally of Ermengarda of Narbonne (*cf.* p. 37 above).

Raimon de Toloza. Count Raimon V, 1148–94. Jeanroy (*op. cit.*, I, p. 160) states that in the second half of the twelfth century the Counts of Toulouse together with the Dukes of Aquitaine were the most powerful lords in the Midi, having extended their lands and substantially increased their wealth. The court of Raimon V and that of Raimon VI (1194–1222) were both among the most splendid in the west and therefore attracted a great number of troubadours. Boutière and Schutz (*op. cit.*) and Favati (*op. cit.*) see a reference to Raimon V in the *Vidas* or *Razos* of the following troubadours, apart from Peire Rogier: Bernart de Ventadour, Bertran de Born, Folquet de Marseille, Arnaut de Mareuil and Peire Vidal. The *Histoire générale de Languedoc* (VI, p. 162) lays great emphasis on the encouragement which Raimon gave to Provençal poetry: "Jamais la poésie provençale ne fut en si grand honneur que du vivant de Raimond V et jamais aucun prince ne favorisa tant que lui ceux qui la cultivaient'.

(12) *el hi estet*. Boutière and Schutz omit *el*. It seems preferable to include it, however, as it is offered by all four MSS.

mas . . . definet. In each case Appel chooses the reading of AB (*e . . . fenic*). It appears reasonable, however, to retain the equally acceptable versions of E, particularly in view of the usual support of R (*cf. N'Anfos de Castela* above).

l'orde de Granmon. About 1076 Etienne de Muret, born in Thiers in the Auvergne, founded a community of hermits on the mountain at Muret near Limoges. After his death in 1124 they installed themselves at Grandmont in the commune of Saint-Sylvestre, also fairly near Limoges. Etienne's adoption of the austere rule of the Cantabrian monks no doubt accounted for the severity of the rule followed by the *Grandmontains*, or *Bons-hommes*, as the members of the Order came to be known. The rule, which was approved by Pope Adrian IV in 1156, was based on two main themes: poverty and solitude. The members were apparently well known for their virtue and the simplicity of their life. Their reputation for humility is reflected in the following reference, quoted by Appel, from Gaucelm Faidit's *S'om pogues partir son voler*:

> Vas midonz sui de franc saber,
> plus humils d'un frair de Granmon,
> et ill m'es d'orgoillos parer
> si que, qan la prec, no'm respon.

(*Cf.* Mouzat, *Les Poèmes de Gaucelm Faidit*, 65, ll. 56–59.)

The Order must have already been flourishing by the time Peire Rogier entered it, in that by 1170 there were as many as sixty communities. However, during the thirteenth century and part of the fourteenth the Order was troubled by internal quarrels, particularly between the *frères convers*, charged with the administration of temporal affairs, and the *clercs*. A serious division also arose between the *frères anglais* and the *frères français*. In 1317 Pope John XXII reformed the Order by reducing the number of communities, which then stood at 149,* to

---

* There were also in existence at that time three communities in England and two in Spain.

thirty-nine and by converting Grandmont into an abbey, which he placed at their head. Perhaps an important contributory factor in the Order's decline, apart from its internal dissensions, was the Hundred Years War, during which the abbey and the other convents were extensively ravaged. In 1245, Pope Innocent IV mitigated the Order's severe rule. As a reaction a section of the Order, led by a Father Frémont, broke away in 1642 to establish their own communities of *l'Etroite Observance*. Approval for the suppression of the Order was given in 1772 by Pope Clement XIV.

(For these notes on the Order reference has been made to the following works: Dom J. Becquet, *Les Institutions de l'Ordre de Grandmont au moyen-âge*, Mabillon, 1952, pp. 34-6; E. Darras, *Le Prieuré Grandmontain de Notre-Dame des bonshommes du Meyrel-lez-Maffliers, 1169-1791*, Pontoise-L'Isle-Adam, 1928, pp. 9, 11-12, 18-19; Canon Farcy, *Une Page de l'histoire de Rouen—Le Prieuré de Grandmont des origines jusqu' à nos jours*, Rouen, 1934, pp. 15-19; R. Farnier, *La Condition juridique des personnes et des biens de l'Ordre de Grandmont des origines au XVIIIe siècle*, Limoges, 1913, pp. 17, 22, 24-39; *Larousse*, III, p. 857; *Nouveau Larousse Illustré*, IV, p. 930.)

Poems

I AL PAREYSSEN DE LAS FLORS (356, 1)

Eleven MSS. A 108 (308); B 108 (p. 696) (Mahn, *Gedichte*, 1401); C 195; D 3–7; E 173; I 12; K 2; M 196; R 26–224; Peire Breumon c84 (125); anonymous ω59 + 66 + 59 (p. 577).

Editions. Raynouard, *Choix*, III, 27; *M.W.*, I, 119; Lavaud, *Troub. Cant.*, II, p. 408; Riquer, *Lírica*, p. 221.

Classification. All the MSS have the same order of stanzas and contain the complete poem, with the exception of c, in which stanzas II and III and the *tornada* are missing, and ω which is fragmentary.

Two main groups are to be observed: ABDIK and CR, the division being clearly marked in 13, 23, 27, 28 (*querra–queira*), 48, 50. Within the first group, which is by far the more consistent and stable of the two, two sub-groups are apparent: AB and DIK. The close connection of the first pair is borne out in 16 ($\bar{q}$), 19, 27, 50, 51, 52, while DIK share variants in 2 (*lalbre–larbre*), 26 (*pauc*), 27 (*se il mais*, etc.), 30 (*tot*), 37, 50, 51, 52. IK follow their normal practice of forming a further subdivision, cf. 15 (*vei*), 17, 19, 27, 51 (*mal*).

EMcω each fluctuate considerably in their relations with the two main groups. M appears to have equal connections with both. It joins the first in 27 (*rancura*), 28 (*qerra*), showing a further link with DIK in 26 (*pauc*) and with AB in 19. On the other hand, its connection with CR is borne out in 23 (*que*), 27 (*si'l sap mal*), 50 (*rogier*).

E joins ABDIK in 27 (*rancura*), 48, apart from DIK in 26 (*pauc*), 27 (*sil mais*). Although Appel is perhaps justified in noting that its link with R in 12, 28 is less important, it appears, on the whole, to belong at least as much to the CR tradition as to the ABDIK tradition. It shares readings with C in 22 (*camor*), 51 (*longuas*), CRc in 28 (*queira*) and with ACMRcω in 23 (*que*) in opposition to BDIK.

E and M are quite often in agreement, cf. 6 (*que*), 13, 17, 26 (*plac–plag*) (with cω) and 26 (with DIK: *pauc*), 27 (with ABDIK: *rancura*).

c appears generally to identify itself with the CR group, although it joins DIK in 2.

The intricate relationship of M and c with the other MSS and that of MRc with each other pose a problem similar to that confronted in VI. Although all three, particularly R, have strong individualist tendencies, they are allied in 16 (*qe*), 23 (*que*), 27 (*sil sap mal*), 30. Further links exist between Mc in 25 (*sestrais–sistrais*), 30, Rc in 25 (*dona*), 27 (*natura–nabdura*), 38, and MR in 1, 22 (*tal*), 34 (*suefre–suefri*).

ω, which was not at Appel's disposal, is fragmentary and, on the evidence available, cannot be classified precisely with either of the two main groups. It is linked with the first in 28, 48 and again with DIK in 2 (*lalbre–larbre*), while it joins CR in 23 (*que*), 27 (*sil sap mal*). An affinity with c is also apparent, *cf.* 2, 26 (*plag*).

Base and orthography. C.

I Al pareyssen de las flors,
quan l'albre·s cargon de fuelh,
e·l temps gens'ab la verdura
per l'erba que creys e nays;
doncx es a selhs bon'amors,   5
qui l'an em-patz ses rancura,
q'us ves l'autre non s'erguelha.

II Bos drutz non deu creir'auctors
ni so que veiran sey huelh
de neguna forfaitura,   10
don sap que sa dona·l trays;
so que dis qu'a fait alhors
creza, si nonca lo jura,
e sso que·n vi dezacuelha.

III Qu'ieu vey de totz los melhors   15
qui senpr'en devenon fuelh,
qu'enqueron tan lur dreytura
tro que lur dompna·s n'irays.
E·l ris torna·ls pueys en plors;
e·l folhs per mal'aventura   20
vai queren lo mal que·l duelha.

IV Qu'amors vol tals amadors,
que sapchon sufrir erguelh
en patz e gran desmezura;
si tot lor dompna·ls sostrays,   25
paucs plagz lur en si'honors,
quar si·l sap mal ni s'atura,
ylh querra tost qui l'acuelha.

V	Per aquest sen suy ieu sors,	
	et ai d'amor tan quan vuelh,	30
	quar s'elha·m fay gran laidura,	
	quant autre·s planh, ieu m'apays.	
	Si tot s'es grans ma dolors,	
	sofier tro qu'elha·m melhura	
	ab un plazer qual que·s vuelha.	35
VI	Mais vuelh trenta dezonors	
	q'un'onor, si lieys mi tuelh,	
	q'ieu suy hom d'aital natura,	
	no vuelh l'onor que·l pro lays.	
	Ni ges no·m laissa·l paors,	40
	don mos cors non s'asegura,	
	qu'ades cug qu'autre la·m tuelha.	
VII	De mon dan prec mos senhors,	
	mas l'amor de midons vuelh,	
	e que·l prenda de mi cura,	45
	que trop es grans mos esmays.	
	Molt mi fera gran secors,	
	s'una vetz per aventura	
	mi mezes lai o·s despuelha.	
VIII	*Peir Rogier* li quier secors,	50
	e si·l mals longuas li dura,	
	pauc vivra qu'ades rauguelha.	

Variants. The illegible parts of ω are indicated by - - -, except where otherwise stated. The first thirteen lines in E are mutilated. The following is what remains of ll. 1–3: — de las flors — lbres cargon — l, el tems gē — verdura. *The words and parts of words missing in the subsequent lines are indicated by* +.

I. 1, *Initial A missing B*, eral *M*, er *R*; pareissen *ABM*, pareisen *DK*ω, parissen *I*, pareysson *R*, pariscen *c*. 2, qan *ADIKMc*, qñ *B*, can *R*; lalbreis *AB*, larbres *M*, lalbre *DI*, larbre *K*ω*c*; cargatz *R*, charguon *c*; de] del *DIK*ω*c*; foil *c*, fueilh *M*, fueill ω, fuelhs *R*, fuoill *ABDIK*. 3, tems *R*; gensa *D*, genssa *AB*; ab] a *c*; gen sap reverdura *R*; gen sap la freidura ω. 4, lerba q + *E*; qe *KM*ω, qi *c*; creis *ABDEIKM*ω*c*; nais *ABDEIKM*ω*c*. 5, *lacking* ω; doncs *ABDIK*, don *M*, adoncs *c*, + *E*; cels *Mc*, celz *AB*, sels *DEIK*; a. s.] aysel *R*; bona amors *B*; amors + *E*. 6, *lacking* ω; qe *M*, que *E*, q̄ *A*, qi *c*; la *c*, lam *D*; en *ABEIKMc*; paz *BMc*; q. l'a. e. p.] quera partitz *R*; ses + *E*. 7, *lacking* ω; cuns *DEc*, cus *IKR*; vas *ABDIKMRc*, + *E*; no *EMR*;

s'ergueilla *E*, s'orgoilla *BIc*, s'orguoilla *AK*, s'orguolla *D*, sescuelha *R*, s'ergoilha gueilha (*both probably by the same hand*) *M*.

II. Lacking in ω *c*; *the following is what remains of ll. 8–11 in E*: —re auctors ni so q̄— (n)eguna forfaitura, don —l trais. 8, bons *B*, mos *I*, os *K* (*initial* m *added by different hand*); drurz *K*; creira *D*, creire *ABIKM*, creyr *R*; autcors *M*, autors *ABDIK*. 9, que *lacking D*, qe *M*, q̄ *BIR*; veyran *R*; sei *DKM*, siei *ABIR*; hueilh *M*, huoill *AB*, oill *DIK*. 10, forfaçura *M*. 11, dom *D*; qe *I*, q̄ *BDR*, de *M*; domnal *K*, dompnal *ABI*, donnal *M*, dōnal *D*; trais *ABDIKM*. 12, qe *KR*, q̄ *ABD*; ditz *ER*; c' *ADEIKR*, q' *B*; fayt *R*; s. qa dich qe fach *M*; ailhors *M*, aillors *ABDEIK*. 13, cresa *M*, crezā *R*; noca *EM*; c. si tot non l. j. *CR*; loi *E*; l. j.] latura *R*. 14, eso *ABDEIKMR*; q̄ *R*, qel *M*, qen *AB*, q̄n *D*; dejacueilla *E* (*the* j *is not entirely clear*), desacoilla *B*, desacuelha *R*, desacuoilla *ADIK*, li des (c)ueilha *M*. (*The last six letters appear to have replaced an earlier reading, which is erased, and to have been added at the same time as* gueilha *in* l. 7. *The letter immediately preceding them is probably* c *but is not entirely clear*.)

III. 15, qu'ieu vey *lacking* ω; qeu *c*, qieu *ABM*, que *D*, queu *I*; vei *IKc*, vi *ABDEMR*; toz *DKω*; meilhors *M*, meillors *ABDEIKc*, meill - - - ω. 16, - - - semp - - - d. ω; qe *Mc*, q̄ *AB*; sempren *AM*; s. e.] sens en *c*; devenen *M*, deveno *c*; foill *Bc*, fueil ω, fueilh *M*, fueill *E*, fuoill *ADIK*; que afolan lur capduelh *R*. 17, qe enqero *c*, qenqeron *A*, qenq̄ron *B*, q̄nqeron ω, qe qeron *M*, quenq̄ron *D*, que queron *E*, quim queron *I*, quin queron *K*, car tan q̄ron *R*; tan *lacking c*, tant *ABDIK*; lor *ABDIK*ω*c*; drechura *ABDKM*ω, dreichura *I*, dreitura *ER*c. 18, que *lacking R*, qe *IM*ω*c*, q̄ *BDI*; lor *ABDIK*ω*c*; dompnais *AB*, domnas *Kc*, donas *ER*ω, dōnas *D*, donnas *M*; nirais *ABDEIKM*ω*c*. 19, tornals] ēdeve *R*, torna *ABM*, tornal *c*; pueys *illegible* ω, pois *ABDI*, pueis *EM*, puois *Kc*; en *lacking R*; plor *IK*. 20, els *c*; fals *R*, fols *ABDEIKMc*, sols ω; per] ab *M*. 21, va *DIKMc*, vay *R*; qeren *M*ω*c*, querren *D*, q̄ren *AR*; qeil *AB*, q̄ill *D*, qel *M*ω, q̄l *R*, queill *E*; doilla *c*, dueilla *E*ω, duoilla *ABDIK*, dueilha *M*.

IV. 22, camor *E*, camors *A*, damors *R*, qamors *BMc*, quamor *C*; tal *IMR*. 23, qe *c*, q̄ *MR*, qui *BDIK*; sachon *IK*, sapchan *R*ω*c*; soffrir *BDIK*, sofrir *A*ω*c*; ergueill *E*, ergueilh *M*, orgoill *BI*ω*c*, orguoill *ADK*. 24, em *E*; paz *B*ω*c*; e] en ω; desmesura *ABDIK*ω*c*. 25, lur *ER*, sa *c*; dampnals *DK*, domna *c*, domnals ω, dona *R*, donals *E*, donnas *M*; sentrays *R*, sestrais *IM*, sistrais *c*, sostrais *ABDEK*ω. 26, pauc *DEIKM*; plac *E*, plag *M*ω*c*, plaitz *A*, plaiz *B*, platz *DIK*; lor *ABDIKM*ω, lem *c*; sia *ABCEMc*; atras ni merma sonors *R*. 27, car *ABDKR*ω, qar *I*(?)*Mc*; sil] si *c*; sab *c*; s. s. m.] sis laigna *AB*, se il mais *D*, sil mais *EI*, sil mas *K*; nis] sen [son?] *D*, vis *IK*; atura] rancura *ABDEIKM*, nabdura *c*, natura *R*, satura ω. 28, el *ER*, il *IKM*ω*c*, ill *AB*, yl *D*; qeira *c*, qerra *ABM*ω, q̄yra *R*, queira *CE*; qi *K*ω*c*, q¹ *R*; q. l'] qilh *M*; acoilla *Bc*, acueilha *M*, acueilla *E*ω, acuoilla *ADIK*.

V. 29, aqest *ABKM*ω*c*, aq̄st *R*; sen] son *M*; soi *E*, son *BDIK*ω, soy *R*, sui *AMc*; eu *BDIKM*ω*c*, yeu *R*. 30, *this line lacking in* ω; tant *AB*, tot *DIK*; cant *A*, qant

POEM I 47

BDI, quant *K*; voill *BDIK*, vueill *E*, vuoill *A*; e no sui ges cel qi sueilh *M*; e nō sui ges cel qe soill *c*; e sō totz aitals com suelh *R*. 31, car *ABDIKRω*, qar *Mc*; celam *E*, cellam *M*, selan *R*, sellam *ADIKωc*, silam *B*; fai *ABDEIKMRωc*; lidura *C*. 32, cant *Rω*, qand *AB*, qant *DMc*; autreis *AB*, autre (?)*ω*; plag *c*, plaing *ABDIKω*, plainh *M*; eu *ABDωc*, yeu *R*; mapais *ABDEIKMωc*, mē pays *R*. 33, granz *IKωc*. 34, soffier *B*, suefre *M*, suefri *R*, sufier *DIKω*, sufrir *c*; t. q. e.] tant tro lam *B*, tant qelam *M*; q̄lam *R*, qella *c*, qellam *ω*, quelam *AE*, quellam *DIK*; meilhura *Mc*, meillura *ABDEIKω*. 35, plazers *MR*; cal *ABDEIKω*, cals *R*, qal *Mc*; qeis *AB*, qes *DMωc*, q̄s *R*; voilla *BDIKωc*, vueilha *M*, vueilla *E*, vuoilla *A*.

VI. 36, mas *Iω*; voil *ω*, voill *BDIK*, vueilh *M*, vueill *E*, vuoill *A*, nam *c*; tr---onors *ω*; de senors *c*, desonors *ABDIKM*; camot tenc sim fai secors *R*. 37, cui *c*, cun *ABDEIKω*; honor *ABDIKM*, honors *c*; si---l *ω*; se *M*, sel *DIK*, ses *A*; leis *DEIKMc*, lieis *AB*; me *BMc*; toill *B*, tueilh *M*, tueill *E*, tuoill *ADIK*, noilh *c*; silh de cuy yeu ges nom tuelh *R*. 38, qeu *c*, qieu *BM*, q¹eu *C*, q̄u *AI*, queu *Dω*; soi *ERω*, son *DIKM*, sui *ABc*; de tal *Rc*; natura *illegible ω*. 39, *illegible ω*; n. v. l'o.] q̄ no vuelh ges *R*; non *ABDIKc*; voil *c*, voill *DIK*, vueilh *M*, vueill *E*, vuoill *B*, vuoll *A*; l' *lacking c*; honor *c*; qel *ADKMc*, q̄l *BR*; pros *R*; lais *ABDEIKMc*. 40, jes *ABω*; non *M*, nō *Dc*; laissail *AB*, laisal *EIKRω*, laissel *M*. 41, dom *D*; cor *c*; no *DEIMR*; savegura *M*. 42, cades *ABDEIKRω*, qades *Mc*; cuich *A*, cuig *Bc*, tem *R*; cautre *ADEIKRω*, qaultre *c*, qautre *BM*; lem *M*; toilla *c*, tueilha *M*, tueilla *Eω*, tuoilla *ABDIK*.

VII. *Lacking c. The stanza is mutilated in E. The following remains:* de mon dan—or de midons — cura, que tro—lt mi feira —entura mi —. 43, seignors *ABω*, seingnors *DIK*, seinhors *M*. 44, lamors *D*; midonz *ABDIKω*; voill *BDIKω*, vueilh *M*, vuoill *A*. 45, qel *Mω*, qeill *A*, q¹lh *R*, quill *B*; preigna *AB*, preingna *IK*, preingua *D*, prenga *Mω*, aya *R*; mi *illegible ω*. 46, qe *M*, q̄ *ABIR*; granz *IKω*; esmais *ABDIKM*, es--- *ω*. 47, mot *Rω*, mout *ABDIKM*; fara *ω*, feira *ABM*; gen *C*; socors *ABDIK*. 48, ves *DIKM*, vez *B*; vetz per *illegible ω*; p. a.] ab nueg escura *C*, senes falsura *M*; sim laisses de nueg escura *R*. 49, meses *AB*, mezeis *DI*; ois *AB*, on *D*; despoilla *BDI*, despeuilha *M*, despuoilla *AK*, desp--- *ω*; esser lay ō se despuelha *R*.

VIII. *Lacking ωc. The tornada is mutilated in E. The following remains:* Peire rotg(i)—guas li dura —. 50, Peire *ABCDIKM*; rogiers *DIK*, rotgiers *AB*; Peirotgier *R*; qer *M*, qier *AB*, q¹er *R*; socors *ABD*. 51, e] car *R*; mal *CIK*; loindās *M*, longeitz *AB*, lengues *I*, longues *DK*, gayre *R*. 52, vievra *R*; cades *ABDIK*, pueys nō *R*, qestiers *M*; jaus ueilha *M*, lacuelha *R*, rançuoilla *AB*, rauzuoilla *DIK*.

Metrical scheme. Seven *coblas unissonans* of seven lines and a *tornada* of three lines following the scheme of the last three lines of the stanzas:

$$a_7 \ b_7 \ c_7' \ d_7 \ a_7 \ c_7' \ e_7'$$

(Frank: 838: 1). There is one other example of this scheme (Jaufré Rudel: Pillet and Carstens, 262, 5).

Notes

Pattison (*R. d'Orange*, p. 57 and p. 136) suggests that the common literary theme of the troubadours expressed in the poem, whereby humble resignation and patience are recommended to the lover, may well be parodied by Raimbaut d'Orange's *Assatz sai d'amor ben parlar* (No. XX, pp. 134–5). In this poem, which is one of Raimbaut's *gaps*, the troubadour satirises lightly the accepted code of love by offering advice exactly contrary to it.

6 *em-patz*. The hyphen is employed to denote that the *n* of the original *en* has been assimilated by the following labial (*p*). (*cf. Anglade*, p. 188.)

7 *s'erguelha*. Raynouard translates as 's'irrite' (*Lex. Rom.*, IV, 385). Levy, however, rejects this meaning in favour of 'is proud, stubborn' (*S.W.*, V, 520) which seems preferable here.

9 *sey*. The strong form of the possessive adjective is normally accompanied by the definite article. The two exceptional cases are: (i) when it is used as a predicate pronoun (see IV, l. 55: *mieus*) and (ii) when it appears, as here, in the nominative masculine plural form (*cf. Altprov. Elem.*, p. 78).

12 *dis*. Appel adopts the reading of ER (*ditz*), the more usual form of the present tense, which is required here before *qu'a fait alhors*. It seems reasonable, however, to retain *dis*, offered by all the other MSS except M, which is independent, as it is an acceptable alternative form of the third present indicative. (*Cf. Grandgent*, p. 47; *Prov. Chr.*, 105, l. 14.) Appel's view of the word is not always consistent, however. He employs it as the present in VII, 12, and, on the other hand, regards it as a significant variant to *ditz* in some cases but not in others (*cf.* IV, ll. 10, 36; V, l. 29).

13 *si nonca*. Appel chooses the reading *si tot non* offered by CR only. The equally acceptable version of the ABDIK group is, however, preferred here in view of the support given by EM, which are generally more inclined to CR (see 'Classification').

16 *fuelh*. The reading offered by all the MSS except R, which has an independent line. No other example has been found of this form of the adjective *fol*. It is used here to fit in with the rhyme scheme and it is interesting to note that it corresponds with the *fuelh* occurring two stanzas earlier, just as *vuelh* in l. 30 does with *vuelh* in l. 44.

Lavaud prefers the version of R (*que afolan lur capduelh*) the meaning of which, however, remains uncertain. He proposes two possible interpretations: 'Who destroy their authority' *or* 'Who lose all possession of themselves.' (*Troub. Cant.*, p. 66.) We have disregarded this reading in view of its independence. It is also worth noting that the presence of *afolan* may suggest that the scribe has been influenced by *fuelh*, given by all the other MSS.

22 *amors*. The usual form of the nominative singular given by most of the MSS is chosen here. CE have the form *amor*, without the *s*, which is possibly a Latinism.

25 *sostrays*. Raynouard (*Lex. rom.*, V, 405) translates the verb by 'abaisser'. The meaning adopted by Levy (*S.W.*, VII, 846) is, however, more suitable in this instance: 'treats badly'. Levy comments at some length upon Appel's reference in the notes to the Italian verb *sottrarre* ('to belittle, defame').

26 *si'honors*. We have followed DIKω in eliding the *a* of *sia* in order to preserve the correct number of syllables in the line. *Cf.* note to II, ll. 7 and 10.
27 *s'atura*. ABDEIKM all have *rancura*, which was probably a tempting choice for the scribes in that it matches well with *sap mal*. However, the result is the introduction of a different subject for each verb, whereas *s'atura*, offered by C, and *sap mal* both serve the same subject. Although independent, the reading of C is retained in view of the support offered by the slight variations of Rcω.
   The literal meaning of *s'aturar* is 'to fix, support oneself'. Lines 26 and 27 could therefore be translated as follows: 'May a small quarrel satisfy their honour (lit. 'be honour to them'), for if it displeases her and *persists* she will immediately seek someone who will receive her kindly.' This interpretation seems preferable to that of Lavaud, who keeps *plagz* as the subject of *sap mal* but makes the lady the subject of *s'atura*: 'car si cela lui déplaît et qu'elle s'obstine . . .'
28 *querra*. The reading of ABDIKMω is adopted, as it offers the more usual form of the third person future which the meaning demands (*cf. Altprov. Elem.*, p. 104). CERc have *queira*, which exists as a much rarer form of the future (*cf. Anglade*, p. 343, note 1). It is primarily, however, the normal form of the third person present subjunctive (*cf. Anglade*, p. 342; *Altprov. Elem., loc. cit.*) and may possibly be intended as such in CERc as a result of the influence of the subjunctive *acuelha*, later in the line, and *sia* in l. 26.
29 Raynouard (*op. cit.*, v, 195) translates this line as 'Par ce sens je suis élevé', taking *sens* to mean 'direction' and *élevé* to mean 'brought up'. It seems preferable, however, to interpret it in the following way: 'By this reasoning I am exalted'. This meaning of *sors* (past part. of *sorzer*) is borne out by Levy's *Supplement-Wörterbuch* (vii, 833), in which Kolsen's translation of the word appears to be appropriate: 'gehoben, in gehobener Stimmung' ('in high spirits'). *Cf. G. de Born.*, 46, l. 73:

> Pois, can fui d'aqui *sors*,
> Tornei vas leis de cors
> C'ab bos pretz me retrais
> Mans bes que pois m'esfrais
> . . .

and Ricketts, *G. de Montanhagol*, ii, l. 11 (p. 49, translation and note, and pp. 52–3). It is also worth noting that Lavaud's translation is fairly close to this interpretation of the line: 'Grâce à cette sagesse, je suis placé au faîte'.
31 *laidura*. The reading offered by all the mss except C, which is independent here (*lidura*).
39 The omission of the conjunction *que*, introducing a consecutive or comparative clause, is frequent in Old Provençal. (*Cf. Altprov. Elem.*, pp. 133–4.) See also III, l. 60; VII, l. 41; IX, l. 17.
44 *vuelh*. See note to l. 16.
47 *gran*. C is again independent (*gen*). All the other mss have *gran*. There is perhaps evidence here of the practice of C's scribe of attempting to improve on the reading available to him (see pp. 32–3 above). It is quite possible that he chose *gen* in order to avoid the repetition of *gran*, which appears in the previous line. It could well be, however, that the repetition of *gran* was intentional and was meant by the poet to produce an antithesis.

48 *per aventura.* The reading of the majority of the MSS has been chosen. CR have *ab(de) nueg escura* and M is independent. *Per aventura* ('by chance') is the standard reading which one would normally expect after such expressions as *s'una vetz.* The more imaginative version of CR is perhaps the work of the intelligent scribe of C, who would be eager to avoid a cliché of this sort. See note to l. 47.

50 *Peir Rogier.* The metre requires the whole name to amount to three syllables only. The reading of R is the only one with the correct number but is slightly defective (*Peirotgier*). All the other MSS have *Peire*, thus offering four syllables. A slightly amended version of R is therefore adopted. The spelling of *Rogier* without the *s* is retained in view of the support given by CM. Further justification for this spelling is provided by the MS readings in II, l. 64. (See note to this line.)

Appel prefers to adapt the reading of ABE (*Peire Rotgiers*) and DIK (*Peire Rogiers*) in order to retain the *s* of the more usual nominative form.

He states (p. 72) that the form *Peir* is found in St John's Gospel as a nominative alongside *Peire* in the accusative. He compares the word to *fraire, paire.* These were in fact among words which, in certain dialects, particularly in the Haut Limousin and in Gascony, lost the need for the supporting vowel, perhaps as a result of their use as proclitics. The *r* also often disappeared, resulting in *Pei* (*Pey, Pé*), *frai, pai, mai. Cf.* the Gascon *Sempé* (< *Sanctum Petrum*). (*Cf.* Anglade, p. 123; Grandgent, p. 35.)

51 *mals.* The more usual nominative form offered by the majority of the MSS is adopted. CIK have *mal.* For the conversion of Latin neuter nouns to masculine *cf. Altprov. Elem.*, p. 67, and Grandgent, p. 85.

52 *rauguelha.* For discussion on the etymology of this word, which we translate as 'has the death rattle', *cf.* Appel's note (p. 73), Levy, *S.W.*, VII, 48, and Meyer-Lübke, *Romanisches etymologisches Wörterbuch*, p. 588.

II TAN NO PLOU NI VENTA (356, 8)

Nine MSS. C 195; D 3–8; I 13; K 2; M 194; R 27–226; G. de Bornelh A 23 (41 and *Archiv.*, 51, 20); N 177d (176–266); anonymous ω 66 + 59 + 66 (p. 577).

Editions. Raynouard, *Choix*, III, 29; *M.W.*, I, 120; Lavaud, *Troub. Cant.*, II, p. 414.

Classification. All the MSS have the same order of stanzas except for D, in which the third stanza appears at the end of the poem.

CN are the only MSS which contain the whole poem. The others have the following omissions. Rω: sixth stanza; M: seventh stanza; D: both *tornadas*; AIKM: second *tornada*.

ω is, to some extent, illegible and fragmentary.

The MSS may be divided into three groups: DIK, AN, CMRω. The MSS of the first two groups follow a more consistent pattern than those of the third group.

DIK share readings in 3, 5, 15 (*part*), 41, 46, 47, 49, 51, 53 (*contra*), 58 (*nis*). IK form a sub-group, *cf.* 26, 30, 35 (*qui*), 64 (in opposition to all the other MSS) and 9, 21, 22, 49.

POEM II

AN are in agreement in 19, 40, 58, and their relationship is confirmed by the fact that they both attribute the poem to Giraut de Bornelh although, as Appel points out, they contain the first *tornada* with the reference to Peire Rogier. They are allied with the first group in 4 (*chantar*), 50 (*quant*), 52 (*cuich–cug*).

The relationship of CMR with each other and with the other MSS is far more intricate, as indicated below:

CMR: 21
  MR: 7 (*qem*), 9 (*alre*), 15 (order of words), 37 (*qe*)
  CM: 50 (*quen–qe*), 51, 52
  CR: 35 (*navia*)

	CMR	MR	CM	CR
DIK				19 (*guirenta*), 40 (*jauzire*)
AN	64 (*rotgier*, etc)	3	41 (*ni*), 49	
A	5 (*em te* (*rete*)), 15 (*par*)			
N		14 (*li–lin*)	47 (*quel*), 49 (*quab*)	Inclusion of second *tornada*

M and R have strong independent tendencies and, as Appel indicates, they often differ in the same lines both from each other and from the other MSS, while C remains with the majority, *cf.* 4, 7, 11, 13, 22, 24, 40 (*seluy*), 43 (*que*), 44 (*en* (1)).

Support for Appel's view that the fourth stanza, which appears at the end of the poem in D, was added in that MS according to a MS closely related to M may be found in the majority of lines in the stanza (29, 30, 32, 34, 35, 36). Appel goes on to assume that, in view of its link with CM (*creaz qes*) in l. 52 in opposition to AIKN, the same MS was also corrected here at a later stage. It should be noted, however, that this is not the only other instance where D is linked with M, *cf.* 37 (with MR), 54.

ω was not at Appel's disposal. Its precise classification is difficult in view of its association with all three groups and, to a lesser extent, its fragmentary nature. It would appear, however, to tend more to the CMR group and to R in particular than to either of the other two groups. The sixth stanza is missing in both R and ω. It is also significant that, immediately following this stanza, lines 55, 56 appear to be missing in ω and have very independent readings in R. ω is linked with CNR by the inclusion of the second *tornada* all three lines of which it contains, in common with C. It is further allied with C in 60 (*plaiz–platz*) but joins NR to oppose it in

69 (*lui*). Its association, on the other hand, with MSS of the first and second groups is seen in 14 (ACDIK: *len*), 19 (CDIKR: *guirenta*), 29 (DM), 35 (IKNR: *sel*), 36 (D), 64 (IK).

Base and orthography. C.

I   Tan no plou ni venta,
qu'ieu de chan non cossire;
frei'aura dolenta
no·m tolh chantar ni rire,
qu'amors me capdelh'e·m te   5
mon cor en fin joy natural,
e·m pais e·m guid'e·m soste,
qu'ieu non suy alegres per al
ni alres no·m fai vivre.

II   Ma dompn'es manenta   10
de so qu'ieu plus dezire;
del donar m'es lenta,
qu'anc no·n fuy may jauzire;
ben sai que pauc l'en sove,
e ges no·m part joc cominal,   15
qu'ilh pensa petit de me,
et ieu trac per lieys mal mortal,
tal qu'a penas puesc vivre.

III   No trop qui·m guirenta
ni qui m'o auze dire   20
q'un'autra tan genta
e·l mon se li ni·s mire;
ni d'autra non s'esdeve,
mas qu'om digua que re no val,
qu'elha ditz e fai tan be,   25
q'una contra lieys no sap sal;
tal domna fai a vivre.

IV   Si s'en fenhon trenta,
ges per so no·m n'ahire;
cuy que·s vol si·s menta,   30
qu'a mi·s denh'escondire;
qu'adonc sai ieu ben e cre

q'us non a dompna tan cabal,
quan quecx la lauza per se,
que s'el n'avia un'aital 35
ben pogra ses lieys vivre.

V Greu planh mal que'n senta
drutz, quant es bos sufrire,
qu'amors es valenta
seluy que n'es jauzire; 40
erguel no vol ni mante,
ans qui lo·lh mostra, lieys non cal,
que mais n'auri'ab merce
en un jorn qu'en dos ans ab mal
sel qu'ab erguelh vol vivre. 45

VI Si uns s'i prezenta,
que·l denh lonc se assire,
ges no m'espaventa,
qu'ab mi l'ai a devire,
que dona, quant en pretz ve, 50
deu aver fin cor e leyal;
e non crezatz que·s malme
contra son bon amic coral
als dias qu'ay'a vivre.

VII E s'il fai parventa 55
que·l guinh ni·l huel lor vire,
per so no·s guaimenta
mos cors ni·s mand'aucire;
que dompna fai manta re
per que plass'a totz per engual, 60
e quasqun cum li cove
deu aculhir dins son ostal,
s'ab gran bontat vol vivre.

VIII Peir Rogier per bona fe
tramet lo vers denant nadal 65
a sidons que·l fai vivre.

IX Clama li per gran merce
qu'aprenda·l vers denant nadal,
s'ab joy de lui vol vivre.

54   THE POEMS OF THE TROUBADOUR PEIRE ROGIER

Variants. The illegible parts of ω are indicated by - - - except where otherwise stated.
 I. Lines 1-6 *lacking* ω; 1, tant *ANR*; non *ADIKN*. 2, qe *M*, queu *DN*, q̄u *AI*, q¹eu *C*; dun *M*; cant *N*, chant *A*; consire *N*, conssire *ADIK*. 3, f. a.] aura freida *A*, aura freia *MN*, aura frey *R*, freydura *C*; ni lenta *M*. 4, nō *AD*; tol *ADIKMNR*; chantar] gabar *M*, solas *R*. 5, camors *ADIKNR*, qamors *M*; mi *ADKMN*, ni *I*; capdel *MR*, capdell *DIK*, chapdella *A*; c. e. t.] cab dolenta *N*; e. t.] anc se *DIK*, em rete *C*; ten *A*. 6, joi *ADIKMN*. 7, e·m pais *lacking* ω; em gui- - - ω; e·m] el *N*, qem *M*, quem *R*; pays *R*; e. g.] em vest *M*, de joy *R*; guid'] guida *AC*; e·m s.] e s. *C*. 8, - - - per al ω; q̄u *I*, qieu *AM*, que *R*, queu *DN*; no *MR*; soi *N*, son *DIK*, sui *A*, sai *M*, si *R*; alegrar *M*. 9, alre *R*, al reis *IK*; a. n. f.] per alre non sai *M*; nō *DIK*; fa *R*; vievre *R*, viv *illegible* ω.

 II. 10, ma d *illegible* ω, mas *M*; dompn'] domn *KN*, dōn *DM*, dompna *C*, dona *R*ω. 11, d. s.] daiso *M*, des *R*; qu'ieu *illegible* ω, qeu *D*, q̄u *I*, qieu *A*, q¹eu *MR*, queu *N*; pus *R*; desire *ADI*, desirre *K*. 12, s len *illegible* ω. 13, canc *ANR*ω, qanc *IM*; n. f. m.] neys no fuy *R*; fui *ADIKMN*ω; may *lacking M*, mais *ADIKN*, mas ω; jauzire *illegible* ω, jausire *M*. 14, en sai *and* sove *illegible* ω; be *R*; say *R*; qe *M*ω, q̄ *DR*; li *M*, lin *NR*. 15, - - - cominal ω; e. g. n. p.] e. n. p. g. (*order of words*) *M*, e no par de *R*; jes *AN*; par *ACM*; jog *D*; comunal *ADIKMN*. 16, qil - - - ω; qel *M*, quel *DIK*, quil *N*, quill *A*, q¹lh *CR*; penssa *A*, pessa *R*. 17, et ieu trac per *illegible* ω; et *lacking R*; eu *DN*, yeu *R*; trai *M*, tras *R*; lei *N*, leis *DIKMR*ω, lieis *A*; mortal mal *M*. 18, tal *lacking C*; q. a. p. p.] qe nō pos mais *M*; capenas *ADIKNR*ω; posc *DN*, puosc *AIK*; vievre *R*.

 III. 19, non *ADIKMN*ω; trob *AI*, truep *R*, es *M*; qim *AM*ω, q¹m *R*, quin *N*; gairenta *M*, garenta *AN*, girenta ω. 20, ne *MN*; qim *M*ω; o *lacking M*; aize *N*, ause *AM*. 21, cun *MR*ω; atra ω; tan genta *illegible* ω; q̄ tant avinenta *A*, cuna autrentan g. *D*, cuna tretan g. *IK*, cuna trita menta *N*. 22, el mon se li *illegible* ω; se] ses *D* (*it is not clear whether the final s, which is above the line, is by the same hand*); s. l. n. m.] se remire *M*, nos li nes mire *R*; vis *IK*. 23, datra ω; no *R*; sēdeve *R*. 24, mais *A*; com *AIKNR*, cō *D*ω, qom *M*; diga *ADIKMNR*ω; qe *KM*ω, q̄ *DR*; r. n.] leis *M*; ren *ADIKN*ω, res *R*; non *ADIKN*ω. 25, qela ω, q̄la *R*, qella *AM*, quila *I*, quilla *DKN*; diz ω; e. f.] estai *M*; faitz *N*, fa *R*; t. b.] tan de be *C*; tant *A*; ben *D*. 26, cuna *ADIKNR*ω; contrab *IK*; leis *DIKMN*ω, leys *R*, lieis *A*; non *ADIKMN*ω; sab *DIKN*; al *M*. 27, tals *A*ω; dompna *AI*, dona *NR*, dōna *D*, donnā *M*; vievre *R*.

 IV. 28, feignon *D*ω, feingnen *I*, feignnon *KN*, feinhon *M*, freignon *A*; treinta *M*, XXX *R*. 29, jes *ANR*ω; so] tan *DM*ω; no·m] non *N*; no·m n'ahire] nō azire *D*; naire *IKN*, nayre *R*, nazire *AM*ω. 30, cui *AIKN*ω, qi *M*, qui *D*, com *R*; qeis *A*, qes *KM*ω, q̄s *R*; v. s.] voilla *IK*; si *A*. 31, ca *ADIKN*ω, qa *M*; q. a. m.] camās *R*; deing *IKN*ω, deigna *A*, deinh *M*, dieng *D*, dev *R*. 32, c- - - ω; adonc *DM*, cadoncs *AIN*, cadons *K*, e dōcx *R*; say *R*; eu *DIKMN*, yeu *R*. 33, q. u. n. a.] q¹eu nō truep *R*; cuns *D*ω, cus *AIKN*, quns *M*; ha *M*; domna *R*, dona *N*ω, dōna *D*, donna *M*; tant *AN*. 34, quan quecx *illegible* ω; can *IKN*, qan *ADM*, car *R*; qecs *A*, quecs *IK*, q̄cx *R*, quer *N*; q. l. l.] chascus cor lai *DM*, l. lor l. *C*. 35, q̄ *MR*, qui *IK*; s'el n'avia] sēigngues *N*; se *D*, si *AM*, siel ω, silh *C*; nages *DM*, nagues *AIK*ω; una *A*; artal *N*, atertal *R*. 36, ben *lacking R*; poyria *R*; pograb l. *D*ω; sens *N*, ses *lacking M*; lei *IKN*, leis *DM*ω, leys *R*, lieis *A*; vievre *R*.

v. 37, grieu *M*; plain *N*, plaing *ADIK*ω, plainh *M*; qen *A*, qe *M*, que *D*, q̄ *R*, quien ω. 38, cant *NR*ω, qand *A*, qant *DKM*; bons *IKN*ω; soffrire *AD*, sofrire *N*ω, suffrire *IK*. 39, camors *ADIKNR*ω, qamors *M*, qᵃmors *C*. 40, cellui *AKN*ω, celui *DI*, a sel *R*; qi ω, qe *I*, q̄ *ACDNR*; jauzire *illegible* ω, chausire *A*, chauzire *N*; qant hom lleis gent servire *M*. 41, orgoill *AIN*, orguoill *DK*ω, qorgueilh *M*; non *ADIKMN*ω; nil *DIK*ω; e per erguelh nō mante *R*. 42, anz *ADIK*ω; qi *M*ω, q¹ *R*; loil *A*, loilh *M*, lol *DIKNR*ω; l. n.] nō lī *R*; lei *DIK*ω, leis *MN*, lieis *A*; qᵃl *R*. 43, que *lacking M*, q̄ *ADI*; nauria *ACIKM*, conqer (*above the line*) *D*; ab *illegible* ω; mece *D*; car greu cre q̄ sesdeve *R*. 44, qen *AD*, qab *M*; anz *DIK*; q̄ naya mas tormen ab mal *R*. 45, sel cabor- - - ω; cel *AN*, cil *M*, sal *C*; cab *ADIKNR*, qab *M*, que ab *C*; ergueilh *M*, orgoil *IN*, orguoill *ADK*; vol *lacking M*; vievre *R*.

vi. *Lacking R*ω. 46, car silsim presenta *A*, sanz un si presenta *DIK*, esil representa *M*, caisim si presenta *N*. 47, qel *M*, quil *D*, quill *IK*, qem *A*; deing *ADIKN*, deinh *M*; si *ADIKMN*; aissire *D*. 48, jes *AN*; mesparventa *M*. 49, cab *N*, car *DIK*, qab *M*, qan *A*; me *M*; l'ai a d.] lai de vire *IK*, lai de vivre *D*. 50, q̄ *CM*; dompna *AIK*, dōna *D*, donna *MN*; cant *N*, qand *A*, qant *DK*; q. e.] quen *C*, qe *M*; prez *DKMN*; ve] mante *M*. 51, e l.] natural *ADIK*, coral *N*; lial *M*. *In D l. 49 is repeated after l. 51*. 52, creaz *D*, cresaz *M*; c. q.] cuich q̄ lais *A*, cug ques *IKN*; qes *M*, q̄s *D*. 53, c. s.] contral sieu *A*, vas lo sieu *M*, encontra son *N*; bon *lacking M*. 54, a. d.] adias *N*; qu'ay'a] caia *KN*, qaia *A*, qᵃya *C*, can a *I*, caia a *D*, qaia a *M*.

vii. *Lacking M*. 55, *lacking* ω; e *lacking C*; sol q̄ nols contenda *R*. 56, *lacking* ω; qel *AD*, quil *IN*; ging *D*, guing *AIKN*; nils *A*; huoils *A*, oil *N*, oill *DIK*; lor] li *A*; ab q̄ vas lor se vire *R*. 57, - - - nos - - -m̄ta ω; nois *A*; gaimenta *ADIKN*, gaymenta *R*. 58, mos cors - - -sire ω; nil *AN*, nim *R*; ausire *DIKN*. 59, q. dona - - -ta re ω; q̄ *AKR*; ma *C*; domna *KN*, dona *R*, dōna *D*; fa *R*; maingta *A*, man *C*. 60, qe *K*ω, q̄ *R*; plass'a] plaiz a ω, platz a *C*, plassa a *A*; tot *D*; egal *DIKN*, engal *AR*, - - -gal ω. 61, - - -scun - - - cove ω; cascun *DKN*, cascus *R*, chascun *AI*; con *IKN*, cō *D*; lin *R*; conve *I*. 62, acoillir *D*, acuillir *AIKN*, acullir ω; dinz *ADIK*ω; osdal *R*. 63, s'ab] siab *C*, sa *D*, sam *R*; beutat *I*; vievre *R*.

viii. *Lacking D*. 64, Peire *ACIKMN*ω; roger *M*, rogiers *IK*ω, rotgier *A*; Peirotgier *R*. 65, tamet *N*; lo] son *R*; denan *IKMN*ω; d. n.] tot per cabal *R*. 66, sidonz *AKN*ω; qel *AM*ω, q̄l *C*; q. f. v.] clamar merce *R*.

ix. *Lacking ADIKM*. 67, cl *and* li *illegible* ω. 68, caprendal ω; denan ω. 69, joi ω; d. l.] d̄llui ω; lui] lieys *C*.

67–9, *N*:   e clama li vers denan nadal
                    sab joi de lui vol vivre.

R: e prēdal avās de nadal
          sap grat de luy vol vievre.

Metrical scheme. Seven *coblas unissonans* of nine lines and two *tornadas*, each of three lines following the scheme of the last three lines of the stanzas.

$$a_5' \ b_6' \ a_5' \ b_6' \ c_7 \ d_8 \ c_7 \ d_8 \ e_6'$$

(Frank: 411: 2). There is one other example of this rhyme scheme but it has a different syllable arrangement. (Gavaudan: Pillet and Carstens, 174, 11.)

Notes

3 *frei'aura*. The reading of DIK is chosen in order to satisfy the metre requirements. *Freia* must be in a position which allows it to be monosyllabic. This is not possible in the case of AMN (*aura freida/freia*), and R, whilst offering the correct number of syllables, has the masculine and not the required feminine form of *frei* (*aura frey*). Bartsch (*Literaturblatt*, IV, 66) reads the line in R as *aura freydolenta*, a construction which he states is not attested elsewhere but which is grammatically possible. This appears to be a rather forced interpretation, however, particularly as the scribe has clearly separated the two words *frey* and *dolenta*.

It is interesting to note that the reading of C (*freydura*), although independent, is very close to that of DIK. The intelligent scribe may have amended the original *a* of *aura* to *d* in an attempt to improve on the text. (See note to I, 1. 47.)

5 *e·m te*. The reading of C (*e·m rete*) gives the line one syllable too many. The similar version of AMR is preferred to that of DIK (*anc se*), particularly as it appears to be supported by N (*cab dolenta*).

7 *e·m s*. C is the only MS to omit *me*. One would certainly expect it to be included, especially in view of the two preceding instances in the line. C is also the only MS to retain the final *a* of *guida*, which is superfluous as far as the metre is concerned and would not therefore be pronounced, *cf.* I, l. 26. It should be noted that C is inconsistent with regard to the elision of superfluous vowels, *cf.* l. 5: *cabdelh'e·m te*; l. 31: *denh'escondire*; l. 54: *qu'ay'a vivre*; l. 58: *mand'aucire*; etc.

10 *dompn'es*. For the elision of the *a* of *dompna*, see l. 7.

13 *may*. *May* is used here to reinforce *anc no* ('never').

15 *part*. ACMR have the reading *par*. The context requires, however, the normal form of the third person present singular of *partir* (= 'to share') offered by DIKN. (*Cf.* Anglade, p. 284; *Altprov. Elem.*, p. 85; *Prov. Chr.*, p. xviii.)

Bartsch (*op. cit.*, IV, 67) erroneously states that R omits *no*. In fact the reading of R, although independent for this line, includes *no* and contains the correct number of syllables: *e no par de joc cominal*.

16 Bartsch (*loc. cit.*) points out that Appel does not indicate in his variants the reading *quel* offered by DMR. We confirm, however, that it is in fact DIKM which give this reading.

18 *tal*. C is the only MS without *tal* and thus again fails to scan correctly.

22 *se li ni·s mire*. Appel (p. 73) and Lavaud translate *se li* literally: 'laces herself', whereas Levy (*S.W.*, IV, 397) gives the verb a more general meaning, which seems appropriate in this context: 'to dress, clean'. This part of the line would

therefore be translated: 'dresses herself or gazes at herself in the mirror'. Levy (*loc. cit.*) quotes another passage where the same use of the word occurs:

> Non es grans meravelhansa
> S'ieu ne fas lauzor,
> Quar non sai melhor
> Ni·*s lia*
> El mon bellazor
> *Troub. de Béziers*, p. 107, 23

Raynouard's reading of the line must be rejected as erroneous: *e·l mon s'eli ni·s mire* ('. . . au monde se choisit et s'admire') (*Lex. rom.*, III, 430). *Eli* is the normal form of the third person preterite of *elire* (*cf. Anglade*, p. 287) and as such would not be linked here with the present subjunctive *mire*. Furthermore the independent reading of R confirms the choice of *li* as opposed to *eli*: . . . *no·s li ne·s mire*.

25 *tan be.* In C the metre is again disrupted, this time by the insertion of *de* between *tan* and *be*. It is the only MS with this reading.

26 *no sap sal.* This expression is to be translated as 'is not pleasing'. Cf. Levy, *S.W.*, VII, 400, where this meaning is illustrated further in the passage from Duran de Carpentras (Mahn, *Gedichte*, 105, 3) which is also quoted by Appel in his notes (p. 73):

> E qar non vueilh mos chantars *sapcha sal*
> Ni c'om lo deia en nuilha cort grazir,
> I met primier per desasaborir
> Lo vieilh seinhor del Tor, qar ren no val,
> El sirventes tenra n'om per plus grieu.

27 *fai a vivre.* Levy gives *faire a* the meaning 'to be suitable for, worthy of' (*S.W.*, III, 385; *Pet. Dict.*, p. 182). Appel's interpretation of the line (p. 73) seems preferable, however: 'Such a lady makes one fond of living' (lit. 'brings it about that one is fond of living'). *Cf. G. de Born.*, 68, 1. 47.

Lavaud objects to this meaning because *tal* is without the usual nominative *s* and he prefers to make *tal domna* the complement of *fai*: 'Telle dame elle fait (est) pour vivre' (*Troub. Cant.*, p. 67). Grandgent (p. 110) states, however, that in the case of *qualis*, which is inflected like *talis*, 'the feminine singular often dropped its -s, and sometimes took the ending -a (*cal, cala*)'. It is therefore reasonable to assume that *talis* was involved in the same process.

28 Lavaud (*loc. cit.*) translates this line: 'If thirty boast about possessing her'. We prefer, with Appel (p. 73), the alternative, and perhaps more common, meaning of *se fenher* and interpret the line as 'If thirty occupy themselves with her.'

29 Bartsch (*op. cit.*, IV, 67) states that in DN the *n*' before *ahire* is lacking. We confirm, however, that it is included in N. The two MSS have, in fact, different readings for this half of the line. D: *nō azire*; N: *non naire.*

30 *cuy.* Consistent with his interpretation of l. 28, Lavaud (*op. cit.*, pp. 67–8 chooses the nominative *qui* of DM and makes it the subject of ·*s vol* and ·*s menta*: 'Let him lie who wishes to lie'. Preference is given, however, to the dative form offered by all the other MSS except R, which is independent (*com*). The lady thus becomes the subject of ·*s menta*: 'Let her lie to *whomever* she wishes'.

It is probable that M was the only MS which originally had *qui*, as the stanza as a whole appears to have been added in D at a later stage according to a MS close to M (see 'Classification').

34 *la lauza*. Once more the line does not scan correctly in C, this time owing to the insertion of *lor* between *la* and *lauza*. The reading offered by all the other MSS except DM is adopted. It should again be noted that the independent version of DM (*chascus cor lai*) is likely to have existed originally in M only. *Cf.* note to l. 30.

35 *s'el*. C is the only MS with the reading *silh*. It is, however, fairly close to the reading of IKNRω, which is chosen here in preference to that given only by AM (*si*) but supported again by D (*se*). (*Cf.* note to ll. 30 and 34.)

36 Lavaud (*op. cit.*, p. 68) treats *pogra* as the first person and regards *lieys* as the poet's lady. However, like Appel (p. 74), we prefer to give *pogra* the subject *el* in l. 35 and to treat *lieys* and *aital* as one and the same lady.

40 *jauzire*. The reading of CR is retained, as it is supported by the DIK tradition in opposition to that of AN (*chausire*). Appel (p. 41) is of the view that *jauzire* is the reading of the original while the version *chausire* is based on conjecture. It is the latter version, however, which he chooses tentatively to adopt. M is independent here and the reading of ω is illegible.

43 *n'auri'ab*. For the elision of the final *a* of *auria* see note to l. 7.

45 *sel qu'*. C and M have independent readings (*sal-cil*). The normal form of the nominative singular offered by all the other MSS is preferred. For the elision of *e* in *que* see note to l. 7.

50 *quant en*. The version of the first and second groups (ANDIK) is chosen here. The stanza is lacking in Rω, and the respective readings of C (*quen*) and M (*qe*) do not satisfy the metre requirements.

55 The metre is once more upset in C, this time by the omission of *e*. The reading adopted is again that of ANDIK. R is entirely independent, while the line is lacking in ω and the stanza as a whole is lacking in M.

56 *lor vire*. In this kind of context *contra* and *ves* appear to be more commonly employed with *virar*. For the use of the dative, however, *cf.* B. von Vent., 35, ll. 13-15:

> Midons sui hom et amics e servire,
> e no·lh en qer mais autras amistatz
> mas c'a celat los sens bels olhs *me vire*
> . . .

and R. d'Orange, XIII, ll. 28-9:

> Si ja tan mos cors mescaba
> Qu'al meu tort me virez l'escut.

59 *que . . . manta*. C is the only MS with *ma*. *Que* is clearly favoured by all three traditions and is used with *dompna* in the same way as in the corresponding line (50) of the previous stanza.

The monosyllabic form *man*, offered by C later in the line, fails to satisfy the metre requirements.

60 *plass'*. The subjunctive is required in the final clause introduced by *per que* (*cf.* Altprov. Elem., p. 135). The reading of the majority of the MSS is therefore preferred to that of C (*platz*), supported by ω (*plaiz*). Neither version is to be found as a recognised form of the subjunctive (*cf.* Anglade, p. 340; Altprov. Elem., p. 103; Grandgent, p. 129).

61 *quasqun*. Suchier (*Goett. gel. Anzeigen*, 1883, 1342) draws attention to the fact that Appel incorrectly splits the pronoun into two (*quasq'un*). Its existence as one word is fully attested elsewhere (*cf. Pet. Dict.*, p. 70, *Altprov. Elem.*, p. 128, etc.). Grandgent (p. 112) suggests that the word is the result of a fusion of *cada ūs* and **cescus* < **cisqu'unus* = *quisque unus* = *unus quisque*.

63 *s'ab*. For the elision of *i*, see note to l. 7.

64 *Peir Rogier*. This reading is not given by any of the MSS. The version of R (*Peirotgier*) is the only one with the correct number of syllables in the line, all the others offering *Peire*. We have therefore taken the same action as in the case of I, l. 50. For *Rogier* we have adhered to C, which is supported by both MR and AN in opposition to IKω (*Rogiers*) (*cf.* note to I, l. 50). The *tornada* is missing in D.

67–9 Cω are the only MSS which contain all three lines of the second *tornada*. N omits half of ll. 67 and 68 and R the whole of l. 67. R appears, in fact, to have merged ll. 66 and 67 into one (*cf. clamar merce* (R: l. 66) and *clama ... merce* (Cω: l. 67)), whereas in N the scribe has clearly gone direct from the middle of l. 67 to the middle of l. 68.

69 *lui*. The reading of the majority of the MSS which contain this *tornada* (NRω) is preferred to the independent version of C (*lieys*), which does not make as good sense.

III PER FAR ESBAUDIR MOS VEZIS (356, 6)

Ten MSS. C 194; D^a 153–528; K 3; a^1 474 (222); Giraut de Bornelh A 23 (42 and *Archiv.*, 51, 20); B 15 (Mahn, *Gedichte*, 1371); N 178c (177–267)(Mahn, *Gedichte*, 881); Bernart de Ventadour I 13; P. Luzer R 21–178; anon. ω 66 + 59 (p. 578).

Editions. Raynouard, *Choix*, III, 32; *M.W.*, I, 117; Lavaud, *Troub. Cant.*, II, p. 424.

Classification. All the MSS have the same order of stanzas except C and R, in which the order of stanzas III and IV is reversed. In a^1 the positions of 21, 22 and 43, 44 are reversed, as well as the order of 43, 44 in DIK and of 56, 57 in A. They all contain the whole poem except for R, in which both *tornadas* and 31–3 are missing, ABN, in which 43 is missing, and ω, which ends at 22 and is partly illegible.

The main division of the MSS is ABDIKN and CR, as borne out by the order of stanzas and the variants, *cf.* 9, 11, 18, 20, 24, 25, 26, 28, 39, 42, 43, 44, 47, 49, 51, 52, 53, 54. The MSS of the first group divide into two sub-groups: DIK and ABN. DIK have common readings in 9, 13, 22, 26 (*qu'il*) (with Ca^1), 32, 33, 34, 39, 43, 44, 47, 49, 59, 60. IK are, as usual, almost identical, being further linked in 41, 59 and by the inclusion of the section of 37 and 38 which is missing in D but which appears earlier, in the middle of 9, in all three MSS. ABN all attribute the poem to Giraut de Bornelh. They omit 43, which, as Appel points out, was added later in DIK after 44, and share readings in 26, 41 and in 13, 22, 54, 55. Of the three, AB are particularly close, *cf.* the last four lines quoted above and 24, 25, 31 (*joi*) (with a¹), 32 (*ni's*), 34 (*noil o*) (with C), 39, 47, 49 (*nuill*) (with CR), 56, 60 (*mas*) (with C), 65.

The various sub-groups defined above are confirmed in many of the instances where the two main groups are interrelated. Often where DIK have common readings are ABN and CRa¹ joined in opposition (*cf.* 22, 33 (R lacking), 39, 59, 60). In the same way DIK and CRa¹ are allied in many of the places where ABN share variants, *cf.* 13 (*li*), 22, 43, 54 (*dans*), 55 (*tortz*). N stands with them, in opposition to AB, in 24, 56, 65. AB and CR join forces to oppose the other MSS in 49 (*nulh*). Notable examples of links between individual MSS of the two groups are NR (*cf.* 27 (*son*), 53 (*joi*) as well as 13 (with AB)) and CN (*cf.* 32, 57 (*mas*)).

a¹ and ω were not at Appel's disposal. a¹ has associations with both traditions. It joins all the MSS of the first group in 18, 24, 39, 42, 49, 52, 53, 54, revealing further links with two or more of them in 25, 31, 32, 35, 41, 47, 49, 60 and with N in particular in 28 (*tot*), 49 (*tal*). It appears, on the whole, however, to incline to the second group, *cf.* 9 (see note), 26, 28, 43, 44, and above. Ra¹ are further linked in 34, 45, 46, as are Ca¹ in 16 (*quan*), 32 (*nō*). It offers the largest number of independent readings, which are fairly insignificant with the exception of 64 (see note to this line).

From the evidence available ω also appears to fluctuate between both groups. It joins CR in 18 in opposition to all the other MSS, while the reverse is true in 9, 20. In 13 it is linked with CDIK against ABNR and stands with CRa¹ for all of 22, being joined in turn by ABN and DIK.

Base and orthography. C.

I
 Per far esbaudir mos vezis,
 que's fan irat quar ieu no chan,
 no mudarai deserenan,
 qu'ieu no despley
 un so novelh que'ls esbaudey;   5
 e chant mais per mon Tort-n'avetz,
 quar trop dechai
 tot quan vey sai,
 mas lai ab lieys creys joys e pretz,
 per que'l sieus conortz m'es plus bos   10
 que tot quan vey sai entre nos.

II
 De midons ai lo guap e'l ris,
 e suy fols, s'ieu plus li deman,
 ans dey aver gran joy d'aitan;
 a Dieu m'autrey;   15

non ai donc pro car sol la vey?
Del vezer suy ieu bautz e letz;
plus no m'eschai,
que ben o say,
mas d'aitan n'ai ieu joy e pretz   20
e m'en fauc ricautz a sazos
a guiza de paubr'ergulhos.

III De totz drutz suy ieu lo plus fis,
qu'a midons no dic re ni man
ni'l quier gen fait ni bel semblan;   25
cum qu'ilh m'estey,
sos drutz suy et ab lieys dompney
totz cubertz e celatz e quetz,
qu'ilh no sap lay
lo ben que'm fai,   30
ni cum ai per lieys joy e pretz;
ni's tanh que ia'l sapch'enoios,
qu'ieu suy sai sos drutz a rescos.

IV Anc ieu ni autre no'lh o dis,
ni elha non saup mon talan,   35
mas a celat l'am atretan —
fe qu'ieu li dey —
cum s'agues fait son drut de mey;
re no'm qual, que ia l'am eis setz. —
Doncs amarai   40
so qu'ieu non ai? —
Oc, qu'eyssamen n'ai joy e pretz
e son alegres e joyos,
quant res non es, cum si vers fos.

V   Per s'amor viv, e se'n moris,   45
qu'om disses qu'ieu fos mortz aman,
fait m'agr'amors honor tan gran,
qu'ieu sai e crey
qu'anc a nulh drut mais tal non fey;
vos jutgatz, dompn', e destrenhetz!   50
Car s'ieu m'esmay
e si mal tray
ni muer per vos, joys m'es e pretz:
de vos m'es totz mals bes, dans pros,
foldatz sens, tortz dregz e razos.   55

62   THE POEMS OF THE TROUBADOUR PEIRE ROGIER

    VI   Ieu mai que mai,
            ma donn', ieu sai
            que vos mi donatz joy e pretz;
            e vuelh mais morir ad estros
            ia·l sapcha negus hom mas vos.   60

    VII   Bastart, tu vay
            e porta·m lay
            mon sonet a mon Tort-n'avetz;
            e di·m a n'Aimeric lo tos
            membre·lh dont es e sia pros.   65

Variants. *The illegible parts of ω are indicated by - - - except where otherwise stated.*
  I. 1, *no variants*. 2, q̄s a^1, qeis *A*, q̄is *B*; car *ABDIKNRa^{1}ω*; eu *BD*ω, yeu *R*; non *ABDIKNRa^{1}ω*. 3, non *ABINa^{1}ω*; mudara a^1, mudaray *R*. 4, qeu a^1, q̄u *DI*ω, qieu *A*, que *B*, quen *N*; nom *N*, non *AKRa^1*, nō *BDI*ω; desplei *ABDIKNa^{1}ω*. 5, sol *I*, son *ABKNRa^{1}ω*; noel ω, novel *ABDIKNRa^1*; qels *AD*ω, q̄ls *I*, qelz *B*, qils a^1; esbaudei *ABDIKNa^{1}ω*. 6, cant ω, chan *DIKNa^1*; mays *R*; p. m. t. n'a.] navez per mon tort *N*; tortz ω; mavetz ω, naves *R*, navez *DK*. 7, car *ABDIKNR*ω, qar a^1; dechai *illegible* ω, dechay *R*, deschai *B*. 8, can *D*ω, cant *BR*, qant *AKa^1*, quant *IN*; vei *ABDIKNa^{1}ω*; say *R*, zai a^1. 9, mais *IK*; lai *lacking CR*; between lai *and* ab: qeu li dei. cō sagues fag *D*, q̄u (quieu *K*) li dei *IK* (*cf*. ll. 37–8); leis *DIKNa^{1}ω*, ley *R*, lieis *AB*; creis *ABDIKNa^{1}ω*; lai *is placed before* jois a^1; honor *R*, honors *C*, jois *ABDIKNa^{1}ω*; prez *DN*ω. 10, per qel sieus c - - - mes - - - ω; qel *ABa^1*, q̄ls *CD*; seus *N*, sieu *R*; conort *R*, conorz *BK*; pus *R*; bons *IK*. 11, *illegible* ω; que] de *ABDIKN*, qe de a^1; can *D*, cant *NR*, qant *ABKa^1*, quant *I*; vei *ABDIKNa^1*; sai *lacking* a^1, far *ABDIKN*, say *R*.
  II. 12, - - - donz ai lo gab - - - ω; midonz *ABDIKNa^1*; gab *NR*, gap *ABDIKa^1*. 13, e suy *illegible* ω; soi *DKN*, son *R*, sui *ABIa^1*; s'ieu] si *ABNR*, sui a^1; pus *R*; li] len *AB*, lin *N*. 14, - - - gran joi daitan ω; anz *ABDIKNa^1*; dei *ABDIKNRa^1*; joi *ABDIKNa^1*. 15, a dieu - - - ω; deu *N*, dieus *R*; mautrei *ABDIKNa^1*. 16, ay *R*, nai a^1; doncs *ABDIKN*ω, doncx *R*; car] qant a^1, quan *C*; vei *ABDIKNRa^{1}ω*. 17, vez - - - ω; soi *B*, son *DIKN*ω, soy *R*, sui *Aa^1*; eu *ABDIKNa^{1}ω*, yeu *R*; bauditz a^1, bauz *ADKN*ω; leitz *R*. 18, pus *R*; no] nō ω; eschai] eschay *R*, nechai *N*, nescai a^1, neschai *ABDIK*. 19, qe *Ia^1*, q̄ *BR*; sai *ABDIKNa^{1}ω*. 20, m. d'a.] e pero sim *ABDIKNa^{1}ω*; nay *R*; ieu *lacking ABDIKNa^{1}ω*, yeu *R*; joi *ABDIKNRa^{1}ω*; pres ω, prez *DN*. *The positions of ll*. 21, 22 *and* 43, 44 *are reversed in* a^1. 21, fas *DIN*ω, fau a^1, faz *K*; ricaus *DIK*, ricauz ω, richautz *AB*, ricx gaug *R*; saizos a^1. 22, guisa *ABIK*, gu - - - ω; del *DIK*; p. e.] paubre ielos *AB*, paubres geillos *N*; paubre *Da^1*; ergoillous *IK*, orgoillos *Da^1*, orgulhos *R*, orguoillos ω. *The rest of the poem is lacking in* ω.
  III. 23, toz *D*, tutz *N*; son *DIKN*, soy *R*, sui *ABa^1*; eu *BDIK*, yeu *R*; pus *R*; fiz

a^1. 24, cab R, car $ABDIKN$, q̄ a^1; re (ren) *before* midons $ABDIKN$ (ren) a^1 (re); midonz $ABDIKa^1$; n. d. n. m.] plus non deman AB; non $DIKNRa^1$. 25, nul a^1; qeir a^1, qier AB, q¹er R; gen] bel C, ben R, en AB; fag $DKNR$, faich AB, faig I, sail a^1; bel] en AB, gen R; senblan IK. 26, cum *lacking* R, con $DIKN$, on C; q¹eu R, que ABN, qil a^1, quil DI, quill K; estei a^1, estey CR, mestei $ABDIKN$. 27, son NR; druz D; fui a^1, soi R, son $DIKN$, sui AB; a. l.] aillors B; leis $DIKNa^1$, leys R, lieis A; domnei KNa^1, dompnei $ABDI$, dōney R. 28, tot Na^1, toz D; celatz e cubertz (*word order*) $ABDIKN$; cubert a^1, cuberz DN, cubretz K; celans C, selatz IKR, selaz DN; q̄s a^1, qetz AB, q̄tz D. 29, qil a^1, q¹l DI, q¹lh R, quil $ABKN$; non $ADIKNa^1$; sab D; lai $ABDIKNa^1$. 30, qem $ABDa^1$, q̄m D; so q¹eu pēs sai R. 31, *lacking* R; com $DIKN$, con a^1; ai] a C; leis $DIKNa^1$, liei A, lieis B; jois $DIKN$, joi ABa^1, joys C; e] ni a^1. 32, *lacking* R; ni·s] ni N, nim DIK, nō Ca^1; taing $ABDIKNa^1$; q. i.] ia nol a^1; q̄ BI; s. e.] sapcha ni vos CN, sapchel ni vos $DIKa^1$; sapch'] sapcha AB. 33, *lacking* R; qeu a^1, q̄u DI, qieu AB, q¹eu C, queu N; son $DIKN$, sui ABa^1; sos drutz sai (*word order*) DIK; a] en $ADIKNa^1$.

IV. 34, unc N; ieu *lacking* N, eu BD, yeu R; no·lh o]non lo $DIKN$, non loi a^1, non loy R; noil AB. 35, ela R, ella $ABDIKNa^1$; no R; sap DIa^1; tallan R. 36, selat DR, sellat IK; atrestā R, autre tan N. 37, *only* fe D (*the rest of the line has been inserted in the middle of l. 9*); qeu a^1, q̄u I, qieu AB, q¹eu R, queu N; dei $ABIKNa^1$. 38, com sagues fag *lacking* D (*the words have been inserted in the middle of l. 9*); com NRa^1, cō IK; fag $KNRa^1$, faich AB, faig I; mei $ABDIKN$, mi a^1. 39, r. n. q.] e non (nois AB) taing $ABDIKNa^1$; cal R; q̄ R, q̄u DI, qieu ABa^1, queu N, quieu K; l'a. e.] la meissez DK, la meissiez I; eyssetz R, issetz C. 40, doncx R. 41, zo a^1; qe a^1, q̄ BD, q̄u I, que AN, q¹eu C; ay R. 42, hoc BRa^1; qu'e.] eysamen R, catresim DK, catressim AIN, qatressim B, qautressi a^1; nay R; e joi A, joi $BDIKNa^1$; prez DN. *For the position of 43, 44 in* a^1 *see ll. 21, 22 above. In DIK ll. 43 and 44 are reversed in order*. 43, *lacking* ABN; e] en a^1, q̄u I, qieu K, q¹eu D; soi R, sui a^1; jojos $DIKa^1$. 44, q. r. n. e.] si tot non ai $ABDIKN$, qar non es res a^1; can R; re R; con IK, com DNR; ver a^1.

V. 45, viev R; sim $DIRa^1$, sin $ABKN$; muris a^1. 46, com $ABDIKR$, cō N, cum a^1; dises DIK; q̄u DIK, qieu ABa^1, queu N; fos] suy C; amans R, amanz a^1, ham D, haman K. 47, fach B, fag DKa^1, faich A, faig I, faytz R; magra amors AB, magra mortz CR; tant AB; grans R. 48, qeu a^1, q̄u DI, qieu ABK, q¹eu R, queu N; say R; crei $ABDIKNa^1$. 49, canc $ADNa^1$, qanc B, q̄ R, que C; negun $DIKNa^1$, nuill AB; mais tal] major CR, tal Na^1, tant DIK; no D; fei $ABDIKNa^1$. 50, jujatz $ABDIK$, julaz N, jutjatz R, viratz a^1; dompn'] domn K, dompna AC, dompnae a^1, don BR, dōn N; e] ni a^1; destregnetz Na^1, destreignetz AB, destreignez D, destreingnez IK. 51, car] qe a^1; seu N; mesmai $ABDIKNa^1$; quieu (q¹eu R) sen lesmay CR. 52, e] ni $ABDIKNa^1$; trai $ABDIKNa^1$. 53, ni *lacking* N; moer N, mor B, muor A; joi NR, jois $ABDIKa^1$; m'es] mer $ABDIKNa^1$; e *lacking* R. 54, toz DK; bes] bo C, bos R; dairz N, danz $DIKa^1$, dars AB. 55, foudatz $ABDIKN$, soldatz a^1; senz a^1, ses *ABIN*, sezs *K*; tortz] e tortz *D*, tot *N*, totz *AB*; dr. e r.] e dr. r. *C*, e dr. e r. *I*; dreitz *ABa*^{1}, dretz *DIKNR*; e] en *D*; raizos a^1, rasos *I*, raszos *K*.

    VI. *Lacking R. In A ll. 56 and 57 are reversed in order.* 56, en *N*, eu *DIKa*^{1}; qe *Ka*^{1}, q̄ *DI*; del mal qieu ai *AB*. 57, ma] mas *BCN*, mor a^1; donn'] domn *K*, dompn *DI*, dompna *AB*, dompnae a^1, don *N*; ē *I*, eu *BDKNa*^{1}. 58, qe a^1, q̄ *AD*; donas *DIK*, donaz *N*; joi *ABDIKNa*^{1}. 59, e] eu *DIK*; voil *N*, voill *BDIKa*^{1}, vuoill *A*; mais lacking *IK* (*included by a later hand in K*); morrir *K*, murir a^1; ad] a *ABN*; estors *ABIK*. 60, ia·l] gal *DIK*; nigus *N*; mas] ni *DIKNa*^{1}.

    VII. *Lacking R.* 61, Bastard a^1, Castart *N*; vai *ABDIKNa*^{1}. 62, e] em a^1; lai *ABDIKNa*^{1}. 63, mon s.] est s. a^1; tortz *B*; naves *N*, navez *DK*. 64, nameric *A*; tos] cos *D*, ros *C*; e digas nai merce alfos a^1. 65, membreil *Ba*^{1}, membreill *A*, membrel *DIKN*; don *ABDN*; e] i a^1; sia] sera *AB*; quelh membre dont elh sia pros *C*.

Metrical scheme. Five *coblas unissonans* of eleven lines and two *tornadas*, each of five lines, following the scheme of the last five lines of the stanzas:

$$a_8 \ b_8 \ b_8 \ c_8 \ c_4 \ d_8 \ e_4 \ e_4 \ d_8 \ f_8 \ f_8$$

(Frank: 731 : 3). There are three other examples of this rhyme scheme but none of them has precisely this syllable arrangement.

Notes

9 *lai . . . joys.* CR are the only MSS which have *honor(s)* and omit *lai*. The reading of all the others is preferred, as *joy* and *pretz* occupy the same position in the other stanzas. The reading of a^1 probably indicates the influence which both traditions have had upon it. The scribe appears to have begun by following CR in the omission of *lai*, only to include the word later in the line on preferring *joys* to *honors*.

    Joys and *pretz* both form the subject of the verb *creys* although it is singular. This usage is fairly frequent in Old Provençal and may perhaps be explained here by supposing that the two subjects come together to form one idea in the poet's mind. Other instances of this usage are found later in l. 53; V, l. 7; VI, ll. 25–6; VIIIa, ll. 37–8.

10 *que·l.* The meaning demands the normal singular form of the article (·l) (*cf. Altprov. Elem.*, p. 80), which is given by all the MSS except CD and R. The first two have the normal plural form (·ls) and the third is independent (*sieu*).

11 *que . . . sai.* Appel follows CR for *que* and ABDIKN for *far*. It seems reasonable, however, to retain CR for the whole line, as they offer a perfectly acceptable reading. They are also the only MSS which have not avoided what was probably the intentional repetition of l. 8. Bartsch (*Literaturblatt*, IV, 66) draws attention to Appel's apparent inconsistency here whereby he chooses CR in the first instance, only to depart from them later in the line for no obvious reason. In a^1 the presence of both *que* and *de* at the beginning of the line is probably a further indication of the influence of both traditions on this manuscript.

13 *s'ieu.* The version of C is retained, as it is supported by DIKω and probably also by a^1 (*sui*). Appel prefers the reading of ABNR (*si*).

16 *car.* C gives an acceptable reading (*quan*) but is supported only by a¹. It is notable that R joins here all the other MSS, and it is their reading which is therefore preferred.

23-33 It seems reasonable to adopt the stanza order of ABDIKNa¹, more natural than that of CR, in which the position of stanzas III and IV is reversed. The theme of secrecy and discretion in stanza III follows on logically from the poet's humble and tactful attitude of stanza II. It persists into stanza IV, where the *o* in l. 34, to which Appel (p. 74) draws attention, refers to the poet's secret love and its benefits, mentioned in stanza III.

25 *gen f.* C is the only MS with *bel*, being influenced probably by the *bel* which occurs later in the line. We have chosen the reading of DIKNa¹, which appears to be supported by that of AB (*en*) and R (*ben*). R, in fact, contains *gen* in the second half of the line.

bel s. C joins DIKNa¹ for this part of the line, and it is their version which is again preferred. AB repeats *en* and R offers *gen*.

26 DIK have been followed throughout the line in view of the fact that they are joined in turn by ABNR and Ca¹.

(i) *Cum.* The reading given by all the MSS except R, in which the word is lacking, and C which is independent (*on*).

(ii) *qu'ilh.* ABN offer *que*, being supported to some extent by R (*qieu*). The version of DIK is chosen, as it is supported by Ca¹.

(iii) *m'estey.* DIK and ABN again join forces to oppose CRa¹, which omit *me*.

The line is to be translated: 'Whatever attitude she may take towards me' (lit. 'However she may be to me').

28 *cubertz e celatz.* Appel prefers the word order of ABDIKN (*celatz e cubertz*). It seems reasonable, however, to adhere to that of CRa¹, which is equally acceptable, *cf.* B. von Vent., 4, ll. 43-4.

> Mas l'amor qu'es en me clauza,
> No posc *cobrir ni celar.*

C is the only MS with *celans*, for which reason the version of all the others is chosen.

31 *joy.* The normal form of the accusative singular, offered by ABa¹, is preferable here to the plural form (*joys*) given by CDIKN. It is the singular form of the word which appears in the corresponding place in the other stanzas.

It is interesting to note that earlier in the line C has *a*, as opposed to *ai*, contained by all the other MSS. This is perhaps an instance where the intelligent scribe of C, confronted with *joys*, could make sense of the line only by regarding *joys* as nominative singular and amending *ai* to *a*. ('Because of her *there are* joy and worth.') *Cf.* note to I, l. 47.

32 *ni's tanh.* The different readings of DIK (*nim*) and N (*ni*) provide support for that of AB, which is therefore retained in preference to the independent version of Ca¹ (*nō*). R omits ll. 31-3. (There is a misprint in Appel's variants, which classify R firstly with C and secondly with CN.)

sapch'enoios. The reading of AB is adopted, the *a* of *sapcha* being elided for reasons of metre. Appel prefers the spelling *enuios*, although it is not given by any MS. The versions offered by the other MSS (*sapcha ni vos, sapchel ni vos*) may well, in fact, be based on a misreading of the form *enuios*. It is not at all clear, otherwise, to whom *vos* would refer. The only dialogue in which Peire is engaged in this poem is with his lady (ll. 50-60) and with himself.

33 *a rescos*. It seems quite reasonable to adhere to the reading of C supported by B. Appel chooses that offered by all the other MSS (*en rescos*). On investigation, however, it appears that the expression is much more commonly used with *a* than with *en*. Neither in his *Petit Dictionnaire* nor in his *Supplement-Wörterbuch* does Levy mention *en rescos*, whereas *a rescos* is attested in both these works as well as in a number of other places, e.g. B. von Vent., 28, l. 51; Folq. de Mars., VII, l. 49; XV, l. 18; Prov. Chr., 7, l. 10.

39 *eis setz*. Appel tentatively suggests that the words may be equivalent in meaning to the German 'selbsechster'. This German usage consists of combining 'selb' with ordinal numbers to denote that a certain person is one of a certain number. 'Selbsechster' would thus be translated: 'as the sixth' or 'as one of six'. Appel, at the same time, expresses reservations about this interpretation, as he admits that nowhere else has he found *eis* used as a substitute for the pronoun in such an expression. We prefer to regard *eis* simply as an adverb and to translate the expression: 'even the sixth'. The adverbial use of *eis* is attested in *S.W.*, I, 325 (No. 3), *Pet. Dict.*, p. 135, and *Lex. rom.*, III, 98.

Appel also sees difficulties in the word *setz*. He states that *seizen* is the usual form of the ordinal and finds it necessary to justify *setz* by referring to the forms derived from the Latin *sextus* in other Romance languages, e.g. Old French *sist*, Italian *sesto* and Vulgar Latin *sistus*. He makes no mention, however, of the accepted alternative Old Provençal version of the ordinal: *sest* (cf. *Altprov. Elem.*, p. 74; *Anglade*, p. 238). As it is used adjectivally here, the word appears in the nominative form. The omission of the middle *s* follows the general rule whereby in cases where the three consonants *scs* and *sts* come together the first *s* is dropped. Cf. *quisque* + *s* > *quecs*, *Christus* > *Critz*, *estis* > *etz*. (See *Altprov. Elem.*, p. 39.)

In the MSS the two words are joined together. Lavaud, in fact, prefers to regard them as one word with the normal meaning of 'except' and translates the line: 'Nothing matters to me, except loving her henceforth'. He admits, however, that he has found no other example of *eissetz* used with *que* in this way. Levy (*Pet. Dict.*, p. 136; *S.W.*, II, 338) mentions only its use as a preposition, for which it may be followed by *de*.

Suchier (*Goett. gel. Anzeigen*, 1883, 1342) also offers an interesting, but somewhat doubtful, interpretation of *eissetz* in this instance. He states that *issetz* or *eissetz* is a rare Provençal word meaning 'exclusively', 'exceptionally', and derived from the Latin ablative *exceptis*, which in due course came to be used adverbially. He cites the modern version of the word, *eicès*, found in Mistral. We have found the word *eicès* in Mistral's *Lou Tresor doú Felibrige ou Dictionnaire Provençal–Français* (ed. V. Tuby, Paris, 1932, p. 840) but only in a long list of alternative forms, all with the meaning of 'except', among which are *eicèt*, *eiceptat*, *escetat* as well as the original Latin *exceptum*. Reference is also made to the use of the word with *que*.

44 *quant res non es*. Lavaud translates this part of the line 'Alors qu'il n'y a *rien* entre nous'. It seems appropriate, however, to give *res* the meaning of 'truth', 'reality', which is an interpretation of the word proposed, with some reservation, by Levy (*S.W.*, VII, 224):

> E si tot hom lo i fai parven
> Per paor, aquo non es *res*,

> Que, quan hom lo troba en deisses,
> Ab gaug et ab alegrier gran
> Rizon tug, quant el vai ploran.

Mahn *Werke*, I, 379 (R. de Vaqueiras)

46 *fos*. C is the only MS with *suy*. All the others have the imperfect subjunctive form of the verb, which one would normally expect in so far as the verb on which it depends (*disses*) is itself an imperfect subjunctive.

47 *m'agr'amors*. The reading of DIKNa¹ and of AB, which include the superfluous final syllable of *agra*. The slightly different version of CR (*magra mortz*) is probably a result of the influence of *mortz* in the previous line.

49 Appel has followed AB for the first half of the line and CR for the second half (*qu'anc a nulh drut maior non fey*). It seems preferable, however, to employ the version of AB for the whole line, particularly as they are joined in turn by CR and DIKNa¹. Support for *nulh drut* is provided by CR in opposition to DIKNa¹ and for *quanc* and *tal* by Na¹ and DIK (*tant*) in opposition to CR.

Mais is used here to reinforce *anc non* ('never'). *Cf*. II, l. 13.

50 *dompn'*. It is necessary, for reasons of metre, to follow BDIKNR in the elision of the superfluous *a*, *cf*. note to II, l. 7.

51 CR appear to have a corrupt reading (*quieu sen lesmay*). a¹ perhaps reveals a slight link with them by its initial *qe* but remains with all the others for the rest of the line.

53 See note to l. 9.

54 *bes*. CR offer variations on *bon* (*bo–bos*). The reading of all the other MSS is preferable in view of the fact that only nouns are employed in this and the following line.

55 The position of *e* before *dregz* in C makes little sense. All the other MSS have the correct order of words, although *e* appears twice in I.

57 *ma*. The reading of ADIK is chosen here. Those of BCN (*mas*) and a¹ (*mor*) make no sense.

60 *Que* is to be understood at the beginning of the line. Lines 59–60 may thus be translated 'And I prefer to die immediately than that anyone other than you know it'. See note to I, l. 39.

64 *n'Aimeric lo tos*. This is probably a reference to Aimeric de Lara, the son of Ermessinde, Ermengarda's sister, and of Manriquez de Lara, Count of Molina (*cf*. note, VIII, l. 36). As Ermengarda herself had no heirs, she called Aimeric to Narbonne in 1168 in order to prepare him to be her successor (*Hist. gen. Lang.*, VI, p. 70). He appears to share in the government of Narbonne from that time until his death in 1177 (*ibid.*). Evidence available in a legal document of 1176 (*ibid.*) suggests that at that time he was administering the estates of Narbonne as its legitimate ruler, having relinquished the name of Lara for that of Narbonne.

Aimeric's death led Count Raimon V of Toulouse to take steps to assure himself of Narbonne and to prevent Ermengarda from giving it to another of her nephews without his consent. As a result the Viscounts of Nîmes and Carcassonne, the lords of Montpellier and Alfonso II of Aragon pledged support for Ermengarda and swore not to allow the Count of Toulouse or his sons to acquire the town of Narbonne and Ermengarda's domains. It appears that by the end of 1177 Raimon was in control of Narbonne and that between 1177 and 1179 Ermengarda called upon her other nephew, Pierre de Lara (*ibid.*). It is highly probable that Pierre, who took over Narbonne from Ermengarda near the end of 1192 (*ibid.*, VI, p. 151; VII, p. 17), was younger than his brother Aimeric.*

This is one of the few poems of Peire Rogier's for which it is possible to suggest a period of composition. Even then, the most precise conclusion we can reach is that it was written some time between Aimeric's arrival at Narbonne (1168) and his death (1177) (*cf.* Diez, *Leben und Werke*, pp. 80–1). Appel (p. 12), on the other hand, is only prepared to fix the later date of 1177, stating that it is not known whether Aimeric was ever at Narbonne before he was called there by Ermengarda. From the contents of the *tornada*, however, in which Peire reminds him of the duties attached to his position and of the family to which he belongs, it is reasonable to assume that the poem was written during the period when Aimeric was sharing the responsibilities of the government of Narbonne.

tos. The respective readings of C (*ros*) and D (*cos*) are probably the result of scribal errors. All the other MSS have *tos*, except a[1], which has an independent line.

65 *sia.* AB have *sera* and not the subjunctive *sia*, which, like *membre·lh*, is required here after the imperative *di·m*. *Sia* is given by DIKNa[1] as well as by C, which presents, at the same time, an independent and slightly corrupt version of the line. The *que* which should introduce the two subjunctives must be understood here.

IV NO SAI DON CHANT E CHANTARS PLAGRA·M FORT (356, 5)

Nine MSS. C 193 (Mahn, *Gedichte*, 1056); D[a] 153–529; D[c] 255 (141, *AdM.*, 13, 386) (stanzas I and VI); I 13; K 3; M 194 (Mahn, *Gedichte*, 1055); R 26–223; T 210; anon. ω 57 (p. 579).

Editions. Lavaud, *Troub. Cant.*, II, p. 432; Gentile, *Ant. testi*, p. 126.

Classification. Appel did not have D[c] and ω at his disposal. The first contains only two stanzas (I and VI) and the second is illegible in several places. Other MSS have the following omissions: MT both *tornadas*, R the second *tornada*, D l. 38 and part of l. 39, T l. 28 and part of l. 27. R has an independent stanza order: 1, 2, 3, 5, 7, 6, 4, 8.

From the variants two broad lines of tradition emerge: DIK and CMRT, *cf.* 1, 2, 5, 6, 7, 11, 13, 16, 17, 19, 27, 32, 33, 39, 44, 52, as well as the second *tornada* (lacking in MRT). Apart from these instances, DIK are allied in 18 (*jois*), 26 (*lo*).

---

* *Ibid.*, VII, p. 17. Appel (p. 12, note 1) also supports the view of Vaissete, as opposed to that of Salazar, who considers Pierre to be the elder of the two (*Historia genealogica de la casa de Lara*, I, 1694, p. 132). No information is available on the year of Aimeric's birth. According to the *Hist. gen. Lang.* (III, p. 691) his parents were married about 1152 and his father died in 1164 (VII, p. 14). Appel considers that since their short marriage produced a large number of children Aimeric's birth, as that of the eldest, should be fixed in the early part of the 1150s.

They form the more stable group, being joined quite often by one or more of the other MSS. IK are, as usual, particularly close, cf. 2 (*nom*), 3, 6 (*trop ben*), 17 (*vol so*), 19, 20, 21, 26, 30, 38, 39, 42, 43 (*amors* (2)), 52, 54. In a number of these instances D joins MSS of the second group in opposition.

The interrelationship of the MSS of the second group is far more intricate. They divide themselves into various combinations of three and two as shown below:

(a) CMR: 3 (*greus*), 32 (*quan*), 39 (*estara*).
CMT: 6, 7 (*trop*), 17 (*quoras*), 30 (*t'aten*), 38 (*so fara–sofra*).
MRT: 1, 2, 5 (*cubrir*), 13, 43 (*amor* (2)).

(b)	M	R	T
C	16 (*n'es*), 19 (*que rir*).	15 (spelling: *estai*), 18 (*ieu*), 24 (*e-a*), 32 (*vivas*), 52.	17, 26 (*loy-lor*).
M		2 (*saupes*), 33 (*non*), 38 (*dese-desse*).	4, 18 (*mi-me*), 24 (spelling: *es*), 25, 44, both *torn.* lacking.
T		16 (*es*), 18 (*joi*).	

The close relationship of both CR and MT is borne out by those instances where in turn they leave their main group to join DIK. CR are, in fact, allied to DIK in all the lines where MT stand alone. The reverse is true in most of the lines where CR are linked. MT are also in agreement with the first group in 9 (*qe*) and M has further links with it in 17 (*dir ges*), 18 (*jois*), 26 (*lo*), 32 (*vivras*). CRT individually have connections, as well, with the first group. This is particularly the case with C, which is the only MS of the second group to contain the last stanza. All four MSS, especially RT, show signs of independence.

From the evidence available ω appears to be closely related to DIK in opposition to the second group, cf. 7, 44, 52 (*tot lo mon*), 57 (*len*). It also joins CDIK by the inclusion of both *tornadas*.

The relationship of D° with the other MSS is difficult to establish on the basis of the two stanzas it contains. It is linked with DIK, in opposition to the second group, in 1 (*cantars*), 2, 5, 6 (*qe*), 39 and also with CDIKR in 4 (*adoncs*). On the other hand, it separates, with D, from the first group to join the second in 3 (*greus*), 6 (*ben trop*), 39 (*estara*). It shares independent readings with R in 7 and, in particular, with T in 36 (*cor*), 40, 42 (*mensogu(n)a*).

Base and orthography. C.

I
No sai don chant, e chantars plagra·m fort,
si saubes don, mas de re no·m sent be,
et es greus chans, quant hom non sap de que.
Mas adoncx par qu'om a natural sen,
quan sap son dan ab gen passar suffrir,   5
quar no·s deu hom per ben trop esjauzir,
ni ia per mal hom trop no·s dezesper. —

II
Mas tot quant es s'aclina vas la mort:
que prezas tu tot quan fas? Ieu non re. —
Mas so ditz hom, qu'avols es qui·s recre,   10
per qu'om deu far tot bel captenemen,
que no·l puesc'hom mal dir ni escarnir;
aisso dic ieu que no·s deu hom giquir
aissi del tot qui·l segle vol tener.

III
Fort estai be qu'om chant e que·s deport. —   15
Oc, quan n'es luecx ni temps que s'esdeve. —
E quoras doncx? Vols o dir ges per me? —
Sapchas qu'ieu hoc. — Quar us grans jois m'en pren? —
Qar ditz totz jorns que rir vols e bordir;
tol te d'aisso, ia t'er *tost* a murir. —   20
E laissarai per so mon joy-aver?

IV
Si joy non ai, don aurai doncx confort? —
E qual joy quiers? — De lieys cuy clam merce. —
Folhs yest. — Per que? — Per Dieu trebalhas te,
ni per aquo . . . —Fai doncx! — Mas per nien   25
t'en entremetz. — Tu que saps? — Aug lo dir. —
Saps tu que? — Fai! — Laissa me tot guerir. —
Ieu voluntiers, e fai tot ton plazer. —

V
Tost venra temps que conostra son tort. —
Aqui t'aten. — Si fatz ieu per ma fe. —   30
Fas ton talan, mas ieu no cug ni cre
tan quan vivras n'ayas nulh jauzimen. —
Non dis per als mas quar m'en vols partir. —
Ieu hoc, per so quar no t'en vey jauzir. —
E ia saps tu qu'als non ai en poder.   35

POEM IV

VI Mos cors no·m ditz qu'ieu ab autra m'acort. —
    Quar ben as dreg pel gran ben que t'en ve. —
    El'o fara. — E quoras? — Er dese. —
    Ben estara si vers es, mas si·t men,
    tu qu'en faras? — Am mai lo sieu mentir   40
    q'autra vertat. — Mal hi sabes cauzir,
    qu'ieu non pretz ren mesorgua contra ver. —

VII Per s'amor viv, e s'amors m'a estort
    de la preizon, e s'amors m'a mes fre,
    que no·m eslays vas autra, si·m rete;   45
    e per s'amor ai tot mon cor jauzen,
    e·m part d'enueg, e·m platz quan puesc servir;
    e valon mais de lieys li lonc dezir
    que s'avia d'autra tot mon voler.

VIII Lo vers tramet e vuelh que si prezen   50
    mon Tort-n'avetz, si·l play que·l denh auzir,
    que totz lo mons li deuri'obezir,
    qar mai que tot vol bon pretz mantener.

IX E si dons Sanz m'a fag descauzimen,
    mieus es lo dans et er lo·m a sofrir,   55
    et el no·s poc de plus envilanir,
    e per vilan lo deu hom ben tener.

Variants. The illegible parts of ω are denoted by --- except where otherwise indicated. Lines 10–21 are completely illegible and ll. 25–41 are lacking.

1. Lines 1–5 *lacking* ω; 1, on (*initial* n *mutilated*) *C,* non *DIKT*; say *R*; cant *T,* chan *DIK*; cantar *T,* cantars D^c, chantar *MR*; plagrami *T*. 2, sieu *T*; sabes *T,* saupes *MR*; dont *T*; de re *lacking R,* ara *M*; ren *IKT*; nō *D,* non *MRT*; sai *MT,* say *R*; sen DD^cIK; be] re *R*. 3, e. e. g.] e grieus es *M*; et] es *T,* ez D^c; greu *IKT*; cantç *T,* chan *R,* chanz DD^cIK; cant *DRT,* qan D^c, qant *KM*; no *R*; sab *D*; che *T,* qe D^cIM. 4, ma *of* mas *mutilated C*; adonc *MT,* adoncs DD^cIK; com *DIKRT,* qom D^cM; ha D^cM; naturall *T*. 5, can *DRT,* qan D^cIM; sab D^c; son]sun *T*; a. g. p. s.] gen paysser e cobrir *R*; gient *T*; passar *precedes* son *C*; cubrir *MT,* soffrir *DIK,* sufrir D^c. 6, quar no·s deu *lacking* ω; car *T,* qar *M,* qe D^c, que *IK,* q̄ *D*; no·s] nous *T,* noys *C*; hom] ho *T*; b. t.] trop ben *IK*; esgausir *T,* esjausir *M,* es--- ω. 7, ni ia *illegible* ω; gia *T*; i. p. m.] per gran mal D^cR; h. t.] nulhs homs *R*; h. t. n. d.] nos dev trop desesperar *T*; om *M*; trop] fort *DIK*ω; desesper DD^cIKMRω.

II. 8, mas] pus *R*; tut *T*; cant *DRT*ω, qant *KM*. 9, que preza(s) *illegible* ω; que *lacking* R, qe MT, q̄ DI, quan C; presas M, preçatç T; can Dω, cant RT, qan KM; en M, eu DIKTω, quieu C, yeu R; no M. 10, m. s.] e nas T; dis DIK; cavols DIKRT, qavols M; qis M. 11, com DIKRT, qom M; t. b. c.] tan gen contenemen DIK; totç T; bels T; captenimen T. 12, com R, qe MT, q̄ D; nol *lacking* I; p. h.] puesca R; puosc IT; om DIKT. 13, aiso T, aissi C, ayso R, perso DIK; eu DIKT, yeu R; qe MT, q̄ DR; n. d. h.] h. n. d. R; no·s] nous T; om M; gecir T, gequir DR, giqir M. 14, aisi T, aysi R; tut T; qil M, q^{i}l D; setgle I.

III. 15, esta DIKMT; ben DIKT; com DIKRT, qom M; cant T; qes MT, q̄s DR. 16, oc] e T; cant DR, qan M, qant T, quant IK; es RT, ner DIK; loc I, locs DKT, locx R, luecs M; ni] e T; tems R; qe KM, q̄ DIRT. 17, cora DIKR, coras T, qoras M; donc M, doncs DIKT; volo M, vol so IK; d. g.] g. d. CT, dire R. 18, sapchatz IK, sapchaz D, sapciatç T; ceieu T, q̄u DI, qieu M, queu K, ieu C, yeu R; oc DIKMRT; car DIKRT, qar M, q^{a}r C; un R, uns T; g. j.] gioi grans T; gran R, granz D; dols C, joy R; m'en] me T, mi M. 1q, can D, car RT, qan I, quan K; dis DIKMR; tot R, toz D, tutç T; giortç T, jorn R, jornz I, jorz D; cor T, qe M, q̄ DIR; joys R, rirs D, rris I, rri(r)s K (*the r was probably added by a later hand*); v. e.] vol o M. 20, t. t.] tolre IK; daco R, daiso DIKT; gia T; t'er] tes R; tost] obs R, tut T, tot *all other MSS*; morir DIMT, morrir K. 21, laierai T, laissat ai IK, laisserai M, layssaray R; mon] non T; gioi T, joi DIKM.

IV. 22, se T; gioi T, joi DIKMω; hai M; d. a. d. c.] tot naurai doncx honor R; don M, donc IK, doncs DTω; conort C. 23, e cal --- joi --- merce ω; qal M, cal DIKRT; gioi T, joi DIKM; cier T, q^{1}ers R, qers M, q̄rs D, quers IK; lei DIK, leis M, leys R, lieis T; cui DIKMT. 24, *after* fols *the rest of the line is lacking in* ω; fols DIKMRTω; es MT, iest DIK; ce T, qe KM, q̄ DR; per] a R, e C; deu I, dieus T; trabagliar T, trebailhas M, trebaillas DIK. 25, ni *lacking* T; acho D, aco IKR, aiso T, aisso M; fas R, ma T, mas M; donc M, doncs DIKT. 26, entremetes R, entremez DIK; t. q. s.] q. s. t. C; tu] e R, ni IK; q. s.] q̄asab T; qe KM, q̄ D, quē R; lo] lor T, loy C, o R. 27, sap M, sas T; t. q.] q̄ tu D, que tu IK; ce T, qe M; fay R; l. m.] layssam del R; laixa T; t. g.] tutom plaser T (*the scribe's eye has probably jumped from the* tot *of l.* 27 *to that of l.* 28); garir M, guerrir DIK. 28, *cf*. l. 27 T; eu DIK, yeu R; volentiers DIK, volontiers M; plaser M.

V. 29, tost] got I, tut T, tot *all other MSS*; venra] veirai C; tems R; ce T, q̄ DIMR; c. s.] conoisera sun T, contras ton R. 30, a. t.] q̄ res nō tems R; aqi M, aq^1 I, aqieu T; tatem IK, tatent T; fas DIKRT, faz M; eu DIK, yeu R. 31, f. t. t.] aco q̄ dey R; tun T; talen IKT; eu D, yeu R; non DIKMRT; cuc T; crey R. 32, ca T, can R, q̄at M, cō DI, con K; vivas CR, vivra T; naias DIKM, nauras T; nuil I, nuill K, nul DT, null M; gausimen T, jausimen M. 33, no R, nol DIK, non o T, nou C; ditç T, ditz M; car DIKRT, qar M; m'en] me M. 34, eu DIKT, yeu R; oc DIKMRT; car DIKRT, qar M; non DIKRT; veg R, vei DIKMT; gausir T, jausir M. 35, ia *lacking* R, gia T; sap T, sapchas R; t. q. a. n. a. e.] quals ieu non ai ges C; cals DIKRT, qals M; ay R.

VI. 36, cor D^cT; no'm] me R; di D^c, dis DIK; q. a.] canb T; qeu D^c, q̄u DI, qieu M, q¹eu R. 37, car $DIKRT$, qan D^c, qar M; has D^c; dretz M, dritç T; pell M, pels T; grans T; be D^c, bens T; que t'en ve *lacking* D (*the scribe's eye has probably jumped from the* ben *of l. 37 to that of l. 39*), qetemie T; qe D^c, q̄ IR, qi M. 38, *lacking* D (*cf. l. 37*); e. o. f.] no fara D^c; ell M; o] so CM; cora D^c, coras IKM; e. d.] amise D^c, arase IK, er iasse C; e ilh ca fag e fara ioc desse R; el sofra en coras eras be T. 39, ben *lacking* D (*cf. l. 37*); estera IK, istera T; v. e. m. s. m.] ves en marrimē R; ver D^c; es *lacking I*, est K; mas] e DD^cIK; si't] si M; ment T. 40, ce T, che D^c, qen DKM, q̄n IR; a. m.] mais am T; mais DD^cIKM, mays R; seu D^cR. 41, cautra $DIKRT$; m. h.] mas il T; hi] i DD^cIK, y MR; saps doncx C, saubes DIT, saubist R; causir T, chausir D^cIKM, chauzir DR. 42, cieu T, q̄ R, qeu D^c, q̄u $DI\omega$, qieu M; pres $DRT\omega$, prez D^cK; re $D^cR\omega$; mensogna T, mensogu(n)a D^c (*it is not clear whether the letter following* g *is* u *or* n), mensoina ω, mensonia IKM, mesonia D, messonia R; (con)tra ver *illegible* ω.

VII. 43, s'a. (1)] samors C; viev R; s'a. (2)] samor $DMR\omega$, per samor T; maistort T, ma e--- ω. 44, la] gran MT; preiso T, preison IK, preizo R, pre--- ω; e] en T; samor $CMRT$; fr--- ω. 45, q̄--- sim re--- ω; e R, qe M, q̄ DT; enlaix T, eslais $DIKM$; vas *is written twice in* M (*it is not clear whether the deletion indications* (··) *under the first* vas *were made by a later hand*), ves T; altra T; si'm]sem T. 46, --- m. c. j. ω; et D; ay R, hai M; tut T; giaze T (*it is not certain whether the mark above the* e *represents a nasal or is merely intended to be the dot of the* i). 47, e. p. d'e.] platz dompneys C, qū nuecs ω; part] par M; enuoi T; play R, plaz $DM\omega$; can $DRT\omega$, qan K, qant M; puosc IKT; ser--- ω. 48, --- lo l. d. ω; leis M, lieis T, llei DIK; li] los T; desir $IKMT$; e plazom may per ver li siei sospir R. 49, q. s'a. *illegible* ω; ce T, qe M, q̄ CIR; sauria D; tut T.

VIII. *Lacking MT. The following is all that is legible in* ω. Lo vers ---l q̄ si prez--- nav--- deing --- tot lo mon --- obezir. --- manten---. 50, voill DIK; q̄ DIR; presen IK. 51, naves DIK; plai DIK, platz R; q̄l DR; deing IK, dreig D, vuelh C. 52, car R, qui DIK; tot lo (li D)mon DIK; la CR; d. o.] devria servir C; bezir IK. 53, car $DIKR$; mais DIK, mays R; q. t.] dautra C; qe D, q̄ I; tut DKR; prez K; manteneir R.

IX. *Lacking MRT. The following is all that is legible in* ω: --- ma ---escauz--- loma--- el nos poc---anir. ---lan len dev hom ben tener. 54, donsanz IK, donz s. D, dous sautz C; fait DIK; deschauzimen DIK. 55, es] er DIK; danz DIK; soffrir IK. 56, el no's] ylh nom C; de] del DIK. 57, lo] len DIK; hom] len D.

Metrical scheme. Seven *coblas unissonans* of seven lines and two *tornadas*, each of four lines, following the scheme of the last four lines of the stanzas:

$$a_{10} \ b_{10} \ b_{10} \ c_{10} \ d_{10} \ d_{10} \ e_{10}$$

(Frank: 747: 2). The same rhyme scheme as that for *Tant ai mon cor* and six other poems, one of which also has this syllable arrangement (Giraut Riquier: Pillet and Carstens, 248, 29).

Dialogue form. Appel and Lavaud introduce dialogue in the first stanza, making a division at the end of the third line. It appears more reasonable, however, to assume, with both Suchier (*Goett. gel. Anzeigen*, 1883, 1343–4) and Cocito (*Romania (Piccolo)*, p. 230, n.1), that the whole of the first stanza forms one single speech on the part of the poet. If the stanza is in fact broken at this point it means that the practical advice and sceptical remarks, opposing, in the following stanzas, the patient, submissive attitude of the lover, are placed in the mouth of the poet instead of his interlocutor's, as is normally the case.

Suchier (*loc. cit.*) and Cocito (*loc. cit.*) terminate the interlocutor's reply at *fas* in l. 9 and reintroduce the poet with *Ieu non re*. We prefer, however, to attribute the whole of ll. 8 and 9 to the interlocutor, as the poet is unlikely, in view of the more encouraging tone of his remarks in the rest of the poem, to state that he places no value on what he does.

Notes

1–3 It is interesting to note that Raimbaut d'Orange also sings about an unknown subject in No. XXIV (*R. d'Orange*), which Pattison (p. 154) considers to be a parody of Guillaume de Poitier's *Farai un vers de dreyt nien* (A. Jeanroy's edition, No. IV). A similar example is found in *G. de Born.*, 53, ll. 43–4:

> No sai de que m'ai fach chanso
> Ni com, s'altre no m'o despo;

Pattison (*loc. cit.*) points out, however, that in *No sai don chant* and in the poem of Giraut de Bornelh the theme is only mentioned briefly, whereas in the case of the first two it runs through the whole poem.

1 *no*. C is slightly mutilated here: the initial *n* is missing.
4 *mas*. The first two letters are missing in C, again through mutilation.
5 C is the only MS in which *passar* appears before *son*. The word order offered by all the other MSS is therefore preferred. *Passar* means here 'suffering'. Levy (*S.W.*, VI, 120) demonstrates this meaning by quoting the following lines:

> E qui sos joys secretz no sab tenir
> E mals e bes *passar* ab gen cubrir,
> No sec lo cor que far deu fis amans.

(*Deux manuscrits provençaux du XIV*^e *siècle* (J. B. Noulet and C. Chabaneau, Montpellier and Paris, 1888, p. 18). He goes on to quote Chabaneau's explanation of how the word acquired this interpretation: 'Ce verbe . . . est peut-être à distinguer, pour l'origine comme pour le sens, de *passar* = *passer*. *Passar* = *souffrir* se rattacherait à *pati* par le supin *passum*, comme *ausar* à *audere* par *ausum*, *confessar* à *confiteri* par *confessum*, etc.'

POEM IV 75

It is interesting to note the similarity between the second line of the passage quoted above and the version of Peire Rogier's line in MRT, all of which have *cubrir* instead of *sufrir*.

6 *no·s*. This reading is offered by all the MSS except T, which is erroneous (*nous*). It is supported by the version of C (*noys*), which is probably based upon the alternative enclitic form (*nois*).

9 *que . . . ieu*. C offers an acceptable but independent reading (*quan . . . qu'ieu . . .*). The version clearly favoured by both traditions (DIKMT) is therefore preferred. The omission of *que* in R may suggest the normally close link between this MS and C.

11 *tot bel captenemen*. Appel chooses the reading of DIK (*tan gen contenemen*). It seems reasonable, however, to adhere to that offered by all four MSS of the second group and which gives an equally acceptable meaning. For the use of *bel captenemen* and *far captenemen* see respectively G. de Born., 63, 1. 6 and B. von Vent., 27, 1. 2.

13 *aisso*. Appel again prefers the version of DIK (*perso*). There appears to be no reason, however, to depart from the reading of the MSS of the second group. The meaning is again equally satisfactory. *Aisso* refers to the noun clause dependent upon *dic* later in the line and thus corresponds to the same construction based upon *so* in l. 10. *Cf*. B. von Vent., 5, l. 32; 33, l. 5.

The slightly different reading of C (*aissi*) may well be the result of the influence of the same word at the beginning of the following line.

16 *s'esdeve*. As Appel indicates, one would expect the subjunctive mood here rather than the indicative. Schultz-Gora (*Altprov. Elem.*, p. 132) states that certain impersonal constructions, such as *par, par me*, may be followed by either the indicative or the subjunctive but that those expressing necessity or suitability are always followed by the subjunctive.

17 *dir ges*. The order of words offered by DIK is preferred, as they are joined by M. R is independent (*dire*) and CT are therefore the only MSS to have *ges dir*.

18 *s. qu'ieu*. The fact that MT joins DIK here justifies the choice of their reading in preference to that offered by CR only (*s. ieu*).

jois. Appel and Lavaud choose *dols*, which is given only by C. However, MRT are generally close to C in the poem, and in view of the fact that they each join DIK here in offering *jois* it is this reading which is considered more reliable. It is also favoured by both Suchier (*loc. cit*.) and Chabaneau (*RLR*, XXV, 103). The independent version of C may perhaps be the result of an attempt by the intelligent scribe to make sense of a difficult line. (*Cf*. note to I, 1. 47.) Suchier (*loc. cit*.) also observes that C often contains evidence of a revising hand.

The choice of *jois*, however, makes nonsense of the line as it stands in Appel and Lavaud, who attribute the whole of it to the interlocutor. The solution lies, as Suchier (*loc. cit*.) suggests, in breaking the line after *hoc* and regarding the words *quar us grans jois m'en pren* as an interpolation on the part of the poet. The interlocutor then continues in l. 19 with what he has begun to say in the first half of l. 18.

It is interesting to note the intransitive use of *prendre* whereby the subject is a noun of feeling with the person concerned in the dative. *Cf*. the French expression *bien (mal) lui en prend*. Other examples of this construction are found in G. de Montanhagol, III, l. 21; VII, l. 14 (see notes) and in *S.W.*, VI, 514 (No. 19), where Levy gives *prendre* the meaning of 'entstehen', 'ankommen'.

20 *tost*. All the MSS have *tot*, with the exception of R (*obs*). The word appears to make little sense in this context and we have therefore followed Appel in amending it to convey the meaning of 'soon' which is required here.

22 *confort*. As in l. 9, C offers quite an acceptable reading (*conort*) but its independence makes it less reliable than that given by the majority of the MSS. It is notable that, as in l. 9, R, which is normally closely related to C, has an entirely different reading (*honor*).

24 *per Dieu*. The reading favoured by both traditions (DIK and MT) is again preferred to the two similar readings of CR (*e dieu–a dieu*) which, though acceptable alternative exclamations, are clearly independent. For the use of all three expressions (*per dieu, a dieu, dieu*) as exclamations see *B. von Vent.*, p. 362 (glossary).

Both Levy (*S.W.*, II, 188) and Chabaneau (*RLR*, XXV, 103) quote part of this stanza, and regard *per dieu* as being the equivalent of *en perdon* ('in vain'). It is this meaning which is perhaps more suitable here than the exclamatory one favoured by Appel (p. 75) and Lavaud in their translation of this stanza.

Appel's division of ll. 24–6 seems to us, on the other hand, to be more acceptable than that suggested by Chabaneau (*loc. cit.*):

> Fols yest. — Per que? — Per Dieu trebalhas te.
> — Ni per aquo . . . — Fai doncx! mas per nien
> T'en entremetz. . . .

26 *tu que saps*. We adopt the reading of DM, representatives of both traditions. Their order of words is clearly favoured by the diverse versions of all the other MSS, except C, which offers an independent order (*que saps tu*). The choice of *tu*, as opposed to the *ni* or *e* of IK and R, is at the same time justified by the support of CT.

lo. The reading offered by DIKM. Support for it is given by the independent readings of CT (*loy–lor*) in opposition to that of R (*o*).

29 *tost*. All the MSS have *tot*, with the exception of I (*got*). It has been amended to read *tost* for the same reasons as in l. 20.

venra. The reading offered by all the MSS except C, which has the independent *veira*.

32 *vivras*. The fact that DIK and M join forces and are obviously supported by T (*vivra*) justifies the choice of their reading in preference to the independent version of CR (*vivas*). The latter provides, however, an equally acceptable meaning, as both the future indicative and present subjunctive are used after *tan com, tan quan* ('as long as'). Cf. *S.W.*, VIII, 45; *Prov. Chr.*, 7, l. 231; 46, l. 21; 24, l. 35.

It is possible that the reading of CR has been influenced by the present subjunctive *ayas*, dependent upon *no cug ni cre* in the previous line.

33 *non*. The reading of MR is preferred to that of DIK (*nol*), as it is clearly supported by C, which has a scribal error (*nou*), and by T (*non o*).

35 *e ia saps tu*. C is clearly independent in this line. The reading of R (*e sapchas tu . . .*) is closely related to that of all the other MSS, which is therefore preferred.

36 *no'm ditz*. Cocito (*op. cit.*, pp. 230–31, note 15) regards as preferable the reading of R (*mos cors me ditz . . .*). He then goes on to translate l. 37 as follows: 'You are certainly right to do it by the considerable good which may come to you from it.' As an alternative he suggests an ironical meaning: 'You are certainly right to do it in view of the considerable good which comes to you from her whom you love.' We have retained, however, the reading of C and the other MSS, which Appel also prefers, particularly as it appears to lend an equally, if not more, ironical interpretation to l. 37: 'My heart does not tell me to come to terms with another lady.' — 'You are certainly right (in *not* doing this) in view of the con-

siderable good which comes to you from her whom you love.' This interpretation is in fact well borne out by the dialogue which follows in the rest of the stanza.

Appel (p. 76) also concludes that l. 37 is intended ironically. He offers a helpful explanation of the presence of the causal *quar* at the beginning of l. 37 in suggesting that it is preceded in the poet's mind by an unexpressed clause such as 'I agree with you'.

38 *el'o*. We have adopted the reading of IK. That of CM (*el so*) gives the more usual form of the masculine pronoun and not the feminine one which the sense of the line demands. The version of T (*el sofra*) appears to be based on it while D° is slightly more independent (*no fara*). The whole line is independent in R and lacking in D. It is likely that the scribes of C and M originally overlooked the possibility of an elision and read the version of the IK tradition as *el o*, not *el'o*. It is worth noting, however, that the scribes of IK generally pay careful attention to the demands of the metre and often make any necessary elisions.

er dese. The reading of M is adopted. Appel (*loc. cit.*) considers that the original MS had *erasse*, which is not actually given by any of the existing MSS but which is fairly close to the reading of IK (*arase*) and that of C (*er iasse*). Appel presumably regards the word as an alternative form of *eras, aras* but admits that he has been unable to find an example of it elsewhere.

The choice of the reading of M seems justified in that it gives quite an acceptable meaning ('It will be at once') and is supported by R, although this MS is independent for the rest of the line. Lavaud (*Troub. Cant.*, p. 69) and Suchier (*op. cit.*, 1344) also prefer this reading. Lavaud does not mention, however, the support of R but erroneously ascribes to it, as well as to DT, the reading *erasse*. In fact T offers *eras be*, while the line as a whole is missing in D.

41 *autra vertat. Autra* has here a genitive meaning: 'The truth of (i.e. from) another'. *Cf.* VI, l. 28. It should be noted, however, that the normal genitive form of the word is *autrui* (*Altprov. Elem.*, p. 127), the use of which before both masculine and feminine nouns is well attested: *cf. Prov. Chr.*, 81, l. 7; *B. von Vent.*, I, l. 28; 7, l. 29; 23, l. 8; *G. de Born.* (glossary); *G. de Montanhagol*, III, l. 50; XIV, l. 28.

The use of *autre, autra* with a genitive meaning does not appear to be very common: no reference is made in *S.W., Pet. Dict., Lex. rom.*, or in any of the grammars listed in the bibliography. Examples may be found, however, in *B. von Vent.* (see 31, l. 30; 33, l. 10; (17, l. 57?)). Attention should also be drawn to Appel's note in *B. von Vent.* to l. 32 of No. 42 (*car anc me pres d'autrui amor enveya*). He interprets *autrui amor*, the reading of one of the MS groups, as meaning 'love for some other', without specification of sex. However, as it is clearly a question of 'love for another *lady*' he considers the alternative reading, *autr'amor*, to be the more natural. One can thus conclude that he regards *autra* as the straightforward feminine alternative to the invariable form *autrui*.

sabes. The reading of KMD° is preferred to the independent version of R (*saubist*) chosen by Appel. They offer one of the forms of the second person present indicative (*cf. Anglade*, p. 345; *Prov. Chr.*, p. xxxiv), which appears to be just as suitable here as the preterite and is supported by the alternative form given by C (*saps doncx*). Moreover, in view of the normally very close relationship between I and K, it may be assumed that further support for the reading of KMD° is provided by the similar version of DIT (*saubes*). The latter would itself, however, be unacceptable here either as a first or a third person imperfect subjunctive or as an alternative form of the second person plural preterite (*saubetz*), since the dialogue in this poem is conducted entirely in the second person singular.

43 *p. s'amor*. We adopt the reading of all the MSS except C (*s'amors*), the scribe of which may have been influenced by the nominative form of *amor* later in the line.

44 *s'amors*. CMRT have *s'amor*. The normal form of the nominative singular, employed in the second half of the previous line, is, however, again required here (*cf.* note to I, 1. 22). It is in fact offered by IK as well as by Dω, which in the previous line gave *s'amor*.

47 *e'm part d'enueg*. C is the only MS not to offer this reading. Its independent version (*em platz dompneys*) may possibly be owing to the fact that the scribe's eye was distracted by *em platz* appearing later in the line.

51 *denh*. The reading of IKR, supported by that of D (*dreig*), is chosen. The *tornadas* are lacking in MT, and C is independent (*vuelh*). Normally where MT stand alone CR join DIK (see 'Classification'). It is therefore significant that here R should separate from C in order to ally itself with DIK.

As the subjunctive form is required, it is likely that the version *vuelh* in C was intended to be read as *vuelh'*, the final *a* being elided before the following vowel.

52 *li deuri'obezir*. *Obezir* is given by DR and was clearly intended in IK (*bezir*). This reading is therefore preferred to the independent one of C (*servir*) on the same grounds as indicated in l. 51.

The verb may be used either transitively or intransitively. Levy (*S.W.*, v, 443) quotes examples of both cases. It is, however. the dative *li*, given by DIK, which is adopted and not the accusative *la* of CR. One may in fact discount the presence of *la* in C, as the accusative is in any case required for the transitive verb *servir*.

53 *mai que tot*. The reading of C (*mai d'autra*), though perfectly acceptable from the point of view of meaning, is independent. The version offered by all the other MSS is therefore chosen.

54 *dons Sanz*. The reading of D supported by that of IK, in which the two *ss* have merged into one (*donsanz*). C probably has a scribal error (*dous sautz*).

Lavaud (*Troub. Cant.*, II, p. 441, notes) suggests that the person concerned is one of the Castilians who would have probably accompanied Aimeric, Ermengarda's nephew, to Narbonne (see III, l. 64, note). Lavaud's view lacks supporting evidence but would seem to be based on the quite reasonable assumption that *dons Sanz* was at the time in the same place as *Tort-n'avetz*, to whom the troubadour requests, only three lines earlier, that the poem be sent. If Lavaud's theory were correct the poem would probably belong to the same period of composition as III (*cf. loc. cit.* above).

Anglade ('Les troubadours à Narbonne' in *Mélanges Chabaneau*, p. 740, note 1) considers that it might be a question of Sancho III of Castille, son of Alfonso VII, born in 1130, who reigned 1157–58. Bergert (*Damen*, p. 8, note 2), however, appears to be justified in rejecting this view. He points out that one would expect the king's title to be employed. Besides, more significant is the fact that the contents of the *tornada* do not match at all the usually generous descriptions of Sancho's character. (*Cf.* Zenker, *Peire von Auvergne*, p. 26, and Milà, *De los trovadores*, p. 81.) It would also suppose that Peire had paid two visits to Castille, the one before 1158 and the other, which is the only one reported in the *Vida*, fairly near the end of his life.

Perhaps a more acceptable theory, particularly in view of the dates involved, is that the Sancho to whom Peire alludes here is the brother of Alfonso II of Aragon on behalf of whom he ruled Provence from 1181 to 1185. No clue is given as to the nature of the wrong which Peire has suffered. However, the tone of the *tornada* would certainly be in keeping with what is known of Sancho, who, during the short period in which the government of Provence was entrusted to him, exploited the country to his own advantage and to the detriment of Alfonso (*cf.* Hoepffner, *Le Troubadour Peire Vidal*, p. 39). In a *tornada* addressed to Alfonso Peire Vidal refers to Sancho's misgovernment in the following way:

> Francs reis, Proensa·us apella
> Qu'En Sancho la·us desclavella
> E gasta·us la cer'e·l mel
> E sai tramet vos lo fel.
> [Avalle, *Peire Vidal*, II, pp. 315–16 (No. XXXVI)]*

If the person to whom Peire Rogier alludes is Sancho it would be reasonable to assume that the poem was written at some stage during his reign. In that case Peire's career would have extended a little beyond the approximate limit (1180) which is generally attached to it. (See p. 13 above, note 1.)

It is possible that the author of the *Vida* identified *dons Sanz* with Sancho and used this reference as the sole basis for his statement about Peire's visit to the court of Aragon. The reference is, however, too brief and too vague for such a suggestion to be regarded as anything more than conjecture.

55 *mieus*. See note to I, l. 9.
56 *et el no·s poc*. The reading of DIK is chosen, as the reflexive use of *envilanir* is better suited to the sense of l. 57 than the independent, but in itself acceptable, reading of C (*et ylh no·m poc*): 'And he could not degrade *himself* more, and one must certainly consider him to be base.'

V TANT AI MON COR EN JOY ASSIS (356, 9)

Eight MSS. C 194; D^a 154–530; D^c 255 (142, *AdM.*, 13, 386) (stanzas II and IV); E 174; I 13; K 3; M 196; anon ω 66 + 59 (p. 576).

Editions. Raynouard, *Choix*, III, 34; *M.W.*, I, 122; Lavaud, *Troub. Cant.*, II, 440.

Classification. All the MSS have the same order of stanzas, and apart from ω and D^c, which are fragmentary, contain the whole poem. The MS variants reveal two clearly defined groups: DIK and CEM, standing opposed in 5, 9, 14, 23, 32, 33, 38, 41, 43, 48. DIK are further linked in 26, 32 (*qem*), 50 (*s'en*), as are CEM in 28 (*senhor*) and 45 (spelling: *veirai*).

* Avalle (*loc. cit.*) observes that in her article 'Pour la chronologie de quelques chansons de Peire Vidal' (*Annales du Midi*, LV, 513–14) Rita Lejeune regards these lines as a reference to the alliance which Sancho made in 1184 with the republic of Genoa against his brother, Alfonso, and which decided the latter to deprive him of the government of Provence in the following year.

Within the first group the normally close relationship of IK is once more evident (*cf.* 6, 15, 20, 28, 30, 32, 36 (*qu'ieu*), 37, 38, 45 (spelling: *verrai*)) while D quite often joins the second group (*cf.* 6, 15 (*joy*), 28, 29 (with E only), 30, 37 (*cal*), 45 (spelling: *veirai*) and 46 (*te*), 50 (*gen*)(both with C only)).

The relationship between the MSS of the second group is considerably more intricate, as shown below:

CE: 13 (*tost*), 15, 26, 30 (*pauz'e*), 48 (*guart lo cors*), 50 (*si*).
CM: 32 (*que*), 37 (*qual*).
EM: 19, 26 (*tan*), 33, 48.

This group is, on the whole, the less stable of the two, all three MSS associating themselves at times with the first group. E joins the latter in 32 (*qem*), 36 (*qu'ieu*), 37 (*tal*), as does M in 15, 26, 50 (*s'en*). C, however, appears to be the nearest of the three to the DIK group, and is in fact supported by it in all four instances where EM stand alone.

ω and D° were not at Appel's disposal. ω, in which the first three stanzas are lacking, has an equal link with both traditions. It joins the first in 23, 26, 28, 33 (*caissi*), 43, 45 (spelling: *en p.*) and the second in 30 (*pauz'e*), 33 (*qu'en*), 37 (*qual*), 41 (*o‘us*), 48 (*cō si*), 50 (*si*). It also shares individual variants with E in 27 (*ha–a*), 29, 50, and with M in 27 (*fieus*), 48 (*gar lo (el) sieu cors (cor)*).

D° contains the second and fourth stanzas only, and on the evidence available its classification is difficult. It joins the first group in 23, 26 (both with ω) and the second in 9 (*lavol*), 14, 28. It has further links with IM in 13 (*tot*), with M alone in 24 and with Eω in 27 (*ha*).

Base and orthography. C.

I
   Tant ai mon cor en joy assis,
   per que no puesc mudar no·n chan,
   que joys m'a noirit pauc e gran;
   e ses luy non seria res,
   qu'assatz vey que tot l'als qu'om fay   5
   abaiss' e sordey' e dechai,
   mas so qu'amors e joys soste.

II
   Lo segle es aissi devis
   que perdut es quant l'avol fan,
   mas ab los pros vay pretz enan;   10
   et amors ten s'ab los cortes,
   e d'aqui son drut cuend'e guay,
   perque·s te joys que tost non chai,
   qu'estiers d'els mais hom no·l soste.

III Si·l joys d'amor no fos tan fis,   15
     ia non agra durat aitan;
     mas no y a d'ira tan ni quan,
     que·l dans n'es pros e·l mals n'es bes
     e sojorns, qui plus mal en tray;
     demandatz cum! Qu'ie·us o diray: 20
     quar apres n'aten hom merce.

IV   Pauc pren d'amor qui no sofris
     l'erguelh e·l mal e·l tort e·l dan,
     qu'aissi o fan selhs que re n'an;
     guerra·m sembla, qu'amors non ges,   25
     quan son li mal e sai e lay,
     e non ai dreg e·l fieu qu'ieu ay,
     s'al senhor don mov, mals en ve.

V   Amors ditz ver et escarnis,
     e dona pauz' e gran afan   30
     e franc cor apres mal talan;
     huey fai que platz, deman que pes. —
     E doncx que·n diretz qu'ayssi vay? —
     Que costa? Que tot torn'en jay,
     pueys apres no y a re mas be.   35

VI   Membra·m aras d'un mot qu'ieu dis. —
     E qual? — No vuelh qu'om lo·m deman. —
     No l'auzirem doncx? — Non onguan;
     no·us er digz ni sabretz quals es. —
     No m'en qal, qu'atressi·m vivray. —   40
     Si·us vivetz o·us moretz, so say,
     no costa re midons ni me.

VII Mon Tort-n'avetz en Narbones
     man salutz, si tot luenh s'estai,
     e sapcha qu'em-breu la veyray,   45
     si trop grans afars no·m rete.

VIII Lo senher, que fetz tot quant es,
     guart lo cors de lieys cumsi·s fay,
     qu'ilh mante pretz e joy veray,
     quan tot' autra gens s'en recre.   50

Variants. *The illegible parts of ω are indicated by* - - -. *The first ten lines in E are mutilated. The words and parts of words missing are indicated by* +.

I. Lacking ω. 1, ta(nt) + *E*; m. c. e. j.] e. j. m. c. *E*; joi *DEIKM*; aisis *E*. 2, qe *DM*; nō *DIKM*, n(o) + *E*; puosc *IK*. 3, qe *M*, q̄ *E*; joi *D*, jois *EIKM*; ma no(irit) + *E*. 4, lui *DEIKM*; ceria *E*; res + *E*. 5, quas(satz) + *E*, qassatz *M*, asatz *K*, assatz *DI*; vei *DEIKM*; q̄ *DIKM*; qom *M*, com *DEIK*; fai *DEIKM*. 6, abaiss'] abjass *IK*, baissa *M*, (abai)sse + *E*; sordey'] sordei *DIK*, sordeia *M*, sor(dege) + *E*; decai *D*. 7, mais *IK*; qamors *M*, camors *DEIK*; jois *DEIKM*; soste + *E*.

II. *Lacking* ω. 8, lo + *E*, le *D^{c}M*; segles *DD^{c}KM*, setgles *I*, se(tgles) + *E*; aisi *E*. 9, qe *D^{c}IM*, q̄ *D*; quant + *E*, can *DIK*, qan *D^c*, qant *M*; laol *DIK*, llavol *D^{c}M*. 10, m. a.] qab *D^c*; vai *DD^{c}EIK*, vei *M*; (pr)etz + *E*, prez *M*, bos prez *D^c*; ennan *D*. 11, ez *D^c*; ten] plen *D^c*; sap *E*, se ab *C*; los] lors *D^c*. 12, daqi *D^{c}M*; son] sōill *D^c*; cuend'] coind *D^{c}M*, cueind *E*; gai *DD^{c}EIKM*. 13, perches *D^c*, perqes *M*, perq̄s *D*; ten *DIKM*; j. q. t.] qe del tot *D^c*; joi *E*, jois *DIKM*; q̄ *DM*; tot *IM*, toz *DK*. 14, qestier *D^c*, qestiers *KM*, q̄stiers *DI*; del *CD^{c}E*, dell *M*; mais] mō *M*; nols *DIK*.

III. *Lacking* ω. 15, joi *DE*, jois *IKM*, joy *C*; non *DEIKM*. 16, ga *D*; aitant *M*, un an *E*. 17, noia *DEIK*, noilha *M*; tant *M*; can *D*, qant *M*. 18, qel *K*, q̄ll *M*, q̄l *D*; danz *DIK*; ell *M*. 19, e. s.] esenhor *E*, ell seinhor *M*; sojornz *IK*, sojorz *D*; qi *IM*; e. t.] enten *E*; trai *DIKM*. 20, demandas *E*, demandanz *IK*, demandaz *M*; com *E*, con *K*, cō *DI*; qu'ie'us] qes *M*, q̄us *D*, queus *IK*; ho *E*; dirai *DEIKM*. 21, car *DIK*, qar *M*; natent *DIK*.

IV. 22, pauc - - - ω; paluc *D^c*; qi *M*, q^1 *C*; non *DD^{c}IK*; soffris *IK*, sufris *E*, suffris *D^c*. 23, lergueilh *M*, lergueill *E*, lorgoill *DD^{c}I*, lorguoill *K*, - - -ill ω; e. m. e. t.] e. t. e. m. *DD^{c}IKω*; ell m. *M*; el t.] e *D*, ell *M*; ell d. *M*. 24, caisi *Eω*, caissi *DIK*, qaissi *D^{c}M*; ho *E*; ffan *D*; cill *D^{c}M*, sels *DEIKω*; qe *DMω*, q̄ *I*, qui *D^c*; r. n'a.] remā *D^c*; re] ren *Mω*. 25, gerram *D^{c}M*, gueram *Iω*, guerran *E*, qerram *D*; senbla *D^{c}ω*; camor *DEIK*, camors ω, qamor *D^{c}M*; no *D^c*; n. g.] noi es *E*; jes ω. 26, can *Dω*, qan *D^c*, tan *EM*; li *lacking DD^{c}IKMω*; mall *M*; e. s. e. l.] de s. e de l. *DD^{c}IKMω*; ssai *D^c*; lai *DD^{c}EIKM*, llai ω. 27, a ω, ha *D^{c}E*, hai *M*; dreig ω; feu *D^c*, feus *M*, fieus ω; qeu *D^c*, q̄u *DIω*, qieu *M*; ai *DD^{c}EIKMω*. 28, seigner ω, seignor *D*, seingner *IK*, seingnor *D^c*, seinhor *M*; mal *M*.

V. 29, amor *DEω*; dis *DIKω*; escharnis *D*. 30, dona] do *D*; pauz'e] paus e *Dω*, paus en *IK*, pauza e *C*, pauzab *M*; affan *D*. 31, tallan ω. 32, huei *EM*, oi *IKω*, or *D*; fa *DEIK*; que (1)] qe *M*, q̄ *C*, q̄m *DEω*, quem *K*, quē *I*; plaiz ω, plaz *M*; dema *E*; que (2)] qe *M*, q̄m *DEω*, quem *K*, quē *I*. 33, donc *Mω*, doncs *DIK*, donx *E*; qen *M*, q̄ *D*, que *IK*; direiz ω, direz *DM*; caisi *Kω*, caisim *E*, caissi *DI*, qaissim *M*; vai *DEIKMω*. 34, q̄ *M*, q^1 *D*; qe t. *KM*, q̄ t. *DI*; t. e. j.] jorn enai *M*; tor- - - j. ω; jai *DEIK*, jais ω. 35, pos *M*, pueis *DEω*, puois *IK*; y] i *DEIKMω*; ha ω; ren *DIKω*, res *M*; mais *DIK*; *in D an* s *may possibly be indicated at the end of* be, *but the MS is not clear.*

VI. 36, a. d'u. m.] d'u. m. a. *M*; ara *DIK*ω; q̄ *M*, q̄u *I*ω, q̄us *D*, quē *C*. 37, cal *D*ω, qall *M*, tal *EIK*; non *DIKM*ω; voil *I*, voill *DK*ω, vueilh *M*, vueill *E*; com *DEIK*ω, qom *M*, quo *C*. 38, nō *IK*ω, nom *D*, non *EM*; donc *M*, doncs *DIK*ω, donx *E*; oga *D*, ogan *IK*ω, ugan *M*. 39, no·us] non *M*; ditz *IKM*, diz *D*ω; sabres *DEIK*ω, sabrez *M*; cals *DEI*ω, qalls *M*; ses *E*. 40, cal *DEIKM*ω; catresim ω, catressim *DIK*, cautressim *E*, qatressim *M*; vivrai *DEIKM*ω. 41, vivez *DIKM*ω; o·us] e *DIK*; mores *E*ω, morez *DIK*, murez *M*; sai *DEIKM*ω. 42, non *DIKM*ω; ren *DIK*ω; midonz *DIK*ω.

VII. 43, naves *DIK*ω, navez *M*; en] e *DIK*ω. 44, maint *M*, me *C*; saluz *D*ω; loing *DIK*ω, loinh *M*. 45, qem *M*, qen ω, q̄n *DI*, quen *EK*; veirai *DEM*, verai *K*ω, verrai *I*. 46, granz *DIK*ω; affars *DK*; n. r.] nomen te *C*, nom te *D*.

VIII. 47, le *M*; seigner ω, seingner *DIK*, seinher *M*; qe ω, q̄ *DI*, qi *M*; fes *DEIKM*ω; cant *D*ω, qant *M*. 48, g. l. c. d. l.] salv e gart son cors *DIK*, gart el sieu cor *M*, gar lo sieu cors ω; gart *E*; de lieys *lacking E*; cō si ω, cōsis *D*, consis *IK*, com (cō *M*) si se *EM*; fai *DEIKM*ω. 49, qil *D*ω, q⁴l *DM*, quil *IK*, quill *E*; manten *DM*ω; prez *DM*ω; joi *DEIKM*ω; verai *DEIKM*ω. 50, cant *D*ω, qant *KM*, quant *I*, e quant *E*; tot' *lacking E*ω; gen *CD*, genz *IK*, ienz ω; s'en] si *CE*ω.

Metrical scheme. Six *coblas unissonans* of seven lines and two *tornadas*, each of four lines, following the scheme of the last four lines of the stanzas:

$$a_8 \; b_8 \; b_8 \; c_8 \; d_8 \; d_8 \; e_8$$

(Frank: 747: 4). The same rhyme scheme as that for *Non sai don chant* and six other poems; none of them, however, has this syllable arrangement.

Notes

7 See note to III, l. 9 (second paragraph).
8 *segle*. The spelling offered by *C* is retained. The normal form of the nominative singular (*segles*) is given by all the other MSS except E, which is mutilated. However, the word is among those neuter nouns which retained their gender for a long period and often had no final *s* (*cf*. Grandgent, p. 91; Anglade, pp. 221–2). The choice of the neuter form is further justified by the absence in l. 9 of a nominative *s* in *perdut*, the reading offered by all the MSS.
11 *s'ab*. We have followed DEIKM in eliding the superfluous *e* for reasons of metre, *cf*. II, l. 7.
14 *d'els*. The DIK group has *d'els* and *no·ls*, while CEMD° offer *d'el* and *no·l*, neither group giving a completely satisfactory reading of the line. The meaning requires *d'els* and *no·l*: 'For no other apart from them (*drut*) upholds it (*joy*).' This reading is in fact chosen by both Appel and Lavaud.
   soste. The reading of all the MSS is retained here. Appel (p. 76) feels, however, that an amendment is necessary (*mante*), as *soste* has already been employed as a rhyme word in l. 7.
15 *joys*. The more usual form of the nominative singular ending in *s*, offered by IKM, is preferred to *joy*, found in CDE. *Cf*. note to VII, l. 5.

24 *selhs*. Appel chooses the more common form of the nominative plural (*cill*) given by MD°. The retention of *selhs* offered by C and all the other MSS seems justified, however, in that there is adequate evidence that it is an acceptable alternative form of the nominative plural (*cf. Grandgent*, p. 109; *Prov. Chr.*, p. xvi; *Lex. rom.*, III, 104).

30 *pauz'e*. For the elision of the *a cf.* II, l. 7 (note).

32 *que*. The word is employed here as the equivalent of *so que* ('that which, what') (*cf. Altprov. Elem.*, p. 136), in the same way as *qui* is often used to mean 'he who', etc (see glossary).

It should be noted that *platz* is in the indicative mood, while *pes* is in the subjunctive: 'It (Love) does today what *is* pleasing and tomorrow what *may be* troublesome.'

36 *qu'ieu*. CMD each have different readings, the first two of which (*quē-q̄*) would be acceptable from the point of view of meaning. The one reading offered by all the other MSS (EIKω) is, however, preferred here.

37 *qu'om*. The reading of all the MSS except C, which probably has a scribal error (*quo*).

44 *man*. C has *me*. Its scribe appears to have regarded *salutz* as the second person singular present subjunctive of the verb *saludar* and *me* as the direct object. The direct form of address for *Tort-n'avetz* in this line does not correspond, however, with the use of the third person in the remainder of the stanza. All the other MSS have *man* except M, whose reading is nevertheless closely related (*maint*).

45 *em-breu*. *Cf.* note to I, l. 6.

46 *no·m rete*. The reading of C (*no m'en te*) would be quite acceptable but the version clearly favoured by both traditions (IKEMω) is preferred. D is independent (*no·m te*).

48 Appel has followed the reading of DIK for this line (*salv e guart son cors c. f.*). There appears, however, no reason to depart from C. In the first half of the line it is clearly supported by the slightly diverse readings of EMω in opposition to DIK and in the second half it is joined by DIK, with the other MSS again differing only slightly.

C is the only MS of its group to contain an entirely satisfactory version of the line. E and ω do not scan correctly, and M contains the accusative form of *cor* ('heart') instead of the invariable *cors* ('person, body'), which has retained the *s* of the Latin neuter accusative: *cors < corpus. Cf. temps < tempus, latz < latus*, etc (see *Altprov. Elem.*, p. 68; *Grandgent*, p. 72).

50 *s'en r*. The reading of DIK has been chosen in view of the fact that it is joined by M in opposition to CEω (*si r.*). Of the latter three MSS, ω does not scan correctly through the omission of *tot'* which it shares with E. C, on the other hand, contains *tot'* and is linked with Eω only for the second half of the line. It has with D the incorrect form of the nominative singular (*gen*), unless the line is intended to be read *gens i recre* and not *gen si recre*, as given by the scribe.

VI GES NON PUESC EN BON VERS FALLIR (356, 4)

Twenty-three MSS. A 107 (307); C 194; D 3–9; I 13; K 3; M 195; R 6–21; T 209; c 86 (131); Jaufre Rudel S 180–114 (p. 167); anon. O 43 (69).

The quotations from the *Breviari d'Amor* (Azaïs' edition):

Lines 31,619–34 (stanzas VI and VII).
Lines 29,825–32 (stanza III).

(A)   205 verso (st. III)
        216 recto (st. VI and VII)

(B)   212 verso (st. III)
        224 recto (st. VI and VII)

(C)   213 verso (st. III)
        225 recto (st. VI and VII)

(D)   166 verso (st. III)
        St. VI and VII missing.

(F)   212 recto (st. III)
        223 verso (st. VI and VII)
        Line 31,619 missing.

(G)   ? verso (st. III)
        ? recto (st. VI and VII)

(H)   212 recto (st. III)
        223 recto (st. VI and VII)

(I)   221 verso (st. III)
        234 recto and verso (st. VI and VII)

(K)   210 recto (st. III)
        219 recto (st. VI and VII)

(L)   219 verso and 220 recto (st. III)
        222 recto (st. VI and VII)

(M)   232 recto (st. III)
        244 verso (st. VI and VII)

(N)   216 verso (st. III), line 29,828 missing.
        227 verso and 228 recto (st. VI and VII)

Editions. Raynouard, *Choix*, V, 331 (stanzas I, VI, VII only); Raynouard, *Lex. rom.*, I, 327; *M.W.*, I, 123; Balaguer, *Los trovadores*, III, 358; Bartsch, *Lesebuch*, p. 63, and *Chrest.*, col. 87; Lavaud, *Troub. Cant.*, II, p. 448; Gentile, *Ant. testi*, p. 128; Piccolo, *Primavera*, p. 98; Riquer, *Lírica*, p. 224.

Classification. From the stanza order three main groups are apparent. Further subdivisions may be made on the basis of the number of stanzas.

1. A   1 – 3 5 4 6 7 *torn.*
   DIK   1 – 3 5 4 6 7 –

2. CS   1 2 3 4 5 6 7 *torn.*
   O   1 2 3 4 5 6 7 –
   T   1 2 3 4 5 – – –

3. M   1 2 5 – 3 6 7 –
   R   1 2 3 6 – 7 4 –
   c   1 2 5 – 6 7 3 –

The MS variants bear out the relationships indicated by the stanza analysis. The opposition between the first and second groups is particularly marked by the omission in the first group of stanza II and by the fourth stanza (*cf.* 26, 27, 28, 29). The grouping of ADIK is also confirmed in 1, 2, 6, 9, 18, 19, 21, 24, 33, 34, 37, 40, 41, 46 (*sofre*), 47 (*non–nō*), 49 (*nai*), 52, 55. The close relationship of DIK can be seen in 25, 28, 32, 40, 43, 44, 46, 47, 48. IK form as usual a further sub-group (3, 7, 18, 21, 54).

The relationship of COST is confirmed by 2, 18, 19, 21, 24, 25 (*mal*), 30, 31, 33, 34, 40. Within this group CS are in agreement, particularly in 8, 23, 27, 60, and are the only MSS containing the whole poem. They are joined by A in the inclusion of the *tornada*. O is fairly close to CS. It contains the entire poem apart from the *tornada* and is linked with them in 11, 12, 13, 14, 15, 27, 32, 37, 44, 46, 47, 48, 49, 52, 55. It is occasionally associated, however, with ADIK (1, 2, 8, 23, 41). T, although a member of group two, is more distantly related to it than O. It joins CS in 1, 2 (*quieu*), 23, CO in 19 (*quel*), and O again in 6, 27 (*cor*), 34. Like O it has occasional agreements with the first group (27, 37). The interrelationship of the MSS of the second group is generally well illustrated in stanza II, missing in ADIK: for ll. 11, 12, 13, 15 COS are grouped together, with T showing slight differences but being obviously related to them.

MRc form a far less stable group. All three, particularly c, are strongly individualistic, and their relationship both with each other and with the other MSS is extremely complex. They share variants in 8, 13. Their interrelationship elsewhere can be summarised as follows. MR: 15, 41 (*plains–plans*), 52 (*crei*); Mc: 13, 41, 43 (with O), 48 (*fas*), omission of stanza IV; Rc: 24 (*vay*), 42, 48 (*si*) (with S).

The accompanying table attempts to set out the relationship of the three MSS with those from each of the first two groups. Notable links with individual MSS of both groups include RT (5, 13 (*qe*), 26), RS (43 (*qieu*)), Dc (54 (*sit*), 55).

Stanza IV is missing in M and c and is placed at the end of the poem in R. Appel's theory seems to be quite acceptable, namely that, since R is in obvious agreement with ADIK in this stanza, the stanza had originally been missing in R and was added later according to a MS of the ADIK tradition. The instances where R agrees with ADIK (26, 28, 29 (*autre*)) are ones in which the opposition between the groups COST and ADIK are very pronounced. It is evident, however, from 25, 27, 29 (*bels*), 30 and 32 that R was not added according to any of the four MSS which are now at our disposal.

	M	R	c	MRc	Mc	Rc
ADIK	18, 23, 24, 55(*e*), 1 (with O), 37 (with T)	18 (*far*), 26, 28, 29, 47 (*non-nō*)		21 (*ben leu*), 46 (*sofre*)	24 (*sai ben*), 49, 2 (*que*) (with O)	
DIK/IK	3	54			48	
COST	40	24 (*me say*)	2 (*nulh*)	6 (*totz-tot*), inclusion of stanza II	18 (*traire*), 19 (*del mon*), 33, 34	18, 24
COS	11, 12	14, 27, 32 (*aquels-aicels*), 48, 49	37 (*mas*), 55	44, 47 (*as*) (with A), 52 (*era*, etc)	47 (*no y*)	46 (*clama'l*), 55 (*mas-mays*)
COT				19 (*quel*)		
CST		2 (*quieu*)				1
CS		8		6 (*totz*)		

Appel also suggests that the third stanza had originally been missing in MRc, pointing out that it appears at the end of the poem in c. It should also be noted that it follows the fifth stanza in M. It seems fairly clear that in M the stanza was added according to a MS of the ADIK tradition (*cf.* 18, 23, 24), as Appel supposes. Appel quotes l. 19 (*del mon*) as evidence that the model for M was not one of the four surviving MSS of this tradition. Lines 18 (*traire*) and 19 (*qel*) could also be mentioned in this respect. There is little evidence to support Appel's theory that the third stanza was added in R and c according to a MS related to the COST group. The two MSS are fairly independent in this stanza. Although they both join COST in most of 18 and are linked individually with them in 19, 24, they also join (with M) the first group in 21 (*ben leu*) and 24.

It is interesting to note that in stanza II, which is missing in ADIK, the link between M and the COST group is fairly pronounced (*cf.* 11, 12, 15), while R and c both offer a number of independent readings. Similarly, in stanza V, which is lacking in R, c is plainly independent (*cf.* 35, 36, 37, 40), whereas in these first three lines and, to a certain extent, in 40, M follows all the other MSS. It therefore appears, on the whole, that M is the least individualistic of the three and, although obviously related to R and c, is more dependent than they are upon the two main MS traditions.

Although the MSS of the *Breviari d'Amor* have links with groups two and three, particularly in stanzas VI and VII, they are to be identified on the whole with the first group. (A), (B) and (F) are very closely related throughout.

Base and orthography. C.

I
Ges non puesc en bon vers fallir
nulh'hora qu'ieu de midons chan;
cossi poiri'ieu ren mal dir?
Qu'om non es ta mal essenhatz,
si parl'ab lieys un mot o dos, 5
que totz vilas non torn cortes;
per que sapchatz be que vers es,
que'l ben qu'ieu dic tot ai de liey.

II
De ren als no pes ni cossir
ni ai dezirier ni talan, 10
mas de lieys quo'l pogues servir
e far tot quant l'es bon ni'l platz;
qu'ieu non cre qu'ieu anc per als fos
mais per lieys far so que'l plagues,
que be sai qu'onors m'es e bes 15
tot quan fas per amor de liey.

III
Ben puesc los autres escarnir,
qu'aissi'm suy sauputz trair'enan
que'l mielhs del mon saupi chauzir;
ieu o dic e sai qu'es vertatz; 20
ben leu manz n'i aura gelos
que diran, 'Mens e non es res';
no m'en cal ni d'aco no m'es,
qu'ieu me say cossi s'es de liey.

IV Greus m'es lo maltraitz a sufrir   25
    e·l dolors, qu'ay de lieys tan gran,
    don no·m pot lo cors revenir;
    pero no·m platz autr'amistatz,
    ni mais joys no m'es dous ni bos,
    ni no vuelh que·m sia promes,   30
    que, s'ieu n'avia cent conques,
    ren no·ls pretz mais aquels de liey.

V   Bona dompna, soven sospir
    e trac gran pen'e gran afan
    per vos, cuy am mout e dezir;   35
    e quar no·us vey, non es mos graz;
    mas si be m'estau luenh de vos,
    lo cor e·l sen vos ai trames,
    si qu'aissi no suy on tu·m ves,
    [el ben qu'ieu ai totz es de liey.]   40

VI Ailas! — Que plangz? — Ia tem murir. —
    Que as? — Am. — E trop? — Ieu hoc, tan
    que·n muer. — Mors? — Oc. — Non potz guerir? —
    Ieu no. — E cum? — Tan suy iratz. —
    De que? — De lieys, don suy aissos. —   45
    Sofre. — No·m val. — Clama·l merces. —
    Si·m fatz. — No·y as pro? — Pauc. — No·t pes,
    si·n tras mal. — No? — Qu'o fas de liey.

VII Cosselh n'ai. — Qual? — Vuelh m'en partir. —
    No far! — Si faray. — Quers ton dan. —   50
    Que·n puesc als? — Vols t'en ben jauzir? —
    Oc, mout. — Crei mi. — Era diguatz. —
    Sias humils, francs, larcx e pros. —
    Si·m fai mal? — Sufr'en patz. — Suy pres? —
    Tu oc, s'amar vols; mas si·m cres,   55
    aissi·t poiras jauzir de liey.

VIII Mon Tort-n'avetz mant, s'a lieys platz,
     qu'aprenda lo vers, s'el es bos;
     e puois vol que sia trames
     mon dreit-n'avetz lai en Saves: 60
     Dieus sal e guart lo cors de liey.

Variants. I. 1, des *O*; e. b. v. n. p. *ADIKMO*; no *R*; posc *OS*, puosc *ADIKT*; e *T*; bo *R*; failhir *M*, faillir *ADIKOSTc*, falhir *R*. 2, nuil *O*, null *STc*, al *ADIK*, sel *R*; n. h.] aloras *M*; ora *ADIKSTc*; qeu *S*, qieu *T*, q¹eu *R*, qe *MOc*, que *DK*, q̄ *AI*; midon *O*, midonz *ADIKS*, midos *T*; cant *T*, chant *Oc*. 3, coissi *M*, consi *IK*, cosi *T*, e com *c*, e cum *A*, com *D*, cō ē *R*; poiri'] poiria *C*, pori *S*, poria *T*, poyrie *R*; poiri'ieu] poiria hom *A*, poiria *IKM*, poirian *c*, poirio *D*; eu *OS*, yeu *R*; ren] doncx *R*, ges *T*. 4, com *AIKORST*, cō *D*, qom *M*, qe hon *c*; tan *DIKMORSTc*, tant *A*; ensegnas *T*, ensegnatz *O*, ensegnaz *S*, enseignatz *AD*, enseingnatz *IK*, enseinhatz *M*, ensenhatz *R*, ensenhaz *c*. 5, si] sil *T*; p. a. l.] de lieis parla *A*; parl'] parll *M*, parla *Tc*; am *RT*; lei *OS*, leis *DIKMc*, lieis *T*; un] .1. *R*; mutç *T*; dus *T*. 6, ce *T*, qe *DMOSc*, q̄ *ACR*; tot *OR*, toz *Sc*, tut *T*, ses *ADIK*; vila *R*, vilan *OT*, vilans *ADIKMc*, villans *S*; no *O*; tor *T*. 7, qe *MOSc*, q̄ *IR*, o *T*; s. b.] sai e cre *c*; sapcha *IK*, sapchaz *DMS*, sapciat *T*, saschaz *O*; ben *ADIKMOST*, totz *R*; ce *T*, qe *KMOSc*, q̄ *DR*. 8, q. b. q.] tot qant eo *O*; cel *T*, qel *AIMSc*, q̄l *R*; bes *MRc*; cieu *T*, qeu *Sc*, q̄u *IK*, qieu *A*, q¹eu *MR*, queu *D*; ai tot *CS*, ai totz *R*, es tut *T*, tot es *c*; lei *OS*, leis *Mc*, liei *AT*, lieis *R*, llei *DIK*.

II. Lacking *ADIK*. 9, re *R*; non *MSTc*; pens *MOSc*; consir *STc*, cosir *O*. 10, ay *R*; desirer *O*, desirier *RST*, dezirer *Mc*; talen *T*. 11, mais *c*; d. l. q. p.] com lieys pusca gen *R*, qel pogues en grat *c*; lei *OS*, leis *M*, lieis *T*; qol *M*, col *S*, cō il *O*, con la *T*; poges *MT*; servr *T*. 12, et *S*, ni *O*; t. q. l'e. b.] so q̄l es bel *R*, tot calies ops *T*, e dir tot qant leis *c*; qan *MO*, qant *S*; il es *O*, lles *M*; bo *M*; nil *lacking c*; play *R*, plaz *STc*. 13, qeu *OSc*, qieu *M*, q¹eu *C*, qe *T*, q̄ *R*; no *S*; crei *T*, cug *M*; qu'i. a. p.] qe per ren *Mc*, q¹eu per res *R*; qeu *OS*, qe *T*; anc] ans *T*; al *O*. 14, mas *MSTc*, mays *R*; p. l. f.] per far tot *M*, qa leis fes *c*; lei *O*, leis *S*, so *T*; s. q.] calieis *T*; zo *OS*; qel *Mc*, q̄l *R*, qe il *O*, qe ill *S*; plages *MT*. 15, q. b. s.] e sai ben *M*, e car say *R*, per qe sai *c*; qe *OS*, cieu *T*; ben *OST*; conors *ORST*, qonors *Mc*; es *M*; bens *T*. 16, totz *M*, tut *T*; can *T*, cant *R*, qan *MSc*, qant *O*; q. eu f. *O*; fais *c*, fatz *T*, faz *MOS*; amo *C*; lei *OS*, leis *Mc*, li *T*, lieys *R*.

III. 17, be (*D*), bem (*B*)(*G*)(*I*)(*M*)(*N*), ieu (*A*); posc *OS*, puech (*C*), puoc (*D*), puosc *ADIKT*, pusc *c*, dey *R*; altres *T*, autras (*N*); escharnir *O*(*D*). 18, qu'a. s. s.] car aissim saubi *ADIK*(*A*)(*B*)(*C*)(*D*)(*F*)(*G*)(*H*)(*I*)(*K*)(*L*)(*M*)(*N*), qar en aissim saupi *M* [*the individual variants within this group are as follows:* car *ADIK*(*B*)(*C*)(*F*), quar (*A*)(*D*)(*G*)(*H*)(*I*)(*K*)(*L*)(*M*)(*N*); aisim *K*, aissim *ADI*(*A*)(*B*)(*F*)(*H*), aichim (*G*)(*I*)(*M*), aychim (*D*)(*N*), ayhin (*C*), ayssim (*K*)(*L*); sabi (*C*)(*K*), saubi *ADIK*(*A*) (*B*)(*D*)(*F*)(*H*)(*L*), saupi *M*(*G*)(*I*)(*M*)(*N*)]; caisim *OT*, caysim *R*, qaissim *Sc*; soi saubuz *S*, soy saubutz *R*, sui saubuz *c*, soi sabuz *O*, soi sabutz *T*; traer *S*, traire *MTc*, trar *O*, far *ADIKR*(*A*)(*B*)(*C*)(*D*)(*F*)(*G*)(*H*)(*I*)(*K*)(*L*)(*M*)(*N*); anan *IK*, avan *D*(*A*)(*B*)(*D*)(*F*)(*G*)(*H*)(*I*)(*N*), avant (*K*)(*L*), enant *c*, enantz *T*, ennaut (*C*). 19, cel *T*, qel *MOc*, qe *S*, q̄ *A*, que *DIK*(*A*)(*B*)(*C*)(*D*)(*F*)(*G*)(*H*)(*I*)(*K*)(*L*)(*M*)(*N*); meils *IKc*, miegll *T*, mieills *A*, mielh *M*(*D*), miels *D*(*I*)(*K*)(*M*)(*N*), mielsh (*C*), mielz *OS*; d. m.] q̄ tuich *A*, q̄ tuit *D*, qua tug *N*, que totz (*H*), que tuch (*D*), que tug (*A*)(*B*)

POEM VI 91

(C)(F)(G)(I)(K)(M), que tugz (L), que tuit IK; saubi ADIKOSTc(A)(B)(C)(D)(F)
(H)(K)(L); causir T(H), cauzir (A)(B)(C)(F)(G)(I)(K)(L)(M)(N), chausir AMS,
sernir O; q̄ de totas ay lo cauzir R. 20, *lacking* (N); eo O, eu ADIKSc, eus R, hieu
(H)(I)(M), qeu T, yeu (G), yo (D); o] me (M), mo (C)(G)(H)(I)(K)(L), vos T; e]
quar (A)(B)(C)(D)(F)(G)(H)(I)(K)(L)(M); say R (C)(D)(K)(L); ce T, qes MOSc, q̄s
DR; vertadz c, veritat (K), veritatz (G), vertat O (B)(F)(H)(I), vertaz S. 21, b. l.]
pero COS; be (A)(B)(F)(H)(K), hieu (N); m. n'i a.] ni aura mainz A, ni aura mout
M, ni aura de (A)(B)(F); mainz D, mayntz (D), mans R, menz O, mot (C)(G)(K),
motz IK (H)(L), moutz (I)(M)(N); agra (C), auras (N), haura (H); gellos O, gilos
DIKR (A)(B)(C)(F)(H)(I)(L)(M)(N), ianglos c; pero ben conosc cemort maural
gelos T. 22, qe Tc, q̄ R, qi MOS, quem (G)(H)(I)(K)(L)(M)(N), quen (A)(B)(C)(F),
quim (D); daran (C), diram (N), dirā D; meins T, men (H)(I), ment M, mentz A,
menz DIKSc, mez O, neys (K); e] o (N), qe c, res (H); es] os (K); res *lacking* (N),
gies T. 23, *lacking* O; non I; cal *lacking* D, qual (A)(B)(C)(D)(F)(H)(K)(L); ni] que
(A)(B)(F); daço D, daiso A, daqel M, daquo (A)(B)(C)(D)(F)(G)(H)(I)(K)(L)(M)
(N); n. m'e.] non es (C); m'e] menes (K), mens (N); daisso (daiso S) nom cal ni
nom es ges CS, daiso non cal ni non es res T, a me q̄ cal ni q¹ns dās mes R, mi que
cal qe dels nō ies ges c. 24, cieu T, qeu IOSc, q̄u A, qieu M, q¹eu R, queu D, quieu
en (A)(B), quyo (D); m. s.] sai ben ADIKMc (A)(B)(C)(D)(F)(G)(H)(I)(K)(L)(M)
(N) [*the individual spelling variants within this group are as follows:* sai ADIKMc
(A)(B)(F)(G)(H)(I)(M), say (C)(D)(K)(L)(N); ben ADIKc, be M(A)(B)(C)(D)
(F)(G)(H)(I)(K)(L)(M)(N)]; mi OS, mo T; sai OST; comsi O, consi DIK, cosi
RT(C), cum me c, qaissi M, quossi (K); s'es] es AD(A)(B)(C)(D)(F)(G)(H)(I)(K)
(L)(M)(N), vai c, vay R; lei OS, leis Mc, leys R, liei T, lieis (A)(F)(G)(H)(I)(M),
lies (B), lieys (C)(D)(K)(L)(N), llei DIK.

IV. *Lacking Mc.* 25, greu CDIKST, grieus O; los D; mal trac T, mal trag C, mal
traz S, mals traitz DIK; soffrir DKOS, sofrir AIT; mot mes greus la fā a sufrir R.
26, eill A; dolor RT; cai DIKT, cay R, qai AOS; de] per ADIKR; lei DIKOS, ley
R, lieis AT; mot R, mout ADIK. 27, nō D; n. p. l. c.] lo cors (cor T) nom pot
ADIKT, no poc lo cor O; ō nos pot mos cors esjauzir R. 28, platz] plai OST;
p. n. p. a.] per nuill (nuil D) plai dautras (ni lautr DIK) ADIK, per plag de nulh
autr R; amistat OR, amistaz S. 29, n. m.] autre R, cautre ADIK; giois T, jois
ADIKOS; m'es] mer T; dolz S, doutz AT, douz DIKO, bels R. 30, non ADIKST;
vogll T, voill DIKS, vuel O, vuoill A; cem T, qem O, iam ADIK, me R, qen S.
31, ce T, qe OS, e ADIK, car R; seu AOS, si ieu C; .c. CDIK, .m. R; concis T,
conqes OS. 32, re T, res R; no'ls] nol O, non T; pres DIKOR, prez S; mais
lacking O, mas ADIKST, mays R; aicels O, aqels S, als q̄ T, cel cai K, cels qai A,
sel cai DI; de *lacking* T; lei OST, liei A, lieys R, llei DIK.

V. *Lacking R.* 33, b.] dousa DIK, doussa A; domna IKc, dōna D, donna A,
dopna T; soven *lacking* I, sovenz O, per vos C; s.] planc e sospir O. 34, en ADIK;
trag c; (1) gran] greu CDS, grieu IK; pena e ACMOTc; (2) gran] grand c, grant M,

greu *OT*; affan *DIKS*. 35, p.] de *T*; cui *ADIKMOST*; molt *S*, mult *O*, tant *M*; desir *ADIKOST*; e qar plus soven nous remir *c.* 36, e. q.] e ca *T*, qe si *M*; car *ADIKOS*; noˑus] nos *MO*; vei *ADIKMOST*; no *T*; gratz *ADIMOT*; ben sapchatz qe nō es mos graz *c.* 37, mas] e *ADIKMT*; se *S*; ben *DIKST*, tot *M*; mestauc *ADIK*, mistauc *T*; liogn *T*, loing *ADIKOS*, lueinh *M*; mas pero ades soi ab vos *c.* 38, lo] qel *c*; vos] vo *C.* 39, caici *O*, caisi *I*, caissi *ADKc*, caitç *T*, qaici *S*, qaissi *M*, qᵃissi *C*; non *ADIKMOST*; soi *STc*, son *DIKM*, sui *AO*; hon *c*, ou *S*; cum *S*, tu *M*; vos *K*.

40, *A*: el bes q̄u ai tot ai de liei
    C: el ben qˡeu ai totz es de liey
  DIK: els bes q̄u (quieu *K*) ai totz ai delleis (dellei *IK*)
  OS: e zo (et cho *S*) qeu ai tot es de lei
    T: e so qiu ai es tut de lei
  M: mas so qe tu veis tot es de leis
    c: qe tot es en poder de leis

vi. Lacking *T*(*D*). 41, *lacking* (*F*); ailass (*I*)(*M*), aylas *MR*(*C*)(*K*)(*L*)(*N*), hailas *S*, jalas *O*; qe *MSc*, q̄ *DOR*, quer (*N*), quet *C*(*A*)(*B*)(*C*)(*H*)(*I*)(*K*)(*L*)(*M*); plaing *ADIKOS*, plains *M*, plang *c*, planh (*A*), planhs (*B*)(*G*)(*H*)(*I*)(*M*), plans *R*(*C*)(*K*)(*L*), playns (*N*); i. t. m. *illegible* (*I*); ge tem *c*, gie ten (*A*), ia ten (*C*), ieu cug (*B*), laissim *C*, la tem *S*, qe tems *M*, temi *R*, ya tem (*N*); morir *ADIKMOSc*(*A*)(*B*)(*G*)(*H*)(*K*)(*L*)(*M*)(*N*), muri *R*. 42, qe *IMOSc*, q̄ *AR*, quez (*C*)(*G*)(*I*)(*K*)(*L*)(*N*), enez (*M*); ass (*M*), has (*H*); e *lacking* *O*(*N*); i. h. t. *illegible* (*I*); i. h.] o eu *c*, o ieu *R*(*A*)(*B*)(*F*); eu *DIKS*, hieu (*H*)(*K*)(*L*)(*M*)(*N*), yeu (*G*); oc *ADIKM*(*C*)(*G*)(*H*)(*K*)(*L*)(*M*)(*N*), ohc *S*, vioc *O*; tant *c*. 43, qe *MOc*, qeu *S*, qien *A*, qˡeu *R*, que (*K*)(*N*), quem (*B*)(*C*)(*L*), queu (*G*); mor *AOS*, mue (*A*)(*B*), mueir *M*, muir *c*, muor *D*, vive (*F*); mors *lacking* *S*; o. n.] ieu oc *M*; hoc *O*, ohc *S*; n. p. g. *illegible* (*I*); no (*H*); poc *O*, pods *c*, pos (*C*), pot *S* (*F*)(*G*), poz *M*, puosc *A*; carir *O*, garir *AMS*, gerir (*N*), guarir *c*, guerrir *DIK*, aver guerir (*K*). 44, i. n. e. c.] *lacking* *DIK*; eu *OSc*, hieu (*G*)(*H*)(*I*)(*M*) (*N*), yeu *R*; non *MOSc*; e. c.] per q̄ *R*; e] o *O*, si (*C*); co (*C*), com *OS*, que (*K*), qom *M*, quo (*G*)(*H*)(*I*)(*L*)(*M*)(*N*); tant *c*, no tan (*K*); soi *DS*(*A*)(*B*)(*H*), son *IK*(*F*), soy *R*(*C*)(*K*)(*L*), sui *MOc*(*G*)(*I*)(*M*); iratz *illegible* (*I*), irat (*C*)(*K*), iraz *Sc*, yratz *R*; tant fort en sui morns et iratz *A*. 45, qe *KMOSc*, q̄ *DR*; la (*H*), lei *OS*, leis *Mc*, lieis *A*(*A*)(*B*)(*F*)(*G*)(*I*)(*M*), liey (*C*), lleis *DIK*; dond *A*, on *M*; soi *DSc*(*A*)(*B*)(*F*)(*G*)(*H*) (*I*), son *IKM*(*K*)(*M*)(*N*), soy *R*(*C*)(*L*), sui *AO*; aissos *illegible* (*I*), aichos *c*(*A*)(*B*)(*F*) (*G*)(*M*), aisos *O*, aychos (*C*)(*N*), aysos *R*, aysshos (*L*), ayssos (*K*). 46, soffra *O*, sofra *S*, sofri *C*, sueffre *M*(*H*)(*I*)(*L*)(*M*), suefre *R*(*C*)(*G*)(*K*), suefri (*A*)(*B*)(*F*), sufre *IK*, suffre *D*, suofro (*N*); noˑm] non *M*, nō *DOc*; clam *DIK*, clama *A*, clamail *OS*, clamailh (*M*), clamalh (*A*)(*B*)(*F*)(*H*)(*I*), claman (*G*), clamar *M*(*K*)(*N*), elamal (*C*); merces *illegible* (*I*), merce *R*(*A*)(*B*)(*F*), merses *c*. 47, si *S*; fas *DIKRc*, fauc (*A*)(*B*)(*C*) (*F*)(*G*)(*H*)(*I*)(*K*)(*L*)(*M*)(*N*), faz *OS*; noi *MOSc*(*A*)(*B*)(*F*)(*G*)(*H*)(*I*)(*M*) [in *M* the letters ia *stand above* oi *of* noias], non *ADIKR*; ai *DIK*, has (*H*)(*N*), hass (*I*)(*M*); paoc *S*, pau (*B*); noˑt pes *illegible* (*I*), e n. p. (*K*). 48, s. t. m. *lacking* O; si *RSc*, que (*N*); no qu'o fas] no quas (qasO) fai *CO*, nocas fa *R*, no qas faz *S*, no qua o fas *c*; non *IK*; co *ADIKM*, que (*A*)(*B*)(*C*)(*F*)(*K*)(*L*); ffas (*K*), fai *A*(*I*)(*M*), fay (*N*); lei *OS*, leis *Mc*, leys *R*, liei *A*, lieis (*A*)(*B*)(*F*)(*G*)(*H*)(*I*)(*M*), lieys (*K*)(*L*)(*N*), llei *DIK*, lyeys (*C*).

VII. *Lacking* T (*D*). 49, cocel (*A*), cocelh (*B*)(*F*)(*G*), conseil O, conseilh *Mc*, conseill *ADIKS*, cosseilh (*I*)(*M*)(*N*), cossel (*C*); n'ai] ai *COS*, ay *R*, nar (*G*), nay (*C*)(*K*)(*L*)(*N*); cal *ADIKOR*(*A*)(*B*)(*F*), qal *M*, qals *S*, qar *c*, que (*K*); voill *DIKS*, vueilh *M*(*I*)(*M*), vuel O, vuhel (*C*), vulh *c*(*B*), vuoill *A*. 50, non *DIKMRS*; fan (*A*), fara *S*, fas *c*, fay (*C*)(*L*), ffay (*K*); farai *ADIKMSc*(*B*)(*G*)(*I*)(*M*), faras (*A*)(*F*), farray (*K*)(*L*), ferai O, fai (*H*), fay (*C*); qeis *c*, qers *ADMOS*, q¹ers *R*, querss (*I*)(*M*), quiers (*C*)(*L*), no quiers (*K*); ton] tan *c*. 51, qem *MS*, qen *AIOc*, quem (*A*)(*K*), nō *R*; p. a.] posca (*C*); posc *M*, puos *A*, puosc *DIK*, pusc *OS*; als *lacking* *D*, may *R*; vol O, vos (*C*)(*K*); te (*G*); bon *D*, mot *R*; chausir O, gausir (*H*), gauzir *A*(*K*), jaurir (*C*), jausir *MS*. 52, hoc *Sc*(*C*)(*K*); doncs *R*, molt *S*(*A*)(*B*)(*F*), mot *DO*(*H*) (*K*)(*L*); c. m.] crem (*K*); cre *ADIKOSc*(*A*)(*B*)(*F*), crey *R*(*C*)(*L*)(*N*); me *ADIKRc*; ara *c*, aram *AIK*(*A*)(*B*)(*C*)(*F*)(*G*)(*H*)(*I*)(*K*)(*L*)(*M*)(*N*), arā *D*, aras *MR*; digadz *c*, digas (*C*)(*L*), digatz *ADIMOR*(*A*)(*B*)(*F*)(*G*)(*H*), digaz *KS*, diguas (*I*)(*K*). 53, si als *S*, siaz O; humil (*H*), humielhs (*K*); f. l. e] l. f. e *c*(*A*)(*B*)(*C*)(*F*)(*G*)(*H*)(*I*)(*K*)(*L*) (*M*)(*N*); frain *D*, franc (*C*)(*H*), francx (*K*)(*L*), francz (*N*), frans O; larc (*H*), larcs *ADIKS*(*A*)(*F*)(*G*)(*I*)(*M*)(*N*), largs *M*, laros O, larx (*C*), larxc (*K*). 54, siˑm] e sim *IKR*(*A*)(*B*)(*C*)(*F*)(*G*)(*H*)(*I*)(*K*)(*M*)(*N*), e ssim (*L*), e sit *A*, sin *S*, sit *Dc*; fa (*A*)(*B*)(*F*), fan *S*(*K*), fay *R*(*L*)(*N*); mal] tort *M*; s. e. p.] sobre (*A*)(*B*)(*C*)(*F*)(*L*), sobres (*K*), suofre (*G*)(*H*)(*I*)(*M*), sofre (*N*), suefri *R*; sufr'] fueffr *M*, soffre *D*, sofr *KOS*, sofre *I*, sofrel *A*; em *IK*; pas O, pauc *c*, paz *MS*; s. p.] sos pes *R*, *lacking* (*K*); soi *ADIKOSc* (*G*)(*H*)(*I*)(*M*), som (*A*)(*B*)(*F*), son *M*, soy (*C*)(*L*)(*N*); pres *in margin in* (*F*). 55, t. o.] en (*K*), oc tu *R*; tu *lacking c*; oc *lacking* (*C*), hoc (*N*), ohc *S*; si amar *C*(*C*); mas] e *ADIKM*, mai (*A*)(*B*)(*F*)(*G*)(*H*)(*I*)(*M*), may (*L*), mays *R*(*C*)(*K*); siˑm] si men (*A*)(*B*)(*F*); creis *Dc*. 56, aichit (*G*)(*I*)(*M*), aissi *C*(*H*), aisi O, aisit *S*(*A*)(*B*)(*F*), aychit (*N*), ayci (*C*), aysit *R*, ayssit (*K*)(*L*); p. i.] lausar poiras O; porras *S*, poyras *R*(*C*)(*L*)(*N*); gausir (*H*), gauzir *A*(*C*), jausir *MS*; lei *OS*, leis *Mc*, liei *A*, lieis (*A*)(*B*)(*G*)(*H*)(*I*)(*M*), lieys *R*(*C*)(*F*)(*K*)(*L*)(*N*), llei *DIK*.

VIII. *Lacking DIKMORTc*. 57, torna verz *S*; mand *A*, prec *C*; lei *S*, lieis *A*; plaz *S*. 58, caprenda *A*; qu'a. l.] qanprendal *S*; se el *S*, si *C*, sil *A*; bon *A*; e. b.] bos es *C*. 59, e. p.] e si *C*; et *S*; pois *S*; voill *S*, vuoill *A*; qe *S*. 60, dreich *A*; navez *S*, na lieys *C*; e. s.] on ill es *A*. 61, deu *S*; salv *AS*; gart *AS*; lei *S*, liei *A*.

Metrical scheme. Seven *coblas unissonans* of eight lines and a *tornada* of five lines, following the scheme of the last five lines of the stanzas:

$$a_8 \ b_8 \ a_8 \ c_8 \ d_8 \ e_8 \ e_8 \ f_8$$

(Frank: 464: 1). According to Frank, the poem is the only example of this rhyme scheme.

Notes

3 *poiri'ieu*. The reading of C is supported by the slightly different readings of ORST. The other MSS do not offer a consistent alternative reading. The *a* of *poiria* needs, however, to be elided in order to satisfy the metre requirements; *cf.* II, l. 7 (note).

8 *tot ai*. CRS give *ai tot(z)*, the order of words being supported by T (*es tut*). The order of words offered by ADIK is preferred, however, particularly as it is supported by Mc and O, which is normally closely related to CS (see 'Classification').

16 *amor*, C contains a scribal error (*amo*). All the other MSS have *amor*.

18 *sauputz*. Although accepted as an alternative form of the more normal past participle, *saubut*, the word in fact breaks the rules of phonetics: the *p* between two vowels vocalizes into *b* (*cf. Altprov. Elem.*, p. 42; *Anglade*, p. 137). It is probably here a question of a Latin influence.

19 *saupi*. *Cf.* note to l. 18. The normal first person preterite form of *saber* is *saup* < *sapui* (*cf. Altprov. Elem.*, p. 99; *Anglade*, p. 308) but *saubi*, *saupi* exist as rare forms (*cf. Anglade*, p. 308; *Grandgent*, p. 144).

'*l mielhs*. This is an example of the neuter *mielhs* used adjectivally with reference to a person. *Cf.* R. de Vaqueiras, Epic Letter, III, ll. 30–1:

          E vos mandetz cinq escudiers muntar,
          de tot lo mielhs que vos saupes triar,
          ...

See also *Literaturblatt*, XV (1894), 191, in which A. Stimming cites other examples, and *Altprov. Elem.*, p. 123.

21 *ben leu*. The reading of the ADIK group is chosen. In this stanza, which Appel considers may have originally been missing in MRc (see 'Classification'), we find that M has been added according to the ADIK tradition, whereas Rc generally offer independent readings or are individually linked in turn with both traditions. It is significant, therefore, that in this line Rc both join ADIKM in opposition to COST.

23 For this line the reading of ADIK is again chosen in preference to that of CST. The line is missing in O. M retains its relationship with ADIK. Rc, although independent, appear to be nearer to ADIK than to CST (*cf.* note to l. 21). Appel (p. 76) suggests that the omission of the line in O might indicate a mutilation in the common original of the COST group.

24 *me say . . . s'es*. Appel chooses the reading of ADIKM (*sai ben . . . es*). For the first half of the line (*sai ben*) c joins this group, whereas R joins COST. However, c is perhaps more closely related to COST than is at first apparent in that the use of *me vay* in the second half of the line in both c and R may well be due to the influence of the earlier *me sai* of the COST tradition. This strong suggestion of support on the part of Rc justifies the retention of the reading of COST.

25 *Greus . . . maltraitz*. Their spelling *greu* indicates that the scribes of CDIKST were influenced by the impersonal expression *greu m'es*, in which the neuter form of the adjective is often employed; *cf. Altprov. Elem.*, p. 71; *Grandgent*, p. 96. (According to Grandgent, the normal nominative form ending in *s* is also used in these constructions.) By offering the accusative form *maltrag* and thereby providing a direct object for *sufrir* CT are, however, the only MSS to follow through the

impersonal use for the rest of the line. The other MSS give variations of the normal form of the nominative singular (*mals traitz–maltraz*). Moreover, in order to justify the use of the impersonal construction, *dolors* in the following line would need to have the normal accusative form, as corresponding to *maltrag*, and offered by RT only.

We have followed Appel in preferring for this line the version of AO, representatives of both traditions. The nominative form *greus* is thus used to serve both subjects, *maltraitz* and *dolors* (in l. 26): 'Suffering and grief are hard for me to bear.' (*Cf.* note to III, l. 9.)

In not adding *s* after *mal* the scribes of AOS have regarded *maltraitz* as forming one word. This view is supported by Levy (*Pet. Dict.*, p. 234).

Lavaud (*Troub. Cant.*, p. 70) erroneously groups Mc with DIK as the MSS which he states Appel follows for his reading *mals tragz*. Both MSS, in fact, omit the whole of this stanza.

27 *no'm pot lo cors*. Appel prefers the order of words given by ADIK (*lo cors no'm pot*). T joins them here while being firmly linked with COS in the rest of the stanza. It has been noted under 'Classification', however, that of the four MSS of the second group T is the most distantly related.

It seems reasonable to retain here the version of COS, particularly as R, although having a slightly different reading, supports them in the order of words, whereas elsewhere in this stanza it is generally attached to the ADIK group. The stanza is missing in Mc.

28 *autr' amistatz*. See note to IV, l. 41.

31 *s'ieu*. C has *si ieu*. It is necessary to follow all the other MSS in eliding the *i* for reasons of metre. *Cf.* II, l. 7 (note).

33 *soven*. C is the only MS with the reading *per vos*. The version clearly favoured by all traditions (ADKMSTc), and which also produces the alliteration *soven sospir*, is preferred here. O is independent, the stanza is missing in R, and the relevant part of the line is omitted in I.

34 *gran pen'e*. The reading of AMOTc is preferred to that of CS (*greu*), shared by DIK. Where the two main traditions are in opposition earlier in this line (*e–en*) and in l. 33, Mc identify themselves with the COST group. It is notable, therefore, that in this instance they depart from CS in order to follow the other two MSS of this group, OT. The support of A provides further justification for this reading. The appearance of *greu* later in the line in OT might be the result of the influence of the earlier *greu* in CS.

The *a* of *pena* is superfluous from the point of view of the metre and is therefore elided. *Cf.* II, l. 7 (note).

37 *mas*. The reading of COSc, the meaning of which is quite acceptable, is retained in preference to that of ADIKMT (*e*), chosen by Appel. It is significant that c supports COS at this point while offering an entirely independent reading for the line as a whole, as elsewhere in the stanza (*cf.* ll. 35, 36, 40). See 'Classification'.

38 *vos*. C contains a scribal error (*vo*).

39 *Tu*. In addressing his lady elsewhere in the stanza Peire employs the normal second person plural. A change to the second person singular from the plural does sometimes occur in Old Provençal, but normally only in a narrative poem (*cf. Altprov. Elem.*, p. 129). *Tu* is therefore taken here to denote a different person in the form of Peire's interlocutor.

40 Appel appears to have been justified in not including this line. He considers (p. 76)

that one would expect it to read something like *Lo sens qu'ieu ai totz es ab liey*, and points out that most of the MSS merely offer a remodelling of l. 8. The independent version of M seems, in fact, to be the only one approaching this meaning.

Lavaud (*Troub. Cant.*, pp. 70–1) does not follow any of the MSS but goes as far as including (in brackets) *mas* at the beginning of the line, in order to express the contrast he says one would expect after l. 39, and *de liey* at the end, on the grounds that they are the words which constitute the refrain in all the other stanzas. Suchier (*op. cit.*, 1883, 1344), in fact, proposes the following reading, having regard to the refrain: *Mas luenh de ti e pres de liey*.

ADIK form one group and OST another. M is fairly close to OST, while c is more independent. The scribe of C appears to have followed the ADIK tradition for the first half of the line and the OST tradition for the second half.

It is interesting to note that the plural form *els* offered by DIK may suggest an attempt on the part of the scribes of these MSS to correct the grammar of A (*el bes*) by making *bes* accusative plural.

41 *que*. C is the only MS with the reading *que't*. The reading offered by all the other MSS except T, which has ll. 41–61 missing, is therefore preferred. *Planher* is used transitively here, with *que* as the direct object. CMR are the only MSS with the correct form of the second person singular (*plangz*) (*cf.* Anglade, p. 339).

ia tem. The reading of ADIK is chosen in view of the fact that they are joined by O and S (which has a scribal error, *la tem*). Independent versions are offered by C (*laissim*), Mc (*qe tems-ge tem*), and R (*temi*).

46 *sofre*. The normal form of the imperative singular found in most of the MSS (*cf.* Anglade, p. 293) is preferable here to either of the readings offered by the COS tradition. C has *sofri* and OS have *soffra*.

48 *No?–Qu'o fas*. The reading of DIKM has been adopted in preference to the less satisfactory one of CORS (*no quas fai (fa) (faz)*). The respective readings of A and c (*noquo fai–noqua o fas*) show a tendency towards both groups. The MSS of the *Breviari*, on the other hand, incline towards the version of DIKM. They have either *no quo* or *no que*, and all except three offer *fas*.

49 *n'ai*. The grouping of the MSS follows a pattern similar to that of the previous line. The reading of the first group is preferred to that of CORS (*ai*) in view of the support given by Mc.

55 *s'amar*. C has *si amar*. For the elision of the *i cf.* l. 31 and II, l. 7 (note).

56 *aissi·t p*. We adopt the reading offered by the majority of the MSS. ADIK are joined by all three MSS MRc as well as by S, while C (*aissi p.*) is supported only by O which is independent for the rest of the line.

It is worth noting, however, that both readings are equally acceptable, as *jauzir de* may be used with or without the reflexive form in this context (*cf.* B. von Vent., 9, l. 41; 25, l. 22 (*j. de*); 18, l. 22 (*se j. de*)).

57 *mant*. C has *prec*. The reading given by AS is chosen, as it seems significant that S should support A after being linked with C for most of the remainder of the poem. In the *tornada* as a whole S plays an important part in being often the deciding factor in the choice of readings.

58 *s'el es bos*. The reading of S, supported by A (*s'il es bon*), is preferred to that of C (*si bos es*) in order to meet the demands of the rhyme scheme. The *e* of *se* needs to be elided, however, for reasons of metre. Appel's version (*s'il es bos*), which Suchier (*loc. cit.*) prefers to express as *si l'es bos*, is not given by any of the MSS but appears to be a corrected form of A.

59 *e puois vol*. S again joins A in opposition to C (*e si vol*). Their reading is therefore again preferred.

60 *dreit-n'avetz*. The version of AS is once more chosen in preference to that of C (*dreit na lieys*). It was probably intended that *dreit-n'avetz* should correspond to *tort-n'avetz* in l. 57. No clue as to the identity of *dreit-n'avetz* has been found.

en Saves. The reading of C is retained here, as it is supported by S in opposition to A (*on ill es*).

Savès was probably a small district in the present day Departments of Gers and Haute-Garonne between Samatan and the Isle-Jourdain. Although it originally fell under the jurisdiction of the Counts of Toulouse and, in fact, gave its name to one of the archdeaconries of the church of Toulouse, it appears to have belonged, as early as the twelfth century, to the Counts of Comminges. (*Cf. Hist. gen. Lang.*, III, pp. 70, 336, 375; XII, pp. 161, 200, 241.)

61 *sal*. Appel has chosen the reading of AS (*salv*). The spelling of C is, however, quite acceptable. After *l* and *r* the *v* hardens to *f* or is dropped: *salve(t)* > *salf* (or *sal*). (*Cf. Altprov. Elem.*, p. 45; *Roncaglia*, p. 76.)

VII ENTR'IR'E JOY M'AN SI DEVIS (356, 3)

Ten MSS. A 108 (309); C 195; D 3–10; E 174; I 14; K 3; M 196; R 27–225; T 211; a¹ 473 (221).

Editions. Raynouard, *Choix*, III, 36; *M.W.*, I, 118; Lavaud, *Troub. Cant.*, II, p. 456.

Classification. All the MSS have the same order of stanzas and contain the complete poem with the exception of DEIK, in which l. 3 is missing, and MTa¹ which omit the fifth stanza. Appel did not have a¹ at his disposal.

The MSS fall into two main groups: ADEIK and CMRTa¹. *Cf.* 3, 4, 5 (*jois-joy*), 21, 27, 28, 31 (*prodans-propdas*, etc), 32 (*loing*, etc–*hom*), 42. The first group proves to be the more stable. DIK form a sub-group (*cf.* 7 (*iā -iam*), 8 (with MTa¹), 20 (*soll*), 39 (*se*) (with CT)). The particularly close relationship of IK is evident in 10, 22 (*fag*) (with CER), 36, 41 (*nueg*) (with MRT). ADE have common readings in 36 (*pres*) (with CR), 38, 41 (*nuoitz*, etc) (with Ca¹), AD being further linked in 5, 22 (*faitz*, etc) (with MTa¹). The position of E, as Appel suggests, is not altogether clear. It appears to belong basically to the first group but inclines quite often to the second, *cf.* 5 (*joi*), 21 (*dig*), 31 (*propdas*), 32 (*hom*). A similarly separates at times from DEIK to join MSS of the second group. It is the only MS of the first group to contain l. 3. It is linked with CMT in 7 (*sui–suy*) and joins MRa¹ in 39 (*si*), CR in 8 (*sui*, etc) and R in 26 (word order), 34. It is also interesting to note that in stanza v, which is missing in MTa¹, A offers a number of independent readings (*cf.* 25, 26, 28, 30), but insufficient evidence is available to draw any positive conclusions.

CMRTa¹ form a rather more loose grouping than ADEIK. RT both offer a large number of individual variants, while C is the least independent of the five. The mss generally reveal an intricate and complex interrelationship in which the two sub-groups MTa¹ and CR may broadly be distinguished. The various relationship patterns are indicated below:

       MTa¹: 3 (*e bordir*), 4 (*bel*), 24 (*mais*), omission of stanza v.
(With mss of Group 1): 8 (*son*), 22 (*fatz*, etc), 36 (*prop–trop*).
       MT: 23, 24 (*si*), 37 (*qe–ce*), 40, 43.
       Ma¹: 14, 36.
       Ta¹: 32.

       CT: 24 (*quieu* (2)) (with Group 1), 39 (*se*) (with DIK).
       Ca¹: 7 (*dompnay*), 15 (*que* (2)) (both with Group 1), 41 (*nuegz*) (with ADE).
       MRT: 7 (*donna*, etc), 41 (*nuech*, etc) (with IK).
       MRa¹: 24 (*qe* (2)), 39 (*si*) (with AE).
       MR: 15 (*qem*), 24 (*qe* (1)).
       RTa¹: 45 (*que*).
       RT: 21 (*ses–sens*), 32 (*nulh–nul*), 41 (*jorn*).
       Ra¹: 15 (*say*), 34 (*com–qon*).

       CR: 3 (*esbaudir–e esbaudir*), 8 (*suy*, etc), 27 (*mes*), 28.
(With mss of Group 1): 4 (*bon*), 22 (*fag*), 24 (*plus–pus*), 36 (*pres*), inclusion of stanza v.

Base and orthography. C.

  I   Entr'ir'e joy m'an si devis,
       qu'ira·m tolh maniar e dormir,
       e joys mi fai rir'e bordir;
       mas l'ira·m pass'al bon conort,
       e·l joy rema, don suy jauzens   5
       per un'amor qu'ieu am e vuelh.

  II   Dompn'ay. — Non ay. — Ia·n suy ieu fis! —
       No suy, quar no m'en puesc jauzir. —
       Tot m'en jauzirai, quan que tir. —
       Oc, ben leu, mas sempre n'a tort. —   10
       Tort n'a? Qu'ai dig! Boca, tu mens
       e dis contra midons erguelh.

POEM VII

III Bona dompna, per que m'aucis? —
Ara·m podetz auzir mentir,
que re no·m fai per que m'azir. —   15
Non re, si [m'] a per pauc tot mort? —
Ben suy folhs e fatz es mos sens,
quar ia dic so per que la·m tuelh.

IV Molt am selieys qui m'a conquis. —
Et elha me? — Oc, so l'aug dir. —   20
Creirai son dig senes plevir? —
Oc ben, ab sol que·l fag s'acort,
e m'atenda totz mos covens,
e qu'ieu n'aya plus qu'ieu no suelh.

V Per lieys ai ieu joy, joc e ris,   25
mas ara·n planh, plor e sospir;
e·l mals, que m'es greus a sufrir,
torna·m a doble en deport;
pauc pres lo mal que·l bes o vens,
que plus m'en ri que no m'en duelh.   30

VI De luenh li suy propdas vezis,
qu'amicx non pot nulhs hom partir,
si·l cor se volon cossentir;
tot m'es bon quant hom m'en aport;
mais am quan cor de lai lo vens,   35
que d'autra si pres si m'acuelh.

VII Ja non dira hom, qu'anc la vis,
que tan belha·n pogues chauzir,
qu'om no la ve que no s'i mir;
e sa beutaz resplan tan fort,   40
nuegz n'esdeve jorns clars e gens
a selh qui l'esgard'a dreyt huelh.

VIII Lo vers vuelh qu'om midons me port,
e que·l sia conortamens,
tro que·ns esguardem de dreyt huelh.   45

Variants. The first twelve lines in E are mutilated. The following is what remains.
Entrir — man — e dormir. mas — el joi rema do — quieu am evue —. Dompnai

nō ai — quar nomē pues —rai q̃n que tir. oc — tort. tort nai cai d— contra midons ergu—. *Parts of lines lacking elsewhere in E through mutilation are indicated by* +.

I. 1, entre a^1; ira e *AMT*; gioi *T*, joi *ADIKa*^{1}, jois *M*; mant *A*. 2, qu'i. t.] quem tolo *R*; qiraem *M*, qiram *ATa*^{1}, quram *I*; tol *ADIKMTa*^{1}; mangiar *T*; durmir a^1. 3, *lacking DEIK*; e *lacking R*, el *T*; gioi *T*, jois *AMa*^{1}; me *MRT*; fa *T*, fay *R*; rire e *ARTa*^{1}; e b.] esbaudir *C*, e esbaudir *R*. 4, e *MRTa*^{1}; l'] il a^1; p. a.] tol lo *R*; bel *Ma*^{1}, bell *T*; conor *I*. 5, gio *T*, joi *M*, jois *ADIKa*^{1}; reman *AMRTa*^{1}, roman *DIK*; d. s.] de sai *AD*; dun *T*; soi *K*, son *M*, soy *R*, sui *ITa*^{1}; gausen *T*, jausens *M*, jauzenz *DIa*^{1}. 6, u. a.] una mulier *T*; cieu *T*, qeu a^1, qieu *AM*, q̄u *DI*; voigll *T*, voil a^1, voill *DIK*, vueilh *M*, vuoill *A*.

II. 7, domnai *IK*, dompnai *A*, dona *R*, donai a^1, dōnai *D*, donna *M*, donpna *T*; n. a.] i nō ai *D*; no *R*; ai *AIKMTa*^{1}, say *R*; gian *T*, iā *D*, iam *IK*; s. i.] sieu *R*; son *DIKa*^{1}, sui *AMT*; eu *D*, ieo *T*; fins *T*, fiz a^1. 8, non *DIKTa*^{1}; soi *R*, son *DIKMTa*^{1}, sui *A*; car *ADIKMRTa*^{1}; non a^1; pois a^1, puosc *ADIKT*; gausir *T*, gauzir *A*, jausir *M*. 9, tut *T*; gausirai *T*, gauzirai *A*, jauziral *D*, jauziray *R*; can *RT*, qan *ADa*^{1}, qant *M*; co *T*, o *M*, qe a^1, q̄ *DR*. 10, o. b. l.] b. l. o. *IKR*; mas] ma *T*; senpre *ART*, sēpre *I*; cort (?) *R*. 11, t. n'a qu'ai] torna cas *R*; n'a] nai *I*; qu'ai dig] qe hai dig a^1; cai *ADIKT*, qai *M*; dic *T*, ditz *M*; bocha *AT*, booca *R*; mentz a^1, menz *DIK*. 12, ditç *T*, diz a^1; midontç *T*, midonz *ADIKa*^{1}; arguogll *T*, ergueilh *M*, orgoill *Ia*^{1}, orguoill *AD*, orguuoill *K*.

III. 13, domna *IKRa*^{1}, dona *E*, dōna *D*, donna *M*; ce *T*, qe *Ma*^{1}, q̄ *AD*, quieu *R*; mauçis *T*. 14, arm *T*, eram *Ma*^{1}; podes *EMT*; ausir *MT*. 15, qe *MTa*^{1}; ren *ADIKMTa*^{1}, res *R*; no *R*, nō *DM*, non a^1; fas *M*, sai a^1, say *R*; qe a^1, q̄ *AD*; q. m'a.] qem nazir *M*, q̄m ayzir *R*, cieu masir *T*. 16, re *lacking R*, ren *IKa*^{1}, te *D*; si m'a] sia *all MSS*; m'a p. p. t.] agrab pauc del tot *R*; tot *lacking I*; mort *A*. 17, be *R*; suy *lacking T*, soi *DEK*, son a^1, sui *AIM*; fols *ADEIKMRTa*^{1}; e. f.] estatç *T*; es] eis *D*; mon *T*; sen *T*, senz a^1. 18, car *ADIKRTa*^{1}, q̄r *M*; ia *lacking R*, gia *T*; dis *C*, dit *T*; zo a^1, ayso *R*; qe *Ma*^{1}, q^{1}eu *R*; q. l.] qellam *DK*, quellam *IT*; toill a^1, tueilh *M*, tueill *E*, tuoill *ADIKT*.

IV. 19, mot *R*, mout *ADIKMTa*^{1}; celeis *DE*, celieis *T*, celleis *IKM*, cellieis *A*, sela *R*, seleis a^1; qe *Ta*^{1}, q̄ *ADR*, qi *M*, que *EIK*; conqis *MTa*^{1}, conq^s *CR*. 20, e. e. m.] e yeu neys leys *R*; ez *M*; ella *ADEIKMTa*^{1}; zo a^1; s. l.] soill *A*, soll *DIKM*; au *C*; dir *lacking I*, dire *T*. 21, crerai *T*, e creyray *R*; sos *T*; dir *ADIK*, ditz *M*; senes] sens *T*, ses *R*. 22, be *R*; a. s. q. f.] sol cab lo fag *R*; qel *AMT*, q̄l *Da*^{1}; fags *D*, faigz a^1, fait *E*, faitz *A*, fatc *T*, fatz *M*. 23, e] e ce *T*, e q̄m *M*; totz *lacking MT*, toz *K*; convens *T*, covenz *DIKa*^{1}. 24, e] si *MT*; cieu *T*, qe *M*, q̄ *R*, qeu a^1, q̄u *AI*; naia *ADEIKMTa*^{1}; pus *R*, mais *MTa*^{1}; cieu *T*, qe *Ma*^{1}, q̄ *R*, qeu *D*, q̄u *IK*, qieu *A*; nom a^1, non *AKT*, nō *DIM*; soill a^1, sueilh *M*, sueill *E*, suogll *T*, suoill *ADIK*.

V. *Lacking MTa*^{1}. 25, leis *DEIK*, leys *R*, lieis *A*; aic *A*, ay *R*; ieu *lacking R*, eu *IK*; joi *ADEIK*; joc] plazer *R*. 26, a. planh, plor] a. plor plaing *A*, er plor e planc

R; plaing DIK. 27, que *lacking* E, qe K, q̄ DR; mer $ADEIK$; g. a.] grans per R; grieus IK; soffrir DI, sofrir AKR. 28, t. a. d.] tornab la doussor A, mas ab lo be torn C, mas per lo ben torn R. 29, pretz A; qel AD, q̄l IR; be R, bens DIK; ho E, lo R; venz DIK. 30, q̄ ER; pus R; m'en] en A; jau C; q̄ AR; dueill E, duoill $ADIK$.

VI. 31, loing $ADIKa^1$, lonh E, lueinh M, luogn T; soi $DEKRT$, son a^1, sui AIM; prodans $ADIK$, propdanz a^1, prōpdans M, tropda T; vesis T, vezins a^1. 32, qu'a. n.] car no sen R; camic Ta^1, camics $ADIK$, camicx E, qamics M; pot] dol D; nuills A, nuils E, nul T, nulh R, nulls M, nuls $DIKa^1$; hōs M, loing A, loins DIK, om T. 33, cors M; se] si $IKRTa^1$, sin D; consentir $DEIKMRTa^1$. 34, bo E; can R, cant ATa^1, qant $DKMa^1$; com AR, ho T, qon a^1, om M; m'en] me a^1. 35, may R; quan *lacking* M, can R, cant a^1, qan K, qand A; q. c.] cantar T; la R, llai DIK; lo] la M (T *possibly*); venz $DIKa^1$. 36, qe MTa^1, q̄ AR, qui IK; dautre Ma^1; prop $IKMa^1$, trop T; si] qe T; macueilh M, macoill a^1, macueill E, macuoill $ADIK$, macuoll T.

VII. 37, gia T; n. d. h.] om nol dira T; canc AER, ce T, qanc Ka^1, qe M. 38, q. t.] qeram a^1; ce T, qe KM, q̄ ACR; tant A; belam T, belan E, belā R, bellan $AIKM$, bellā D, bellcon a^1; poges MT; chausir MT, jauzir ADE. 39, com $AEIKRT$, cō D, qom M, qon a^1; non $DIKMRa^1$; vei a^1; com A, ce T, qe KMa^1, q̄ DI; no si $+ E$;* non $ADIKMa^1$; s'i] se $CDIKT$. 40, e] car R, en T; beautatz D, beutat MT, beutatz $AEIKRa^1$; r.] ce resplan T; tant Aa^1. 41, nueg(z) $+ E$, noegz a^1, nuech M, nueg IK, nuegs D, nuoc T, nuoitz A; nesdeven AMa^1; giorn T, jornz I, jors M, jorz K; clar T; genz $DIKa^1$, giens T; nueg fa semblar bel jōr e gē R. 42, a. s.] cellui AIK, celui DE; selh *lacking* R, aicel T, cel a^1, cell M; ce T, qe D, q̄ AE, qi Ma^1, q^1 R, que IK; l'e. a. d. h.] la adreg a lhuelh C; la garda R, lesgarda AIK, lesga+(ra) E; ab $ADIK$, de ER; dreg $DEIKMRa^1$, dreich A, dritç T; hueilh M, hueill E, huoill A, oill $DIKa^1$, uoill T. VIII. 43, lo $+ E$, mon a^1; voil K, voill $DITa^1$, vueilh M, vueill E, vuoill A; ca R, com $AEIKT$, con a^1, cō D, qom M; a midons MT, midon A, midonz $DIKa^1$; m. p.] maport A; me *lacking* MT, mi $DEIKa^1$. 44, e que $+ E$; e *lacking* R; cell T, qeil a^1, qeill A, qel M, q̄l DI, q̄m R; s. bos c. R; conortamenz $DIKa^1$. 45, ce T, qe a^1, qens AM, qenz D, quenz IK; (esgar) dem de $+ E$; ergardem M, esgarde D, esgardem AIK, esgardon T, nos gardem a^1; de *lacking* T, en M; d. h.] dreic inogill T; dreg $DIKMa^1$, dreich A, dreit E; hueilh M, hueill E, huoill A, oil K, oill DIa^1; tro que dreg la gardō miey huelh R.

Metrical scheme. Seven *coblas unissonans* of six lines and a *tornada* of three lines, following the scheme of the last three lines of the stanzas:

$$a_8 \ b_8 \ b_8 \ c_8 \ d_8 \ e_8$$

---

* Although it is not clear, the letter immediately preceding mir may well be l and not the i of si. It should also be noted that in a^1 there is an indication that a letter following si has probably been erased.

(Frank: 755: 1). According to Frank, the poem is the only example of this rhyme scheme.

Notes

1 The subjects of *an* are *ira* and *joy*. The line is therefore to be translated: 'Sorrow and joy have so divided me between them.'
   Cf. a similar construction in *B. von Born.*, 13, ll. 8–10 (p. 31):

   > Tot mo sen tenh dintz mo serralh,
   > Si tot m'an donat gran trebalh
   > Entre n'Azemar e'n Richart.

   and in *R. d'Orange*, xv, ll. 1–5 (p. 115):

   > Entre gel e vent e fanc
   > E giscl'e gibr'e tempesta
   > E·l braus pensars que·m turmenta
   > De ma bella dompna genta
   > M'an si mon cor vout en pantais
   > ...

3 *e bordir*. The two infinitives need to be linked by a conjunction. Only C is without a conjunction and R, in remedying this error, produces one syllable too many for the line. The reading of the remainder of the MSS of the second group (MTa¹) is therefore chosen, particularly as it is also offered by A, the only MS of the first group containing this line.

5 *joy*. Appel follows ADIKa¹, which have the *s* of the nominative case (*cf. Anglade*, pp. 219–22; *Altprov. Elem.*, pp. 67–9). The form without the *s* is, however, preferred here in view of the fact that E joins CMRT in support of it. It is possible that *joy* was not entirely governed by the normal declension endings, as the word was borrowed from Northern French, and probably originates from Poitou or Saintonge (*cf. Anglade*, p. 84; *Altprov. Elem.*, p. 25; *Grandgent*, p. 24).

10–11 *n'a tort—tort n'a?* The repetition of these words may well be intended as an allusion to the *senhal Tort-n'avetz* (see section on the *senhal*, pp. 10–13 above).

16 *si m'a. m'* is omitted in all the MSS. We have inserted it in order to complete the sense of the line by providing *morir* with a direct object.

18 *dic*. C is the only MS with *dis*. The others, with the exception of T, which is erroneous (*dit*), give the present tense of the verb, which one would expect here in order to correspond with the sense of the rest of the stanza. The meaning is accurately reflected in Lavaud's translation: 'Car je viens de dire - - -'.

20 *aug*. Appel treats as an essential variant the much more usual form of the first person present indicative, which is given by all the MSS except *C* and which is therefore preferred here (*aug* < *audio*) (*cf. Anglade*, p. 289; *Altprov. Elem.*, p. 92). He chooses the less common, but quite acceptable, version offered by C only (*au* < **audo*). *Auzir* is one of those verbs which show both the form based on the original Latin, with the *e* or *i* following the consonant, and that based on the Vulgar Latin where the *e* or *i* is dropped. Other examples include **credo* > *cre*, *credeo* > *crei*; **vido* > *ve*, *video* > *vei* (*cf. Grandgent*, p. 126).

22 *fag*. Appel has preferred the normal form of the nominative singular given by the varied readings of ADMTa¹ (*faitz*, *fags*, etc). We have adhered to the spelling of

C, which is supported by the more stable readings of EIKR and which offers quite an acceptable form of the nominative singular. In the case of words ending in *g*, *ch*, *h*, the *s* or *z* which followed was sometimes absorbed into the sound of the fricative and thereby disappeared. (*Cf. Prov. Chr.*, p. ix; *Anglade*, pp. 223-4; *Altprov. Elem.*, p. 68.)

25 *ai*. The reading of C and the majority of the MSS is preferred. Appel has chosen the single reading of A (*aic*). If one considers ll. 25 and 26 out of context, the choice of the preterite tense would appear to be quite appropriate as far as the sense is concerned and is perhaps justified by the presence of *ara* in l. 26. Lavaud (*Troub. Cant.*, p. 72) follows Appel's reading whilst expressing reservations about it. It is worth noting, however, that this stanza is very similar in content to the first stanza, in which the present tense is used effectively to emphasise the vacillation between joy and sorrow. For this reason, and in so far as the present tense occurs throughout the rest of this stanza, its retention here seems quite justified. One cannot ignore, either, the doubt attached to the reliability of A in view of its other independent readings in this stanza.

27 *m'es*. Like Appel, we have retained the reading of C, although it is supported only by R and is opposed by all the MSS of the first group (ADEIK) (*mer*). The stanza is missing in MTa¹. The present tense makes better sense here and corresponds with the tense employed in the rest of the stanza. *Cf.* note to l. 25.

28 *torna·m a doble*. The reading of CR (*mas ab*(*per*) *lo be torn e. d.*) is unsatisfactory, as it leaves *mals* in the previous line without a dependent verb. The perfectly acceptable version of DEIK has therefore been chosen. A (*tornab la doussor e. d.*) is independent but it is significantly closer to DEIK than to CR.

30 *m'en ri*. The reading of C (*m'en jau*) seems to be perfectly acceptable from the point of view of meaning but is naturally suspect in that it is not offered by any other MS. All the traditions have *m'en ri*.

39 *s'i mir*. The reading of AMRa¹ is preferred to that of CDIKT. In this instance *se mirar* is to be translated 'to model oneself' (see *Pet. Dict.*, p. 249: 'prendre exemple') and therefore requires *i* in order to complete the sense of the line: 'One does not see her without modelling oneself *on her*.'

It is perhaps significant that A separates here from the first group to join MSS of the second group, as it does on one or two other occasions (see 'Classification').

41 Lines 40-1 are quoted in *Altprov. Elem.* (p. 134) as an example of the frequent omission of the conjunction *que* when it is used to introduce a consecutive or comparative clause. See note to I, l. 39.

42 C offers a corrupted reading for the second half of this line (*a. s. q. la adreg a lhuelh*). We have therefore chosen the version favoured by most of the other MSS of the second group (MTa¹). Although R is independent, it is clearly nearer to them than to C. For the spelling of *dreyt* and *huelh*, however, it seems preferable to retain that adopted by C in l. 45.

Appel's version of the line, which is quite similar, is not contained by any of the MSS but appears to have been established on the basis of both traditions. Appel follows C and the other MSS of the second group for *a selh* and then adopts the reading of ADIK for the rest of the line (*que . . . ab . . .*).

VIII SEIGN'EN RAYMBAUT, PER VEZER (356, 7)

Twenty-two MSS. A 207 (599); C 196; D 136-468; D° 255 (144, *AdM.*, 13,387) (stanzas III, IV, VI); E 175; I 155; K 141; R 6-20; T 189; U 138 (*Archiv.*, 35, 459); a¹ 475 (223); β² 1154 (stanza VI) (Bohs, p. 271; *Denkmäler*, pp. 175-6); Raimbaut d'Orange G 89 (p. 277).

Appel did not employ D° and did not have a¹ at his disposal.
The quotations from the *Breviari d'Amor* (Azaïs' edition):

Lines 32,617-23 (stanza III).
Lines 32,634-40 (stanza IV).

They are not given in (A). (Page missing.)

(B) 229 verso
(C) 231 recto and verso

They are not given in (D). (Ends at 31,461.)

(F) 229 verso
(G) ? verso and ? verso
(H) 229 recto
(I) 242 recto
(K) 227 recto
     Line 32,637 missing.
(L) 237 verso
(M) 251 recto
(N) 234 recto

Editions. Raynouard, *Choix*, IV, 1; *Parn. Occ.*, p. 25; *M.W.*, I, 124; Lavaud, *Troub. Cant.*, II, p. 462.

Classification. The interrelationship of the MSS is reflected to a great extent by the stanza order:

        ADEIKR: 1 2 3 4 7 6 5 torn.
            CT: 1 2 3 5 4 6 7 torn.
             G: 1 2 3 4 6 5 7 torn.
             U: 1 2 3 6 5 4 7 torn.
            a¹: 1 2 7 5 6 4 3 −

It should be noted that G and U have a similar order of stanzas. They also stand with CT in opposition to ADEIKR in the position of stanza VII, while the opposite is true in their reversal of the order of stanzas V and VI.

In view of their position at the end of the poem, stanzas III and IV in a^1 have been examined to see if there is any evidence that they were added at a later stage or if they can throw further light on the relationship of the MS with the others. The same procedure has been adopted in the case of the fourth stanza in U. In neither case, however, is there anything to suggest that their relationship with the other MSS is significantly different from that found in the rest of the poem. The only point probably worth noting is that the readings of the two MSS are particularly close in stanza IV (cf. ll. 22, 24, 25). This stanza also occupies the same position in each MS.

The classification formed by the stanza analysis is borne out by the variants. ADEIKR show themselves to be the more stable group, coming together to oppose the other MSS in 4 (*soi*), 5 (*partrai*), 16, 17 (*car*), 20, 21 (*non ten*), 22 (*et ab*), 29, 30, 43. ADIK are frequently allied elsewhere, being joined in turn by E and R; cf. 5 (*qe*), 13, 28 (*e*), 34 (*cors*), 41, 48 (*qieu*), 52. DIK form a further sub-group (cf. 1, 12, 24 (*gargaz*), 26 (*obs es*), 50), with IK offering, as usual, almost identical readings. They share variants in 27 (with A), 28 (*ni*) (with E), 30 (with R), 32, 35, 46. AD also have a fairly close relationship, cf. 25, 28, 46.

R is the most individualistic of the MSS of the first group. It associates quite often with MSS of the second, cf. 13, 34, 35 (*onor*), 36 (*el*), 46, 48, having notable individual links with C (1, 12 (*sis–si*), 50), T (21 (*condug–conduc*), 24 (*afans*), 28 (*loc–lioc*), 32, 33 (*ni*), 35), a^1 (15, 19). E also occasionally inclines to MSS of the second group (cf. 12 (with T), 28 (*ni*), 36 (*caber*), 41). The two MSS share readings with GU in 24 (*ses–sest*), 32 (*non*), and with CU in 1 (*raimbaut*).

The MSS of the second tradition form a rather more loose grouping to which may be added the defective D^c. $CGTUa^1$ stand together in opposition to the first group in 5, 29, 30, 41, 43, though in all but 5 and 41 they subdivide, offering variations on their common original. In a number of other instances the readings of four of the MSS confirm their relationship and oppose the readings of the first group, cf. 4 (*fi–fis–si*), 16 (*qavez*, etc), 17 (*qe–qez*), 21 (*noies–noia*), 28 (*ni*), 52.

All the MSS of this group, notably T and U, are prone to individualism, but C to a lesser extent than the others. The complex relationship between them is indicated below. The pattern is borne out in a number of those instances where the MSS join the first tradition in groups of two or more.

(a) *Groups of three*

CTa^1: 29(*tal*); TUa^1: 16, 20, 27 (*tol*); CGa^1: 6 (*cossius*)

GUa^1: 6, 13, 34 (*cor*), 43, 45; GD^ca^1: 17 (*con(qant)hom*), 26 (*qe*), 41 (*e*)

(b) Groups of two

	C					
T	5, 9, 13, 18, 22, 43, 48					
		G	T			
U		18 (*chader*), 19 (*com*), 48	10 (*vostri-vostre*), 12, 28 (*vera-verra*), 42, 46 (*voles-vollez*)			
				U		
a¹	14, 40 (*essay*), 46	4 (*qeu*), 5 (*qeu*)	35		22, 24, 25 (*qui*), 30, 40	a¹
Dᶜ		16, 17, 19, 20 (*aqe*), 26, 41				Dᶜ

On the evidence available it is difficult to classify precisely the MSS of the *Breviari d'Amor* in relation to the other MSS. They share variants with each of the two groups in turn as well as with a¹ and Dᶜ.

Base and orthography. A.

> I Seign'en Raymbaut, per vezer
> de vos lo conort e'l solatz
> soi sai vengutz tost e viatz,
> mais que non soi per vostr'aver;
> qe sapcha dir, qan m'en partrai,   5
> cum es de vos ni cum vos vai,
> q'enqeront m'en lai entre nos.
>
> II Tant ai de sen e de saber
> e tant sui savis e membratz,
> qand aurai vostres faitz gardatz,   10
> q'al partir en sabrai lo ver,
> s'es tals lo gaps cum hom retrai,
> si n'i a tant o meins o mai,
> cum auch dir ni comtar de vos.

III
    Gardatz que vos sapchatz tener 15
    en aisso q'eras comenssatz,
    car hom, on plus aut es poiatz,
    plus bas ven, si·s laissa cazer;
    pois dizon tuich qe mal l'estai:
    'Per que fetz, pois era non fai, 20
    q'era non ten conduitz ni dos?'

IV
    C'ab pro maniar et ab cazer
    pot hom estar soau malvatz,
    mas de gran affan es cargatz
    sel que bon pretz vol mantener; 25
    ops l'es qe·s percatz sai e lai
    e toill'e don, si cum s'eschai,
    qan veira qu'er luocs e sazos.

V
    No·us fassatz de sen trop temer,
    per c'om diga: 'Trop es senatz,' 30
    q'en tal luoc vos valra foudatz
    on sens no·us poiria valer;
    tant cant auretz pel saur e bai
    e·l cors aissi fresquet e gai,
    grans sens no·us er honors ni pros. 35

VI
    Si voletz al segle plazer,
    siatz en luoc fols ab los fatz,
    et aqui mezeus vos sapchatz
    ab los savis gen captener;
    c'aissi coven c'om los assai: 40
    l'un ab ira, l'autre ab jai,
    ab mal los mals, ab ben los bos.

VII
    D'aisso vuoill qe·m digatz lo ver,
    s'auretz nom drutz o moilleratz,
    o per cal seretz apellatz, 45
    o si·ls volretz ams retener;
    veiaire m'es al sen q'ieu ai,
    segon q'ieu cuich, mas non o sai,
    c'a dreich los auretz ambedos.

VIII
    Seign'en Rambaut, eu m'en irai 50
    mas vostre respos auzirai,
    si·us platz, anz qe·m parta de vos.

Variants. E is mutilated to some extent, the parts missing being indicated by +. *Lines 19–21 and 29–35 are mutilated in C. We have included what remains.*

I. 1, segner Ta^1, segner en G, seingner DIK, seingnier U, senhen CR, senher E; raimbaut EU, rainbaut T, rambaut A, rābaut G, rambautz IK, rambauz D, reambaut a^1; veder U, veser T. 2, lo] el G; conortz I; solatz + E, solaz G, sollaz U. 3, s. s.] sasoi T; soy R, sui DGa^1, suy C; ça U, chai G, fai a^1, say R; veguz G, vencuz D, venguz U; e *lacking* U; viaz DG. 4, mais] plus A; (qu)e + E, ce T, qe U, q̄ IR, qeu G, qieu Aa^1; non soi + E; no CR; fi CU, fis G, si T, son $DIKR$, sui a^1. 5, q. s. d.] e vuelh saber C, eu voigll saber T; q̄m E, qeu G, qieu a^1, que IK, q̄ AR; sapchatz E; ca T, cant R, qant U, quan CI, (qua)n men + E; irai $GTUa^1$, iray C, partray R, parttai D. 6, c. e. d. v. n.] de vos cones o a^1, de vos qies (quies U) o GU; com $DEIKR$, con T; es] er T; c. v.] comsius a^1, cossius C, cū sios G; com $DEIKRT$, con U; (vo)s + E; vai + E, vay CR. 7, q'e. m'e.] qan menirai U; cenceron T, qar qeron a^1, qenqero G, qenqueron I, quenqeron D, quenqueron CEK, q̄nq̄ron R; m'en] mut T; lai] mās R, sai E; etre T.

II. 8, ay R; senz a^1. 9, e. t. s.] e suy (sui T) tan CT; tan a^1; soi KU, soy R, (s)ui + E; savis + E, savi T; membraz D, menbratz IKT, menbraz U, m̄braz G. 10, cant RT, qan G, qant DUa^1, quant $CEIK$; auray R; vostre T, vostri U, vostros G; faitz + E, faigz Ca^1, faiz DG, fatz RT, faz U; gardat R, gardaz DGU, guardatz C, gar(datz) + E. 11, cal $DEIKRT$, qual C; sabray R, saurai G; lo] bel G, dir C, li (*perhaps*) a^1. 12, (s)es + E, si R, sis C; tals + E, tal TU; caps DIK, gab U, gabs a^1, gap T, guabs R, guaps C; c. h.] cono T; com $DERU$, con IKa^1, quon C; om GU; retray CR, lo fai E, lo faie T. 13, si n'i a tant] on es aitan CT, o senes tan(tant a^1) Ga^1, o (e U) si nes tant RU; se DIK; tant o + E; o] e T; meinhs C, meinz Da^1, mens RT, menz IKU; ho E; mais T, may CR. 14, com $DEIKRU$, con Ta^1, cō G; a. d. n.] ausit nai T; au G, aug $CDEIKRa^1$; dir *lacking* D; ni] e Ca^1; (c)omtar + E, contar TU, cōtar G.

III. 15, garaz G, gardan (L), gardas (I), gardat $C(C)$, gardaz DU, guardatz a^1 (G)(M)(N); q. v.] vos qeus A; qe D^cTUa^1, q̄ GR; v. s. t.] sapchatz mantener R, poscatz mantener a^1; vos] nos (K)(L), not (C); puesca (C)(K), puscas (I), puscat (L), puscatz (B)(F)(G)(H)(M)(N), sapchaz DGU, sapciatç T; t.] retener U. 16, en aisso] + E, aco R, aizo a^1, ençoi U; aicho G, aiso $DIKT$ (B)(F), ayso (C), aysso (I)(K)(N), enaysso (L); cara E, caravetç T, cavetz (B)(F), qar avetz a^1, qavez D^cG, qavez era U, q̄ eras R, qera D, q̄ra I, quara C, quaras (G)(H)(I)(N), que aras (K), quera K, queras (C)(L)(M); comensat (B)(F), comensatz $CD^cEIKRT(C)(G)(H)(I)(M)(N)$, comensaz D, comenzatz a^1, comenzaz GU. 17, qar C, qe D^cGTa^1, qez U, quar $EIK(C)(G)(H)(I)(K)(L)(M)(N)$; h. o.] con hom D^cG, qant hom a^1; hom *lacking* (C), om $T(B)(F)$; o. p.] emqes U; on] o T; pus (C)(K)(L)(M); (pl)us aut + E; es *lacking* U; poiat (F), poiaz DGU, ponsatz (N), puatç T, pugatz (C), puiat (B), puiatz $R(I)(K)(L)$. 18, pus $CR(C)(K)(L)(M)$; b. v.] basset C, bassetse (*or possibly* basietse) T, em bas a^1; bass (M); chay (R), ne (C)(F)(I), nes (N), ve $D^cEU(B)(G)$

(H)(K)(L)(M); si`s] se C, se se T, ses G(I), si a^1, zes U; laicha (G)(M), lais T, laisa EG(B)(F), laisar U, laycha (C)(I)(N), laysa R, layssa (K), layssha (L); (ca)zer + E, caser (H), caszer (L), chader GU, chazer CR. 19, pu(eis) + E, pueg (C), puei (F), pueis a^1(B)(G)(H)(I)(M), pueys R(K)(L)(N); d. t. q.] dich chascus vei G, diz chascus ve D^c; diran U, diso (H), dison DIT, disson K, diszon (L), dizo (C); totz (H), tug ER(B)(C)(G)(I)(K)(L)(M)(N), tuh (F), tuit DIKUa^1, tutç T; qe mal l'estai] cebelistai T; qe *lacking* U, que DEIK(B)(C)(F)(G)(H)(I)(K)(L)(M)(N), q̄ ARa^1; mal] com G, cō D^c, cum U; l'estai] estai Aa^1(B)(F), estay R(C), istay (K)(L), listai (H), listay (N). 19–21, C: pueys dizon tug qu—fetz ara—es cond—. 20, p. q. f. p. e.] aqe folses pois als G, aqest fetç et aras T, aquel fezia mas er U, aqest fes zai era a^1; per] a D^c; (q)ue + E, qe DD^c, q̄ R; fetz + E, fec (K), fes IKR(C), fez DD^c; e (B)(F)(H), et (L), ez (C)(G)(K)(M)(N), per et (I), pos D^cE, puois D, pus R; ara D^c(B)(F), aras E(C)(H)(I)(K)(N), eras R(G)(L)(M); no T(B)(C)(F)(G)(H)(K)(L)(M)(N); fa (B), fay R(C)(K)(L)(N). 21, caras T, qara a^1, qeras G, quaras (C)(H), quera K(B)(F), q̄ra A, queras E(G)(I)(K)(L)(M)(N), q̄ras R; n. t.] noia a^1, noies D^cGT; no D(H); serv U, tan D, te ER(B)(C)(F)(G)(H)(I)(K)(L)(M)(N); (con)duitz + E, conduc T, conduch G, condug R(C)(G)(H)(I)(L)(M)(N), conduh (B)(F), condut (K), condutz IKa^1, conduz DD^c, servir U; dons T.

IV. 22, c'ab *lacking* a^1, ab CGD^{c}T, cam (C), cap R, qab U, qap D(K), quab (G)(I)(L)(M)(N), quan (H), quap IK(B)(F); mangiar T, manzar U; et ab] ab ben C, camben T, e ab gent (gen a^1) Ua^1; e (B)(F)(H), ez D^c(C)(G)(M)(N); ab *lacking* (I), am (C), an (H); giaser T, iaczer (C), iaser U(H), iaszer (L). 23, pod IKU; h. e. s.] estar suau hom C, om suau eser (B)(F); om a^1 (C); esser (C)(G)(H)(I)(K)(L)(M)(N); suau D^cEGRT(C)(G)(H)(I)(K)(L)(M)(N); malvastz (C), malvat (H)(K), malvaz DD^{c}GU. 24, mas] qe Ua^1; grans R, grant G, grantç T; afan CEGUa^1(B)(F)(G)(I)(M), afans R, afantç T; affa (C), affans (K), affar D^c; es] ses D^cEGR(B)(C)(F)(G)(H)(I)(K)(L)(M)(N), sest U; cargastz (C), cargat (H)(K), cargaz U, carguatz CR(M), gargatz IK(I), gargaz DG, quargatz (N). 25, *lacking* (K); s. q. b. p. v.] qui proeza (proesa D(H), proesza (L)) vol AD(C)(G)(H)(I)(L)(M)(N), qui vol proeza (B)(F); cel GTUa^1, selh C; ce T, qe D^c, q̄ CGR, qi a^1, qui U; b. p. v. m.] v. b. p. m. a^1; bo D^c; prez D^cGU; mantenir (L), manter (F). 26, cove C, obs es DIKT, obs la U, cops lies (lhes (B)(F)) G(B)(F), qobs (quobs (N)) es a^1(N), qops les D^c, quob lhes (G), quobs lhes (I)(M), quobs lies (C)(K), quops lhes (H), quops lies (L); obs ER; qe D^cGa^1, qeis A, que (K), queis (F), ques DEKU(B)(C)(G)(H)(I)(L)(M)(N), q̄s CR; parca (G), percas CEIKR(B)(F)(I)(N), percase (K), percass (M), percasse (L), percaz D^cGU, perchatz a^1, perquas (H), perquasse (C), pircaz D; çai U, chai G, say R(C)(I)(K)(L)(N), ssai D^c; lay R(C)(I)(K)(L)(N). 27, e t. e d.] edol ēdos G; e *lacking* U; toill'] cuelha (G), culh (N), toilla AD^c, tol TUa^1, tolha C, tuelh (C)(I)(K)(L)(M), tuelha (B)(F), tuelhe R, tueill E, tuoill D, tuoille IK, velh (H); e *lacking* (G), le (C)(K)(L); do CD^{c}ER(B)(F)(M); s. c.] tut çant T; co R, com DEIa^1(C), cō D^cK; leschai AIK(G)(M), leschay (N), lhescai

(H)(I), sescai D^cT, sescay (C)(K)(L). 28, ca T, can GR, e (B)(C)(F)(G)(H)(I)(K)(L)(M)(N), ni EIK, qant D, quan CU; v. q.] ne veira AD, ve que es C; vera T(C)(K), verra U, veyra R(I)(L)(N); cer T, qe U, qer D^cGa^1, q̄r R, quec (L), ques (H), quex (C); lioc T, loc R(C)(H), locs $D^cGU(B)(F)$, locx (K)(L), luecs Ia^1, luecx C, luex E, luocs (G)(I)(M)(N); ni CD^cEGTU; saisos DT, saizos a^1, saso (H), sasos IK, saysos (N), ssazos (L).

v. C: per ta — no sial — tal lue — sens n— auretz —si fres— er hon—. 29, fasatz EK, fassaz D; s. t.] trop sen D; per cho qeus faichaz plus temer G, perço quos fa a mielz tener U, per tal qevos fassatç temer T, per tal qieu fassatz plus temer a^1. 30, digua E; es] etz A; cenatz E, membratz I, menbratz K, m̄bratz R, senaz D; no seiaz sēpres trop senaz G, non siatç trop prim ni senatç T, non siaz al prim trop senaz U, no(m) siatz al prim truep senatz a^1 (the m of nom is not entirely clear). 31, cen T, quen E, q̄n IR; lioc T, loc IRU, luec Ea^1; valdra G, varra U, vaudra T; foldā G, foldatz RT, foldaz U, foudaz D. 32, o GU; sen RT, senz $DIKUa^1$; noˑus] non EGRU, nos IK; pogra G, poria T, poyria R; valer] pro tener G. 33, t. c. a.] mentre qaurez G; tan EU; qant $DKUa^1$, quan E, quant I; acretz a^1, aures DEIKT, auret R, aurez U; saur] brun U; e] ni RTU; bay R. 34, lacking T; el] e (probably) a^1; cor $GRUa^1$; aisi EU, aysi R; coindet U, fresqet Ga^1; jay R. 35, gran R, granz DGIKU, trop Ta^1; sen RT, senz $DIKUa^1$; noˑus] no U; er honors ni + E; er] es IK; honor GTU, onor R.

vi. 36, volez DD^cGU; al] el $CD^cGR\beta^2$; setgle E; caber $CEU\beta^2$, parer R, plaser T, plaxer G. 37, s. e. l.] ē locs sias R, siaiatç e lioc T, e loc siatz β^2; sias E, siaz DGKU; loc D^cKUa^1, luec CE; fatz β^2, fol U, folhs C, folz D^c; faitç T, faz DGU. 38, e $U\beta^2$, ez D^c; aqi D^cGTa^1, aq^1 R; meseis T, meteis D^cG, meteus Ra^1, meteys $C\beta^2$, metheis U, mezeis DEIK; sapchaz DGU, sapciatç T. 39, a. l. s. g.] gent a. l. s. R; los savis] lasavia T; los] les U; gent U; cabtener E, chaptener DIK, mantener $R\beta^2$. 40, caisi T, caisis E, caissis β^2, qaissi D^c, quaissi C, q̄t totz a^1, q̄ totz R, qe tut U; conve T, conven GU, cove $CDD^cER\beta^2$; cō IUa^1, quom C; asai IT, asay R, assay β^2, essai a^1, essay C. 41, luns ADa^1, lus $CGIKU\beta^2$; a. i.] anbira T; irals ADIK, ira els a^1; e l'a. D^cG; autres $ADIKa^1$, lautres $C\beta^2$; am T; gai a^1, giai T, jay $C\beta^2$, zai U; ab irals us autres ab jay R. 42, ab] a T; mal] mas U; mals] mal T, bos mals a^1; ab ben] et ab bes T, et abes U; ab] a G; be DD^cERa^1, bo β^2; bons T, pros C.

vii. 43, daiso EIK, dayso R; voill DIK, vueill E, vuelh R; q̄m EIR; digaz D, diguatz E; de vos vuelh (voill T) vostre nom saber CT, per vos meteis vodra saber G, per vos metheis (meteus a^1) volrai saber Ua^1. 44, s'] si C; sabrez U, saures EIKT, saurez DG; drut E, druz GU; o]ho E; meilleraz U, moelleratç T, moilleraz D, molheratz C, mulleraz G. 45, p. p. c.] per qal (qual U) nom GUa^1; o]ho ET; qual C, q^{al} R; seres EIK, serez DGU; apelatz EKRT, apelaz GU, apellaz D. 46, o si] el T, ho sils E, o si AD, o U, ols CRa^1, o sis K, ossis I; voles T, vollez U, volres DKa^1, volret R, volrez I; abdos U, am IK, amdos CRa^1, amdui T; retenir T; osambdos los volrez tener G. 47, veizaire U, veyaire R; cieu T, qeu DGa^1, q̄u IU, quieu *CEK*, q¹eu *R*; ay *R*. 48, seguon *U*; q̄ *R*, qeu *D*, que *GU*, quieu *EIK*; cuch *U*, cug *DEIKRa*¹, cuit *G*; non o] nolo *G*, non a *I*; o] ho *E*; say *R*; perso us o dic quar (car *T*) ben o say (sai *T*) *CT*. 49, c'a d.] cadrez *D*, qadrei *G*, quabdreiz *U*; qab *a*¹, qua *C*; drec *T*, dreg *CEIKRa*¹; aures *EIKTa*¹, aurez *DGU*; abedus *T*, ambdos *U*.

VIII. *Lacking a*¹. *Mutilated in E; the following is what remains.* — mas vos — ans q̄m —. 50, segnor *T*, seigner *G*, seingner *DIK*, seingnier *U*, senhen *CR*; raimbaut *U*, raymbaut *R*, raybaut *C*, rainbaut *T*, rambautz *IK*, rambauz *D*; ieu *CT*; min *U*; iray *C*; yemniray *R*. 51, vostra *U*; r. a.] respostra aurai *U*; respost *C*, respot *R*; audirai *G*, ausirai *T*, auziray *R*. 52, s. p. a. q.] enans que iam *C*, enanz q̄me *G*, enas cegia *T*, enabanz qe *U*; si'us] sieus *R*; plaz *D*; ans *IKR*; quem *KR*, q̄m *I*.

Metrical scheme. Seven *coblas unissonans* of seven lines and a *tornada* of three lines, following the scheme of the last three lines of the stanzas:

$$a_8\ b_8\ b_8\ a_8\ c_8\ c_8\ d_8$$

(Frank: 571 : 10). The same scheme as that for Raimbaut d'Orange's *Peire Rotgier, a trassaillir* and five other poems. There are a further seven examples of this rhyme scheme with a different syllable arrangement.

Notes

C has a greater number of independent readings than usual and is also mutilated to some extent. A has been chosen as base, as it contains few independent readings or apparent errors. Often where it is independent its version is quite acceptable.

1 *Raymbaut.* The reading of AG (*rambaut*) and DIK (*rambauz*) renders the line one syllable short. The version of CERU, supported by T (*rainbaut*) and a¹ (*reambaut*), is therefore adopted. *Cf. Vida*, (10) 1 (note).

4 *mais que.* A has an acceptable but independent reading (*plus qieu*), supported only in part by Ga¹ (*mais qeu*). The reading clearly favoured by both MS traditions is therefore considered preferable.

non soi. Vengutz is understood.

15 ff. In advising Raimbaut to 'maintain worth' by not renouncing his generosity and hospitality Peire may well be merely following convention. On the other hand, the advice could imply that Raimbaut is no longer as liberal as he used to be, which would confirm what is known about his relatively poor financial position (*cf.* Pattison, *R. d'Orange*, p. 16 and p. 90, note 1). In the *planh S'anc jorn agui joi ni solatz* (G. de Born., 76, ll. 41–53) Giraut de Bornelh praises in a conventional way Raimbaut's generosity and 'worth' (*cf.* note below to ll. 29 ff). Pattison (*op. cit.*, p. 16, note 37) suggests that this implies that, to some extent at least, Raimbaut followed Peire's advice.

15 *gardatz que vos.* A is independent here (*gardatz vos qeus*). We have therefore chosen again the reading of the majority of the MSS, which is supported partly by Ra¹, independent for the rest of the line.

19 *l'estai.* The dative *l'* which is included in most of the MSS makes the meaning of the

line complete. Its omission in ARa¹ may perhaps be explained by a scribal error resulting from confusion with the *l* of *mal*. Its presence in D°GTU, where it is preceded by words other than *mal*, is perhaps further justification for its retention.

25 *sel que bon pretz*. The reading of AD (*qui proeza*) offers an acceptable meaning, being supported by all the MSS of the *Breviari d'Amor* except (K), in which the line is lacking. We choose, however, the version favoured by the other MSS of the first group in view of the fact that they are linked here with the second group in opposition to AD. *Cf.* note to l. 28.

27 *s'eschai*. The reading of A (*leschai*) is joined only by that of IK. The choice of the version offered by the remaining MSS of the first group (DER) and by the second group is therefore justified here. Moreover, from the point of view of meaning, *s'eschai* ('is fitting') would seem preferable in this context to *eschai* ('falls (to)'), particularly when taken in conjunction with the following line: 'When he sees (lit. 'will see') that it is (lit. 'will be') the (appropriate) place and time'.

toill'e. The superfluous *a* of *toilla* would not be pronounced and is therefore elided.

28 *veira qu'er*. AD are the only MSS with the version *ne veira*. Although it offers a perfectly acceptable meaning, it seems advisable to choose the reading of all the other MSS of the first group (EIKR) in view of the fact that they are joined by D°Ga¹ and, on the whole, by the MSS of the *Breviari*. It is notable too that the readings of CUT, despite their independence, clearly favour this reading. *Cf.* note to l. 25.

29 ff. Pattison (*op. cit.*, p. 21 and p. 40) considers that, in advising Raimbaut to be more foolish and less learned, Peire is alluding, in part, to the obscure learned poems which Raimbaut based on Marcabru's *trobar clus* style and which dated from a period just prior to Peire's visit. Pattison (*loc. cit.*) also sees in this advice a reference to Raimbaut's learned environment. He considers that the language and general style of Raimbaut's poetry suggest that he was a man of considerable learning. *Cf.* note below to ll. 38-9.

The precept of adapting oneself in turn to the respective ranks of those with whom one deals, of being wise with the wise and foolish with fools, was a common one in Old Provençal poetry.* In his *planh S'anc jorn agui ni solatz* Giraut de Bornelh follows the conventional pattern of praise by attributing this ability to Raimbaut:

> A! bels amics ben ensenhatz,
>   Nescis als fatz
> E·drechs e savis als membratz.
>   . . .

(G. de Born., 76, ll. 25-7). *Cf.* above, note to ll. 15 ff.

30 *es*. A is the only MS with *etz*, the second person plural of *esser*. The third person singular form (*es*) adopted by all the other MSS of the first group is preferable here in that the direct speech probably refers to Raimbaut in the third person as in the case of l. 20. The MSS of the second group offer in this line variations of an entirely independent reading.

---

* Appel, in his note to VIII, l. 37 (p. 78), quotes two instances from the poetry of other troubadours. Kolsen, in *G. de Born.*, II, pp. 130-1 (note to ll. 26-7 of 76), names three others. Pattison (*op. cit.*, p. 21, note 1) refers us to D. Scheludko, *Archivum Romanicum*, XI, 278, for many Provençal examples and possible Latin sources of this idea.

36 Appel (pp. 77–8) and Avalle (*P. Vidal*, II, p. 406) draw a parallel between this line and l. 9 of Peire Vidal's poem *Quant hom es en autrui poder*, which reads *car qui vol al segle plazer*. They point out that the division of the MSS between *plazer* and *caber*, at the end of the line, occurs in both poems.

Appel goes on to make further comparisons between the poems: l. 8 of Peire Rogier's poem is identical to the first line of the next stanza in Peire Vidal's; there is a similarity between l. 4 of the former and l. 28 of the latter (*e non ai gran cura d'aver*); the two poems are also closely related in their form.

The contents of the first *tornada* ('Domna, per vos am Narbones—E Molinatz e Savartes—E Castell'e·l bon rei n'Anfos—De cui sui cavaliers per vos.') lead Appel to suggest that Peire Vidal probably addressed the poem to a close relative of Ermengarda of Narbonne* and therefore perhaps modelled it, to a certain extent, on one of the poems of the viscountess's resident troubadour.

38–9 Pattison (*op. cit.*, p. 21 and p. 90, note 1) deduces from these lines that Raimbaut must have welcomed men of learning to his court.

41 *l'un . . . l'autre*. ET, supported by D^c, are the only MSS to offer, in each case, the correct form of the accusative which the meaning demands. It is their version of the line which is therefore adopted.

ADIKa^1 offer the correct accusative plural form of the definite article (·*ls*) before *autres* but earlier in the line have the usual form for either the singular or the nominative plural (*l*') before the accusative plural *uns* (*cf. Altprov. Elem.*, p. 80; Grandgent, p. 101). It is interesting to note that the reading of R is probably an attempt on the part of its scribe to correct this error (*Ab ira·ls us autres . . .*). GU support ADIK in the first instance (*l'us*) and ETD^c in the second (*l'autre*). C is the only MS which is incorrect in both cases (*l'us . . . l'autres*).

44 *drutz o moilleratz*. Like the verb 'to be', *aver nom* is followed by a complement in the nominative case. (*Cf. Altprov. Elem.*, pp. 120–1.)

46 We retain the version of the line clearly favoured by most of the MSS of the first tradition, despite their slight variations. R joins the diverse but obviously related readings of the MSS of the second group (*amdos*, etc).

The actual reading which we adopt is the version of E. Although AD are very close to it, they lack the direct pronoun ·*ls* which *ams* is intended to qualify. It is possible that the scribes of the two MSS regard the word as understood, but such cases would not appear to be very common. The inclusion of the word is further justified here by its appearance, in one form or another, in all the other MSS of both traditions except U.

50 *Rambaut*. The classification of the MSS follows almost the same pattern as in the first line. However, in this case the two-syllabled version of the word offered by AG and supported by DIK (*rambauz*) fulfils the metre requirements of the line and is therefore retained. Of the MSS with the trisyllabic form of the word, R is in fact the only one which satisfies the metre. CTU have one syllable too many.

---

* Ermessinde, Ermengarda's sister, married Manriquez de Lara, Count of Molina. See note to III, l. 64 (*n'Aimeric lo tos*).

VIIIa RAIMBAUT D'ORANGE'S REPLY
PEIRE ROTGIER, A TRASSAILLIR (389, 34)

Eight MSS. A 208 (600); C 196; D 136–469; D^c 256 (167, *AdM.*, 14, 201) (stanza III only); E 175; Rambautz I 155; Rambauts K 141; Raembaut U 139 (*Archiv.*, 35, 460).
Appel did not employ D^c.

Editions. Parn. Occ., p. 52; Raynouard, *Choix*, IV, 3; *M.W.*, I, 73; Appel, *P. Rogier*, p. 64; Lavaud, *Troub. Cant.*, II, p. 470; Appel, *R. von Orange*, p. 19; Pattison, *R. d'Orange*, p. 88.

Classification. All the MSS have the same order of stanzas and contain the complete poem, with the exception of ADIK, in which l. 48 is lacking, and E, a large part of which is mutilated. The MSS may be divided into two broad groups: ADIK and CEU. The first is the more consistent, with all four MSS sharing readings in the following lines and opposed jointly or independently by at least two MSS of the second group: 9, 17, 18, 19, 21 (*venoil*), 30 (*qez eu*), 31, 35 (*puois*), 39 (*servir*), 44 (*q'ieu*), 47 (*degra·m*), 49 (*del*), 50 (*sui bas*), 51. On the other hand, all three MSS of the second group are allied in 1 (C mutilated), 14, 27 (*car*) (all with A) and 9. The opposition between the two traditions is confirmed by the omission of l. 48 in ADIK, mentioned above.

Within the first group DIK form their usual subdivision, *cf.* 1, 5, 11 (*qem*), 13, 20 (*els*), 27, 32 (*es*), with IK showing further links in 3 (*ai*), 12 (*ñ–nō*), 14, 21 (*ditz*), 29, 32 (*totz*), 52 and particularly in 20, 23 (*e–et*), 39, 42, where they stand in opposition to the other MSS. AD, for their part, share readings in 3 (*aic*), 12 (*no·m*), 20 (*puois conogutz*), 21 (*dich–dig*), 23 (*cals*), 32 (*tortz*).

CEU form a more loose and intricate grouping. In his classification of the MSS Appel makes no specific reference to the relationship between C and E. Important links are seen, however, in 11, 13, 21 (*digz*), 31. E is also closely allied to U in 23 (*cal*) (with IK), 48 (*dic*). Special attention should perhaps be drawn to the relationship of U with each of the other two MSS of its group. Pattison regards it as vaguely related to CE. However, apart from being connected both with E and with CE as a whole (see above), it has particularly important links with C, mostly in opposition to the other MSS. *Cf.* 19, 21 (*ven lo*), 35 (*plus*), 39, 44 (*qe*), 49, 50. Appel points out the similarity between the reading of 22 in C and that of 43 in GU in *Seign'en Raymbaut, per vezer*, and considers that the scribe of C must have had the original of U before him. He adds that this would explain many of those instances where they differ both from each other and from the other MSS, that is, where the original of U has contained errors.

All three MSS individually associate themselves at times with the first group, E in particular showing fairly strong links with this tradition, in opposition to the other MSS, *cf.* 17, 19, 20, 25 (*m'o*), 32 as well as 18, 21 (*venols*), 30 (*que*) in which its independent readings are nearer to the first group than to the second. U is connected with MSS of the first group in 11, 47, standing quite close to all four in 40 (*escaeguz*). It stands with A in 20 (*faich–fach*) in opposition to the other MSS. C is allied with AD in 12 (*no·m*), 23 (*quals*) and again with A in 5 (*etz*), the latter two instances being in opposition to the others.

There is insufficient evidence available in the one stanza concerned for us to comment on the relationship of D^c with the other MSS.

Base and orthography. A.

I

Peire rotgier, a trassaillir
m'er per vos los digz e·ls covens
q'eu aic a midonz, totz dolens,
de chantar que·m cuidiei soffrir;
e pois sai etz a mi vengutz,   5
cantarai, si n'ai estat mutz,
que non vuoill remaner confes.

II

Mout vos dei lauzar e grazir
car anc vos venc cors ni talens
de saber mos chaptenemens,   10
e vuoill qe·n sapchatz alqes dir;
e ia l'avers no·m si'escutz,
s'ieu sui avols ni recresutz,
qe pel ver non passetz ades.

III

Car qui per aver vol mentir,   15
aqel lauzars es blasmamens
e tortz e mals enseignamens,
e fa·n als autres escarnir;
q'en dich non es bos pretz saubutz,
mas el faich es puois conogutz,   20
e pelz faitz veno il dich apres.

IV

Per me voletz mon nom auzir,
cals son, o drutz . . . Er clau las dens,

                c'ades poia mos pessamens,
                on plus de prion m'o conssir;   25
                ben vuoill sapchatz que non sui drutz
                tot per so car non sui volgutz,
                mas ben am, sol midonz m'ames.

V   Peire rotgier, cum puosc sofrir
                qez eu am aissi solamens?   30
                Meravill me si viv de vens;
                tortz es si·m fai midonz morir.
                S'ieu muor per liei farai vertutz,
                per qu'eu cre que, si fos perdutz,
                dreitz fora qe puois mi nogues.   35

VI   Era il ven en cor que m'azir,
                mas ia fo q'er'autres sos sens
                c'aitals, e ssos entendemens,
                per q'ieu li dei totz temps servir,
                pel ben qe·m n'es escazegutz;   40
                ja no m'en vengues mais salutz,
                li dei totztemps estar als pes.

VII   Si·m volgues sol tant cossentir
                q'ieu fos totztemps sos entendens,
                ab bels digz n'estera gauzens,   45
                e feira·m ses faitz esgauzir;
                e degra·m ben esser cregutz,
                q'eu non dic tant qe·m fos creguz
                mais del bon respieich don visques.

VIII   Bon Respieich, d'aut sui bas cazutz, 50
                e si no·m ereb sa vertutz,
                per conseil li don qe·m pendes.

Variants. C is mutilated in ll. 1–4 and E in ll. 1–8 and 35–52. The following is what remains. Other mutilated parts are indicated by +.

    C. 1–4: — tras—ir mer —os los — els co — quieu — midons — dolens —m cuygey (de chantar) —.

    E. 1–8: — rotgier —ssaillir — per vos —gz els co—s quieu — midons — dolens —hantar — cugei su— e pos sai — ami ven—utz que —.

    35–52: — fora que —. Araill v— queraut(r) —demens — pel be q— maven—

als pes. Sim v— fos tos (t)— nestera —auzir— nō dic — bon resp(e)—. Lonc r—
non er al— qem pend(e)—.

I. 1, rogiers *DIK*, rugier *U*; trasaillir *DK*, trassillir *U*. 2, ditz *IK*, diz *DU*; e˙ls]
el *U*; convenz *U*, cŏvenz *DK*. 3, qieu *U*, quieu *K*, q̃u *AI*; aic] ai *IK*, fi *U*; toz *DU*;
dolenz *DIK*. 4, qem *DU*, q̄m *I*, qiem *A*; cugei *DIK*, cuigei *U*; sofrir *U*. 5, pos *U*,
puois *DK*, pus *C*; nes *U*, nest *DIK*; vencuz *D*, venguz *U*. 6, chantarai *CIK*,
chanterai *U*; si] sim *C*; estar *A*; muz *DU*. 7, qe *DI*, qieu *A*; voill *DIK*, vuelh *C*;
romaner *DIK*; cofes *C*.

II. 8, *no variants*. 9, qar *U*, quar *CE*; cor *CEU*; talenz *DIKU*. 10, saber] vezer *U*;
captenemens *CE*, captenemenz *DI*, captenimens *U*, chaptenemenz *K*. 11, voilh
U, voill *DIK*, vueill *E*, vuelh *C*; qē *A*, qem *DU*, quem *K*, q̄m *I*, quen *CE*; sapchaz
DU, sapsatz *K*; alques *CDEIK*. 12, laver *U*; no˙m] ñ *I*, nō *K*, non *U*, nous *E*; si']
sia *ACU*; escuz *DU*. 13, s'ieu] sen *U*, sien *DIK*; soi *E*, son *DIK*, suy *C*; recresuz *U*,
recrezutz *CEIK*, recrezuz *D*. 14, que *CEKU*, q̄ *A*; pases *E*, passaz *D*, passe *IK*,
passez *U*.

III. 15, qar *DD*ᶜ, quar *CE*; qi *U*. 16, aquel *DEIKU*, aq̄l *A*, aquelh *C*; lausar *U*;
blasmamenz *DD*ᶜ*IK*. 17, e. t. e] e torn en *C*, et es trop *U*; torz *DK*; mal *E*; en-
segnamens *U*, ensegnamenz *D*ᶜ, enseingnamenz *DIK*, ensenhamens *E*, essenhamens
C. 18, e fa˙n als] es fai als *C*, e fais (fas *E*) nals *D*ᶜ*E*; fai *DIK*; altres *D*; escharnir
*D*ᶜ; e fas vas la gent e. *U*. 19, q'e. d. n. e.] non es en digz *C*, greu er en diz *U*; quen
EK, q̄n *I*; dig *DEIK*, ditz *D*ᶜ; faiz *U*, prez *DD*ᶜ*I*; saubuz *DU*, sauputz *C*. 20,
mais *C*, mals *IK*; el] als *C*, els *DD*ᶜ*EIK*, per *U*; fach *U*, fagz *C*, faitz *D*ᶜ*E*, faiz *D*,
fatz *IK*; est *U*; p. c.] i conegutz *E*, i conogutz *I*, i conoguz *K*, reconeguz *D*ᶜ,
reconogutz *C*, tost conoguz *U*; conoguz *D*. 21, pels *CDD*ᶜ*EIK*, per *U*; fag *U*,
fagz *C*, faigz *E*, faiz *D*, fatz *IK*; ven lo *CU*, venoill *D*, venol *IK*, venols *E*; dig *D*,
digz *CE*, dir *U*, ditz *IK*; appres *D*ᶜ.

IV. 22, mi *U*; volez *DU*; per mi meteys voletz auzir *C*. 23, cal *EIKU*, quals *C*;
soi *E*, suy *C*; ho *E*; drut *E*, druz *DU*; er] ar *E*, e *I*, et *K*; denz *DIKU*. 24, ades
C, qades *U*; pueja *CEU*, puoja *IK*; pensamens *EU*, pessamenz *DIK*. 25, on *lacking*
U; pus *C*; p. m'o] pren en *C*; preon *DIK*; m'o] e mon *U*, me *D*; consir *EU*,
cossir *C*. 26, b. v. s. q.] e dic vos ben quieu *C*; voilh *U*, voill *DIK*, vueill *E*; sapchaz
DU; qe *U*; no *CE*; soi *E*, son *DIKU*, suy *C*; druz *DU*. 27, t. p. s.] pero qan *U*;
quar *CE*, que *DIK*; no *C*; soi *E*, son *DIKU*, suy *C*; volguz *D*. 28, midons *CE*.

V. 29, eire *D*; rogier *CD*, rogiers *IK*, rugier *U*; com *DEU*, con *IK*; posc *I*,
puesc *CEU*; soffrir *D*, sufrir *CE*. 30, q. e.] quades *C*, qeu *U*; que *E*, quez *IK*; ieu
EI; aisi *EU*; solamenz *DIK*. 31, meraveil *K*, meraveilh *U*, meraveill *DI*, meravil
C; s. v. d. v.] siesc vivs (viv *E*) davens *CE*, ses avinens *U*; vi *D*; venz *DIK*. 32,
t. e. s.] en aissim *C*, tort ai sim *U*; torz *D*, totz *IK*; es] er *A*; midons *CEU*; morrir
IK, murir *CE*. 33, seu *U*; muer *CEU*; lei *DIK*, leis *EU*, lieys *C*; vertuz *DU*,
[vertu]tz + *E*. 34, p. q. e. c.] per que eu cre *A*, per quem platz *C*; qeu *DU*, quieu
E; que *lacking A*, qe *U*, q̄ *K*; perdutz + *E*, perduz *DU*. 35, d. f.] dreg agra *C*;

dregs K, dreigs I, dreiz U, drez D; que CDIK, q̄ A; plus CU, pois I; mazires C, menoges IKU, mi noges D.

VI. 36, aral C, eraill D, eral IKU; azir] aizir U. 37, i. f.] ian fan U, si fon D; fon IK; quer CI, q̄r KU; senz DIK. 38, qaitals U, quaitals C; captenemens C, entendemenz DIK, entendimens U. 39, qeu U, q̄u I, quieu DK, q¹eu C; li] loy C; dey C; tot IK, toz DU; s.] grasir U, grazir C. 40, sol p. b. C; q̄e K, quem C, queu I; escaeguz U, escazeguz D, escazutz C. 41, jamais n. m'e. v. s. DIK, jamais nom neschazes s. C, jamais non navenges s. U; saluz DU. 42, dey C; tostemps CIK, toz temps DU; al IK.

VII. 43, s. v. s.] e sim volgues C; sol tant] daitan U; tan CIK; consentir DIKU. 44, qe U, q̄ C, qeu D, q̄u I, queu K; f. t. s. e.] t. f. s. e. C; tostemps CIK, toz temps DU; entendenz DIK. 45, ab] a U; bel U, belhs C; ditz IK, diz DU; jauçens U, jauzens C, jauzenz DIK. 46, feram CDIKU; s. f. e.] senes fag jauzir C; ses] sos ADIU; faiz D, fatz IK, prez U; esjauzir DIKU. 47, degrā I, degran U, devrian C; ben lacking C; creguz DIU, crezutz C. 48, lacking ADIK; quieu C; dic] quier C; tan C; qe·m] ian C; crezutz C. 49, mas CDIKU; del] dum U, dun C; bon] bel U; respet U, respeig DK, respieg CI; don] qem U; visqes DU.

VIII. 50, respeit U, respeiz D, respieg CIK; sui bas] bas son CU; son DIK; cauz U, cazuz CD. 51, no·m] non U; ereb] era U, recep C; vertuz DU. 52, conseilh U, conseill DIK, cossel C; do C; quem CIK, q̄m E; pengues U, perdes IK.

Metrical scheme. Seven *coblas unissonans* of seven lines and a *tornada* of three lines, following the scheme of the last three lines of the stanzas:

$$a_8\ b_8\ b_8\ a_8\ c_8\ c_8\ d_8$$

(Frank: 571:11). The same scheme as that for Peire Rogier's *Seign'en Raymbaut, per vezer* and five other poems. There are a further seven examples of this rhyme scheme with a different syllable arrangement.

Notes

1 *rotgier.* The reading of AE, favoured by Pattison, is preferred. Appel's version (*rogier*) is not offered by any of the MSS but, together with that of U (*rugier*), clearly supports AE in opposition to DIK (*rogiers*).

3 *aic.* The version of AD, supported by IK (*ai*). CE are both mutilated here and, as Pattison (*R. d'Orange*, p. 90) observes, U(*fi*) cannot be trusted very much in view of the number of its independent readings and errors throughout the poem. Appel follows U but is obliged to amend its reading in order to give the normal form of the first person preterite (*fis*).

4 *que·m.* The reading of A (*q'ie·m*) chosen by Pattison would be quite acceptable but in view of its independence is rejected here in favour of that offered by DIKU. It is a pity that CE are mutilated, as they both identify themselves at times with the ADIK tradition (see 'Classification') and might therefore have provided useful guidance on the choice of reading. It is perhaps significant, however,

that U, which also has at times firm links with this tradition, including an important one with A in l. 20 (see 'Classification'), should support DIK here in opposition to A.

5 *etz.* We have adhered to the reading of A in view of the fact that it is joined by C in opposition to DIK (*nest*) and U (*nes*), E being again mutilated. Moreover throughout the rest of the poem Raimbaut addresses Peire by the polite second person plural and not by the singular, perhaps indicating his respect for the older and, at that time, more established poet. (See section on Peire's life, p. 4.)

Appel's version (*n'etz*) is not given by any of the MSS but is obviously close to AC. It might well be based upon U, as *es* is an alternative form of *etz* (*cf.* Anglade, p. 314; Roncaglia, p. 113). However, *es* is also an acceptable form of the second person singular (*cf.* Anglade and Roncaglia, loc. cit.), and U could alternatively, therefore, be linked with DIK.

The absence of C from Appel's variants would suggest that *n'etz* is offered by this MS, but it is quite clear that C joins A in this instance.

6 *estat.* A contains a scribal error (*estar*).
7 *que.* The reading of A (*q'ieu*), though again acceptable, is independent. The version favoured by both traditions is therefore preferred.
12 *si'escutz.* We have followed DEIK in eliding the *a* of *sia* for reasons of metre.
18 *e fa'n als.* We have adhered to A, which is joined by DIK. The readings of CEUD° all differ from each other, while E (*e fas nals*) is at the same time fairly close to ADIK. Pattison's objection (loc. cit.) to the reflexive form of *far* given by CEUD° and chosen by Appel is reasonable. It is more likely that fun would be made of the flattered than of the flatterer.

The reading adopted by Appel (*e fai·s a. e. e.*) is based on those of CEUD° but is not actually offered by any of them.

19–21 *dich, faich,* etc. In l. 19 ADEIK give the singular (*dich–dig*) and CUD° the plural (*digz,* etc). In l. 20 *faich* is in the singular in AU and in the plural in CDEIKD°. In l. 21 U is the only MS with the singular *fag* and is joined by C for the singular *dir–(lo)digz* in opposition to the other MSS.

Appel adheres to the plural for all three lines. It seems reasonable, however, to remain with A for the three lines particularly in view of Pattison's sound assumption (loc. cit.) that, considering the large number of singulars, the original probably had one set of contrasting words in the singular and the other in the plural. Confusion may thus have arisen from the influence of the one set upon the other.

20 *es puois conogutz.* The support of D justifies the retention of the reading of A. The versions of IKE (*esi conogutz/conegutz*) and U (*est tost conoguz*) are fairly close to it, while that of C, preferred by Appel, is more independent (*es reconogutz*).

It is also worth noting that *puois* is more appropriate from the point of view of meaning in that it corresponds with *apres* in the following line.

23 *o drutz* ... Raimbaut probably interrupts his thought here. (See Pattison's note on this line, op. cit., p. 90.) Alternatively, it is possible that a second clause was meant to be understood, as Lavaud in fact suggests in his translation of the line: 'Quel je suis, ou *si je suis* "amant".' We prefer to regard *cals son* as an indirect question, whereas Pattison takes it to be a direct one.

28 *mas.* Appel (p. 79) considers that the word is probably used here with its causal meaning (*cf. Pet. Dict.,* p. 231; *S.W.,* v, 30–1). However, the meaning 'but', favoured by both Lavaud and Pattison in their translations, appears to us to be more appropriate.

29 *rotgier*. The reading of A is retained for the same reasons as in l. 1. In addition, D departs from IK to join C and U in support of AE.

30 *qez eu*. It appears reasonable to adhere to ADIK, which have the form *qez* before the following vowel. Appel selects the individual reading of E (*que ieu*). C and U offer further independent versions.

31 *si viv de vens*. Like Pattison, we have chosen the reading of ADIK favoured by Levy (*S.W.*, VIII, 621). Appel prefers that of C, supported by E (*s'iesc vivs (viv) d'avens*)—translated by Pattison (*loc. cit.*) as 'if I live beyond Advent'—but in his later edition of Raimbaut d'Orange (*Raïmbaut von Orange*, p. 22) he follows ADIK, the version of which he modifies slightly by replacing *si* by *se*.

Lavaud also favours the reading of ADIK, but his interpretation of the line is perhaps doubtful: 'Je m'émerveille de vivre de soupirs.' (*Troub. Cant.*, p. 73)* The similar interpretations of *vens* offered by Levy (*loc. cit.*) and Pattison (*op. cit.*, p. 88, translation) ('nothing'–'thin air') appear to be more appropriate here. The same use of the word is found in l. 24 of Peire Vidal's *Si·m laissava: Que'l segles non es mas vens* (Avalle's edition, XXXII); Raynouard in fact translates the line as 'Le siècle n'est que vent.' (*Lex. rom.*, v, 499.)

Pattison chooses to divide the line into two parts: *Meravill me! Si viv de vens!* ('I am astounded. Indeed, I am living on thin air!'). However, it seems to make as good sense taken as a whole: 'I am amazed if I live on thin air.'

32 *es*. Pattison retains the independent reading of A (*er*). C and U also have independent readings. The version of DIK is preferred in view of the fact that it is supported by E, which often associates itself with this group in opposition to the other MSS (see 'Classification'). The meaning is as acceptable as that of A.

Appel also follows DIKE for this line but does not include the version of A in the variants.

34 A omits *que* after *cre* and provides the correct number of syllables in the line only by not eliding the *e* of the earlier *que*. We prefer the reading of all the other MSS except C, which offers an independent version of the line.

35 We retain the version of ADIK for this line and follow Pattison's interpretation (*loc. cit.*): 'It would be right for me then to harm myself [i.e. to kill myself]'. The verb *nozer* is thus preferred to *enojar*, favoured by Appel, who reads the line as *dreitz fora que plus m'enoges* and translates: 'so würde also meine Dame eigentlich ganz recht daran tun, mich noch mehr als bisher zu quälen' (*Raïmbaut von Orange*, p. 22, note 1). The reading *plus* is given by CU only, which, as we note in 'Classification', are quite often independent in this poem. C is, in fact, independent for the rest of the line.

See Pattison's discussion (pp. 90–1) on Appel's interpretation of ll. 33–5, including the latter's suggestion that the lines may have a humorous basis (*loc. cit.*).

37–8 Although the verb *era* is in the singular, it has as subjects the two nouns, *sens* and *entendemens*. *Cf*. note to III, l. 9.

41 Like Pattison we have retained the reading of A, which, except for the position of *mais*, is supported by that of DIK. C and U are again more independent, and E is mutilated, although what remains seems to indicate a further independent version linked with U. Pattison (*op. cit.*, p. 91) states that Appel follows the majority of

---

* For partial justification of the translation of *vens* by 'soupirs' Lavaud refers to *Prov. Chr.*, 100, l. 40, but in fact Appel tentatively translates *vens* in the passage concerned by 'trieb' ('instinct', 'impulse'). Levy (*S.W.*, VIII, 620) cites the passage and reports Appel's suggested translation.

the MSS. However, the latter's version is not precisely offered by any one of them and appears to be a combination of DIK and U (*jamais no·m n'avengues salutz*).

The line has a concessive meaning, confirmed by the presence of the initial *ia*. Cf. *Altprov. Elem.*, p. 136.

44 *q'ieu*. There seems to be no strong reason to depart from A, supported again by DIK, in favour of CU (*que*) employed by Appel. (E is again mutilated.) The two versions make equal sense.

46 *ses*. Of the MSS ADIKU, K is the only one which appears to offer the correct version, the meaning of which ('without') is given by the independent reading of C (*senes*). E is again mutilated. In ADIU (*sos*) the *e* may have been mistaken for an *o* in copying or may have resulted from confusion between the possessive forms *ses* and *sos*. Anglade (p. 100) refers to *sos* as a possible rare alternative form for *ses*, although he admits to not having found an example.

47 *degra·m*. It seems reasonable to adhere, as Pattison does, to the version of A, joined by DK and perhaps by I (*degrā*). Appel prefers the reading of U (*degra·n*), which is supported by that of C (*devria·n*) and which offers an equally acceptable meaning.

The scribes of C and U presumably treat *degra–devria* as the first person ('I should certainly be believed in this matter (lit. 'concerning this')'), while the reading of ADK consists of an impersonal construction: (lit.) 'It should certainly be believed to me . . .'

48 Pattison (*loc. cit.*) suggests that this line, which is missing in ADIK, may be corrupt. E is fragmentary, but sufficient evidence remains (*nō dic*) for us to link it with U. It is the latter's version which is preferred to that of C (*qu'ieu non quier tan ian fos crezutz*), which Pattison (*op. cit.*, p. 89, variants) inadvertently states is missing.

49 *del*. The reading of A, joined by DIK, is here retained in preference to that of CU (*dun–dum*). The subsequent appearance in U of *bel* instead of *bon* may well in fact have resulted from the influence of the earlier *del* in ADIK. Appel, however, follows C for this line.

The words *bon respieich* form the *senhal* of Raimbaut's lady. They are obviously meant to be an allusion to her, as Pattison makes clear by his use of capital letters (*cf.* note to l. 50).

50 *Bon Respieich*. For discussion on this *senhal* see *R. d'Orange*, pp. 37 ff and 59.

Appel (p. 79) considers that Raimbaut's use of the third person in the *tornada* would suggest that the *senhal* is not intended in this line to denote the troubadour's lady. In his later edition of the poem (*Raimbaut von Orange*, p. 44) he places a question mark after the words and suggests that they do not form an address but are perhaps merely an interrogative repetition of the words in the previous line. Lavaud, on the other hand, considers that Raimbaut is in fact addressing his lady, but only as a witness of his suffering at the hands of another (*op. cit.*, II, p. 477, note 2). It seems fairly clear, however, in view of the reference to the *senhal* in the previous line, that *Bon Respieich*, addressed in the second person, and the lady spoken of in the third person are one and the same, and that both refer to Raimbaut's lady.

Raimbaut mentions, at the beginning of the poem, the promise he has made to his lady to refrain from singing. Pattison indicates other poems which contain a reference to such a restriction imposed upon the troubadour by his lady and places them in approximately the same period (*op. cit.*, p. 40 and p. 90, note 1). One may assume that, having broken his pledge, Raimbaut employs the third person in the *tornada* in a token attempt to conceal the fact that it is his lady to whom he is referring. The reference in l. 49 is, however, intended to remove any doubt about the matter.

It is interesting to note that E gives *lonc r . . .*, suggesting one of the four variants of the *senhal* employed by Raimbaut (see *R. d'Orange*, p. 39).

sui bas. Appel follows the order of words given by CU. Again, there seems to be no strong reason to depart from the equally acceptable order of ADIK.

IX DOUS'AMIGA, NO·N PUESC MAIS (356, 2)

One MS. c 86 (130).

Editions. Chabaneau, *RLR*, xx, 139; Lavaud, *Troub. Cant.*, II, p. 478; Nelli-Lavaud, *Les Troubadours*, II, p. 86.

Authenticity. Appel considers that the form, content and style of the poem all cast doubt upon Peire Rogier's authorship, and he refers to the general unreliability of this MS in the attribution of its poems.[1] It is interesting to note, for example, that the poem immediately preceding *Dous'amiga* in the MS, *Bels Monruels aicel que·s part de vos*,[2] is wrongly attributed to Peire Rogier and that Peire's *Al pareyssen de las flors* is earlier attributed to Peire Breumon.

P. Meyer had previously expressed the view that the poem's form did not provide grounds for attributing it to Peire Rogier.[3] Appel discusses the poem's form in some detail, with particular reference to its unusual rhyme scheme.[4] This is the only instance in the poetry of the troubadours in which the monorhyme of the scheme a a a a a b is masculine in some stanzas and feminine in others.[5] Although the latter part of the poem is lacking, there is clear evidence of an alternating pattern: the masculine rhymes appear in stanzas I, II, and IV, V and the feminine ones in stanzas III and VI.

The contents of the poem are based largely on the theme of *amor de lonh*, examples of which may be found elsewhere in Peire's work.[6] The poem differs, however, from the others in two respects: firstly, while Peire Rogier normally speaks of his absence from his lady in purely general and abstract terms the poet seems, in this case, to be more specific (see ll. 15–18) and to be referring to a particular occasion on which he was separated from his lady.[7] Secondly, the poem shows no sign of departing from its mood of despondency and contains no trace of the note of encouragement and optimism with which Peire normally counters his expressions of doubt and despair. These comments must, however, be subject to the general reservation that they are based not on the whole poem but only on the six stanzas available to us.

As for the style of the poem, while a feature such as the juxtaposition of opposites found in ll. 31-4 is fairly common in Peire's work,[8] nowhere else does he include similes like the one in l. 28 or such detailed personal and natural descriptions as in ll. 21-2 and ll. 16-18 respectively. We have in fact noted above that Peire differs from his contemporaries in beginning very few of his *cansos* (I and II only) with a reference to the season.[9]

Notes

1 *P. Rogier*, p. 68. Pillet and Carstens (p. 312) also doubt the poem's authenticity.
2 Appel includes in his edition of Peire Rogier (pp. 88-94) a critical edition of *Bels Monruels* and discusses its authorship. He states later (*B. von Vent.*, p. 66) that it was not written by Bernart de Ventadour. Pillet and Carstens (p. 54) summarise the diverse views expressed on the authorship and leave the question open.
3 *Romania*, X (1881), 622.
4 *Op. cit.*, pp. 68-9. Appel observes that the use of a small number of rhymes is a feature of popular poetry and of the work of the early troubadours. Lavaud (*op. cit.*, p. 76) does not see here, however, any grounds for doubting Peire's authorship. He suggests that the poet would have been delicate enough to renew his style by adopting, where appropriate, popular devices of this kind.
5 Appel (*loc. cit.*); Jeanroy, *Poésie Lyrique*, II, pp. 74-5, note 6 .
6 *Cf.* VII. We find in VI, ll. 37-9, the idea expressed in ll. 19-20 of this poem, whereby the poet's heart or soul remains with his lady while his body is far away. Lines 19-20 should also be compared with III, ll. 7-9 and 29, 33 for the use of *sai* and *lai*. (See section on Peire Rogier's lady, p. 11.)
7 We refer above (p. 3 and p. 12) to the possibility that the account in the *Vida* of Peire's enforced departure from Narbonne was based in part on the contents of this poem. *Cf.* l. 6 (*e departen nostr'amor*) and l. 23 (*mal o fai qi·ns a partiz*).
8 *Cf.* III, ll. 54-5; V, ll. 29-32; VII, ll. 1-5, 25-30, 41.
9 See section on the order of the poems (p. 30, note 4).

I

Dous'amiga, no·n puesc mais;
mout me pesa qar vos lais,
e (*redol m'en*) et esmais,
e teng m'o a gran pantais,
qar no·us abras e no·us bais   5
e departen nostr'amor.

II

D'aitant (*sabeos*) mon talan,
q'anc femna non amei tan;
e no·us (en) aus far semblan
ni trob per cui vos o man.   10
Vau m'en; a *Dieu* vos coman,
al espirital seinhor.

III Non puesc mudar qe no˙m plagna,
    qar se part nostra compagna;
    eu m'en vauc en terr'estragna;   15
    mais am freidur'e montagna
    no fas *figa* ni castagna
    ni ribeira ni calor.

IV Lai s'en vai mos cors marritz,
    e çai reman *l*'esperiz;   20
    et ai tant los uls fronçitz
    qe m'en dolon las raïtz;
    mal o fai qi˙*ns* a partiz,
    e no˙n puesc aver baudor.

V   Sans e sals for'eu gueritz,   25
    qant serai acondormiz,
    si fos de leis tant aisiz,
    q'en semblant d'una per*n*iz
    li baises sos oils voltitz
    e la fresqetta color.   30

VI Dous estars lai m'es ardura,
    e bons conortz desmesura,
    e sazïontas fraitura,
    e dias clars *noitz* oscura;
    per mon jovent qar pejura   35
    ai marriment e dolor.

Variants. We give below the instances where we depart from the MS, as well as all those readings in the previous editions of the poem which differ from our text. The abbreviations employed for the editions are as follows: *Chab.* = Chabaneau (*RLR*); *Appel* = Appel, *Peire Rogier*; *Lav.* = Lavaud, *Les Troubadours cantaliens*; *Nelli-Lav.* = Nelli-Lavaud, *Les Troubadours.*

I. 1, dousa *c Chab.* 3, redolmein *c*, ve dol[s] m'en *Chab.*, ver dol mein *Lav. Nelli-Lav.* 4, et *Chab.* 5, et *Chab.* 6, departem *Chab.*

II. 7, d'aitan *Chab.*; sabchas *Appel. Lav. Nelli-Lav.*; talant *c*. 8, qe *c Appel. Lav. Nelli-Lav.*; tant *c*. 9, en *lacking c*; semblant *c*. 11, vac *Chab.*, vai *c*; dieus *c Chab.* 12, senhor *Chab.*

III. 13, que *Chab.* 15, terra *c Chab. Appel. Lav. Nelli-Lav.* 16, freidura *c Chab. Appel. Lav. Nelli-Lav.*; et *Chab.* 17, nos *c*; figu *c*. 18, ni] en *Lav. Nelli-Lav.*

POEM IX 125

IV. 20, l'] les c; esperitz *Chab.* 21, uls] cils *Lav. Nelli-Lav.* 23, m. o] ma[s]so *Chab.*; qi'ns] qi us c; partitz *Appel.*

v. 25, fora c *Chab. Appel. Lav. Nelli-Lav.* 27, de leis] d'ela(s) *Chab.* 28, perviz c.

VI. 33, saziontat[z] *Chab.*, sazïontatz *Nelli-Lav.*; fractura *Chab.* 34, c. e noit c; noit *Chab.* 36, et *Chab.*

Metrical scheme. Six *coblas singulars* (plus three which are missing) of six lines:

$$a_7\ a_7\ a_7\ a_7\ a_7\ b_7$$

(Frank: 17, 3). There are three other examples of this rhyme scheme but none of them has this syllable arrangement. It should also be noted that the a rhymes are masculine in the first, second, fourth and fifth stanzas and feminine in the third and sixth stanzas (see section on the authenticity of the poem).

Notes

1 *Dous'amiga*. The final a of *dousa* is superfluous as far as the metre is concerned and would not, therefore, be pronounced.

2 *lais*. A verb of sorrow like *pesar* requires the verb of the dependent clause, introduced by *que*, to be in the subjunctive mood. However, when *quar* replaces *que*, as in this instance, the indicative is employed (*cf. Altprov. Elem.*, p. 133).

3 The MS contains the reading *e redolmein et esmais*. Chabaneau reads in error *redolmen* (*RLR*, xx, 139) which he alters later to *redolmem* (*op. cit.*, xxv, 103). His version of the line (*e ve dols m'en et esmais*) is rejected both by Meyer (*Romania*, x (1881), 622), who regards it as being very forced, and by Appel (p. 79) on the grounds that the subject *dols* should not be allowed to separate *ve* from *m'en*. The version favoured by Lavaud (*e ver dol mein et esmais*—'and indeed I bear sorrow and affliction') seems to be too contrived (see Levy, *S.W.*, II, 266: *faire dol, menar dol* ('to bewail, grieve')).

Appel (*loc. cit.*) tentatively proposes two alternative readings of the line: (i) *e be dol m'en us esmais*, (ii) *e redol m'en et esmais*. It is the latter which we have chosen to include in brackets and which Stengel proposes in his diplomatic edition (*Die altprovenzalische Liedersammlung c der Laurenziana in Florenz*, Leipzig, 1899, p. 72). Although this interpretation is somewhat arguable, it is perhaps the most plausible, differing only slightly from the actual reading of the MS. Appel (*loc. cit.*) suggests that *se redoler* may be analogous to the Italian verb *ridolersi* ('to complain, lament') but we have been unable to find any other examples of the verb with the prefix *re-*. As for *esmais*, he quotes (*loc. cit.*) another instance of the first person singular of *esmaiar* ending in *s* (Mahn, *Gedichte*, 5,331). However, the verb is normally employed transitively or reflexively, and its intransitive use, although it exists,* must be regarded as exceptional.

6 We support Appel's view (*loc. cit.*) that Chabaneau's amendment to *departem* is unnecessary, as the third person plural is quite acceptable: 'They separate *or* one separates (our love).'

---

* Levy (*S.W.*, III, 235) cites an intransitive meaning of *esmaiar* ('timore deficere, desperare') found in E. Stengel's *Die beiden ältesten provenzalischen Grammatiken*, p. 30 and p. 172.

7 *sabeos*. In his diplomatic edition Peleaz reads the MS as *sab cos* ('Il canzoniere provenzale c'' in *Studi di filologia romanza*, VII, 388). Appel (*loc. cit.*) also implies that a *c* may have been intended instead of an *e*. We have, however, made a careful comparison with the scribe's *c*s and *e*s elsewhere and confirm that the reading here is *sab eos*. In view of the doubt attached to the word we have enclosed it in brackets. Chabaneau's explanation of the word, although by no means certain, would appear to be reasonable (*op. cit.*, XX, 139; XXV, 103–4). He regards it as a contracted form of *sabetz vos* (> *sabeus*) and quotes a small number of other examples of such contractions in the poetry of the troubadours. He admits, however, that the process is more common in narrative works than in lyrical poetry and that he has not found a case which can be traced back as far as Peire Rogier's period. The construction found in this poem therefore provides, in his view, a further reason for doubting Peire's authorship. P. Meyer (*Romania, loc. cit.*) also finds it difficult to accept a contraction of this sort in the work of Peire Rogier and, for his part, favours *sabetz* without a pronoun.

The principal objection to the contraction is that the indicative *sabetz vos* would normally be unacceptable as an imperative form of *saber*. Suchier (*Goett. gel. Anzeigen*, 1883, 1344) suggests that, if *sabeos* is to be amended at all, it would be preferable to choose *sapchas* or *sabes*. As the subjunctive mood would be expected (*Altprov. Elem.*, p. 132; *Anglade*, p. 345), Appel and Lavaud boldly amend *sabeos* to *sabchas*. Even if this version were to be adopted, however, the plural form *sabchatz* would perhaps be more appropriate in view of the use of the polite second person elsewhere in the poem.

8 *q'anc. Cf.* note to l. 1 for the elision of the *e* of *qe*.
9 The line as it stands is one syllable short. The inclusion of *en* satisfies the metre requirements as well as completing the meaning of the line: 'And I do not dare to show *it* to you.' All the previous editions include *en*. It is interesting to note the alternative solution to the metre problem which Stengel suggests in his diplomatic edition: *e no[n] u[o]s aus f. s.*
11 *vau*. The MS has the normal form of the first person singular, *vai*, which Chabaneau incorrectly reads as *vac*. We have followed Appel, Lavaud and Nelli-Lavaud in changing it to the usual form of the third person singular (*cf. Altprov. Elem.*, p. 107) required by the meaning.
Dieu. The MS offers the nominative form of the word (*dieus*) which Chabaneau adopts. It is, however, the objective form which is clearly required here after *per*, and which is also adopted in the three other editions.
15 *terr'estragna. Cf.* note to l. 1.
16 *freidur'e. Cf.* note to l. 1.
17 *no fas figa*. The MS has *nos fas figu. Nos* does not make sense, and we have been unable to find an example of *figu* elsewhere. All four editions, together with Raynouard (*Lex. rom.*, III, 322), amend the reading of the line in the same way.
Que is to be understood at the beginning of the line: '*Than* I do fig and chestnut.' For the omission of *que* see note to I, l. 39.

The poem is thought to have been composed at a time when Peire was leaving the Auvergne. Lines 16–18 are seen as expressing the poet's preference for the cold mountains and treeless plateaux of the Haute Auvergne to the valleys or plains of the warm and fertile lowlands. (*Cf.* Lavaud, *Troub. Cant.*, pp. 74–5; Nelli-Lavaud, *Les Troubadours*, p. 86, note; J. Ajalbert, 'Les Troubadours d'Auvergne', *Mercure de France*, CXXXVII (Jan., 1920), 73–4.) See also p. 12 above.

20 *l'esperiz*. The MS has a scribal error (*les esperiz*), probably the result of confusion over *es* at the beginning of the word.
21 *uls*. Lavaud amends the MS reading to *cils*, as it is the word which is normally employed with *fronçir* in such cases. It is possible, of course, that *cils* was originally intended but was changed to *uls* through a copying error on the part of the scribe. Support for this suggestion may perhaps be seen in the existence of the entirely different form of the word (*oils*) later in the poem (l. 29). (*Cf.* Lavaud, *op. cit.*, p. 75.)

We prefer, however, to retain the version *uls*, on the assumption that the poet is using the word here in a loose sense to denote the eyebrows as well as the eyes themselves. It is interesting to note that Levy gives the word *cil* the meaning of 'eyebrow', 'eyelid' and 'eye' (*Pet. Dict.*, p. 77).
22 *raïtz*. We accept the meaning of the word given by Lavaud (*loc. cit.*) ('nerves'), which is an extension of the normal meaning, 'roots'.
23 *qi·ns*. It is necessary to amend the reading of the MS (*qi·us*), which is probably a scribal error, in order to make sense of the line: 'He who has parted *us* (not *you*) . . .'. *qi·us* also produces one syllable too many in the line. All four editions make this amendment. It should be noted, however, that Appel does not include the version of the MS in his variants and that Stengel, in his diplomatic edition, incorrectly reads the MS as *qins*.
25 *for'eu*. *Cf.* note to l. 1.
28 *perniz*. The MS has *perviz*, which is probably the result of an error in copying. This reading is confirmed by Pelaez, Stengel and Chabaneau in their respective editions. Appel, however, mistakenly omits a reference to it in his variants. *Perniz*, which both Chabaneau (*op. cit.*, XX, 140) and Appel (p. 80) compare to the Italian *pernice*, is one of four recognised forms of the same word listed by Levy (*S.W.*, VI, 234). Its appearance in this poem is, in fact, the only example of the form quoted by Levy. The other three forms are *perdritz*, *perditz*, *perlitz*, the last of which is also attested by Chabaneau (*ibid.*; *op. cit.*, IX, 358 (second article on P. Meyer's edition of *La Chanson de la Croisade contre les Albigeois*, reference to l. 4026)).
34 The *e* found in the MS version between *clars* and *noitz* is omitted, as it renders the line meaningless: *es* is understood between *dias clars* and *noitz oscura*, as in the case of the opposites in the previous two lines. The insertion of *e* would also give the line one syllable too many.

All these nouns should be in the nominative case, and the *noit* of the MS has therefore been amended accordingly. (For the formation of the nominative form *noitz* see *Altprov. Elem.*, pp. 68–9.)

Both these amendments are made in all the editions of the poem apart from Chabaneau's, in which the reading *noit* is retained.

There remains one further line of six syllables only which probably begins a seventh stanza: *Parlan vauc fasc forsatz*. Having regard to the space which the scribe normally leaves blank between each of the poems, an examination of the arrangement of the stanzas in the MS would seem to indicate that there is space available for an eighth and ninth stanza and possibly for a short *tornada* of two or three lines.

Glossary

(In the case of the *Vida* the references denote sections, not lines)

a (prep., to, at): Vida, 3, 10, 12; I, 5; II, 31, 60, 66; III, 15, 24, 49, 63, 64; VI, 57; VII, 42; VIIIa, 5; IX, 11. After *aver*: II, 49, 54. After *greus*: VI, 25; VII, 27.
a: see *ab*.
ab (prep., with): Vida, 8, 11 (four times); I, 3, 35; II, 43, 44, 45, 49, 63, 69; III, 9, 27; IV, 5, 36; V, 10, 11; VI, 5; VIII, 22 (although), 37, 39, 41 (twice), 42 (twice); VIIIa, 45. *a*: VIIIa, 3. (see also *ab sol que*.)
abaissar (v. intr., to decline): *abaissa* (3 sing. pres.): V, 6.
abrassar (v. tr., to embrace): *abras* (1 sing. pres.): IX, 5.
ab sol que: see *sol*.
aclinar, s' (v. reflex., to incline, bow): *s'aclina* (3 sing. pres.): IV, 8.
aco (dem. pron., this, that): VI, 23 (see *esser*). *aquo*: IV, 25.
acondormir (v. tr., to send to sleep): *acondormiz* (past. part., m. nom. sing.): IX, 26.
acordar, s' (v. reflex., to agree, to come to terms): *m'acort* (1 sing. pres. subj.): IV, 36. *s'acort* (3 sing. pres. subj.): VII, 22.
aculhir (v. tr., to receive, to welcome (favourably)): II, 62. *acuelh* (3 sing. pres.): VII, 36. *acuelha* (3 sing. pres. subj.): I, 28. *acuilli* (3 sing. pret.): Vida, 4.
ades (adv., always, already, immediately): I, 42, 52; VIIIa, 14, 24.
adonc (adv., then): II, 32. *adoncs*: Vida, 3. *adoncx*: IV, 4.
afan (s. m., grief, suffering, labour): V, 30; VI, 34. *affan*: VIII, 24.
afar (s.m., business): *afars* (nom. sing.): V, 46.
affan: see *afan*.
ahirar, s' (v. reflex., to get angry, annoyed): *'m ahire* (1 sing. pres.): II, 29.
ailas (inter., alas!): VI, 41.
aisir (v. tr., to receive, to welcome) *aisiz* (past. part.): IX, 27.
aissi (adv., thus, so): IV, 14; V, 8, 24, 33; VI, 18, 56; VIII, 34, 40; VIIIa, 30.
aissi (adv., here): VI, 39.
aisso (dem. pron., this, that): IV, 13, 20; VIII, 16, 43.
aissos (adj., m. sing., anxious, disturbed): VI, 45.
aital (adj., f. sing., such): I, 38. *aitals* (m. nom. sing.): VIIIa, 38.
aital (pron., f. sing.): II, 35.
aitan (adv., as much, as long): III, 14, 20; V, 16. *aitant*: IX, 7.
al (def. art. dat., m., to the, at the): Vida, 10 (12); I, 1; II, 54 (= on the); V, 28; VII, 4; VIII, 11, 36, 47 (= according to); IX, 12.

GLOSSARY

als (pl.): VIIIa, 18, 42.
alegres (adj., m. nom. sing., happy, joyful): II, 8; III, 43.
alhors (adv., elsewhere): I, 12.
alqes (indef. pron. neut., something): VIIIa, 11.
alres (indef. pron. neut., anything else): II, 9.
als (indef. pron. neut., anything else): IV, 35; VI, 13. Used adjectivally after *ren* and *que* (= else): VI, 9, 51. See also *per al(s), tot l'als*.
amar (v. tr., to love): VI, 55. *am* (1 sing. pres.): III, 36; IV, 40; VI, 35, 42; VII, 6, 19, 35; VIIIa, 28; IX, 16. *aman* (pres. part.): III, 46. *amei* (1 sing. pret.): IX, 8. *amarai* (1 sing. fut.): III, 40. *am* (1 sing. pres. subj.): III, 39; VIIIa, 30. *ames* (3 sing. imperf. subj.): VIIIa, 28.
amador (s.m., lover): *amadors* (acc. pl.): I, 22.
ambedos (adj., m. pl., both): VIII, 49.
amic (s.m., friend, lover): II, 53. *amicx* (acc. pl.): VII, 32.
amiga (s.f., friend, love): IX, 1.
amistatz (s.f., friendship, love): VI, 28.
amor (s.f., love): Vida, 8; I, 30, 44; III, 45; IV, 43, 46; V, 15, 22; VI, 16; VII, 7; IX, 9. *amors* (nom. sing.): I, 5; II, 5, 39; III, 47; IV, 43, 44; V, 7, 11, 25, 29. *amor* (nom. sing.): I, 22.
ams (adj., pl., both): VIII, 46.
an (s.m., year): *ans* (acc. pl.): II, 44.
anar (v. intr., to go): *vai* (3 sing. pres.): I, 21. *vay* (3 sing. pres.): V, 10, 33; VIII, 6. *vay* (imp. sing.): III, 61. *anet* (3 sing. pret.): Vida, 2.
anar, s'en (reflex., to go away): *m'en vauc* (1 sing. pres.): IX, 15. *vau m'en* (1 sing. pres.): IX, 11. *s'en vai* (3 sing. pres.): IX, 19. *s'en anet* (3 sing. pret.): Vida, 10. *m'en irai* (1 sing. fut.): VIII, 50.
anc (adv., ever): VI, 13; VII, 37; VIIIa, 9.
anc . . . no (adv., never): III, 34. *anc . . . non*: IX, 8. *anc no . . . may* (never): II, 13. *anc non . . . mais*: III, 49.
ans (adv., rather): II, 42; III, 14.
anz qe (conj., before): VIII, 52.
apaysar, s' (v. reflex., to be appeased): *m'apays* (1 sing. pres.): I, 32.
apellar (v. tr., to call): *apellatz* (past. part., m. nom. sing.): VIII, 45.
aportar (v. tr., to bring): *aport* (3 sing. pres. subj.): VII, 34.
aprendre (v. tr., to learn): *aprenda* (3 sing. pres. subj.): II, 68; VI, 58.
apres (adv., after, afterwards): V, 21, 35; VIIIa, 21. (prep., after): V, 31.
aqel (dem. adj., this, that): VIIIa, 16. *aqella* (f. sing.): Vida, 8.
aqel (dem. pron., this one, that one): *aquels* (m. acc. pl.): VI, 32.
aquest (dem. adj., this, that): I, 29.
aqui (adv., here): IV, 30. *aqui mezeus* (at the very same time): VIII, 38. *d'aqui* (for this reason, as a result): V, 12.

aquo: see *aco*.
ara (adv., now): VII, 14, 26. *aras*: V, 36. *er*: VIIIa, 23. *era*: VI, 52; VIII, 20, 21; VIIIa, 36. *eras*: VIII, 16.
asegurar (v. tr., to assure, to protect): *s'asegura* (reflex., 3 sing. pres.): I, 41.
ardura (s.f., intense heat): IX, 31.
assatz (adv., well, indeed): V, 5.
assaiar (v. tr., to deal with): *assai* (3 sing. pres. subj.): VIII, 40.
assire (v. tr., to seat, to establish): II, 47. *ai assis* (1 sing. perf.): V, 1.
atendre (v. intr. and tr., to wait, to expect, to fulfil): *aten* (1 sing. pres.): IV, 30. *aten* (3 sing. pres.): V, 21. *atenda* (3 sing. pres. subj.): VII, 23.
atressi (adv., all the same): V, 40.
atretan (adv., as much): III, 36.
aturar, s' (v. reflex., to persist): *·s atura* (3 sing. pres.): I, 27.
aucire (v. tr., to kill): *·s aucire* (inf. reflex.): II, 58. *aucis* (2 sing. pres.): VII, 13.
auctor (s.m., witness): *auctors* (nom. sing.): I, 8.
aura (s.f., wind): II, 3.
ausar (v. intr., to dare): *aus* (1 sing. pres.): IX, 9. *auze* (3 sing. pres. subj.): II, 20.
aut (adv., high): VIII, 17; VIIIa, 50.
autre (indef. adj., other): *autra* (f. sing.): IV, 41 (from another); V, 50; VI, 28 (of another). *autres* (m. nom. sing.): VIIIa, 37.
autre (indef. pron., m. sing., other, another): I, 7, 32, 42; III, 34; VIII, 41. *autra* (f. sing.): II, 21, 23; IV, 36, 45, 49; VII, 36. *autres* (m. pl.): VI, 17; VIIIa, 18.
autreyar, s' (v. reflex., to give, commit oneself): *m'autrey* (1 sing. pres.): III, 15.
auzir (v. tr., to hear, to listen to): IV, 51; VII, 14; VIIIa, 22. *aug* (1 sing. pres.): IV, 26; VII, 20. *auch* (1 sing. pres.): VIII, 14. *aug* (3 sing. pres.): Vida, 10(8). *auzirai* (1 sing. fut.): VIII, 51. *auzirem* (1 pl. fut.): V, 38.
aventura (s.f., chance, fortune): *per aventura* (by chance): I, 48. *per mal'aventura* (unfortunately): I, 20.
aver (v. tr., to have): II, 51; III, 14; IX, 24. *ai* (1 sing. pres.): Vida, 10(9); I, 30; II, 49; III, 12, 16, 20, 31, 41, 42; IV, 22, 35, 46; V, 27; VI, 8, 10, 49; VII, 25; VIII, 8, 47; IX, 36. *ay* (1 sing. pres.): V, 27; VI, 26; VII, 7 (twice). *as* (2 sing. pres.): VI, 42, 47. *a* (3 sing. pres.): II, 33; IV, 4. *an* (3 pl. pres.): I, 6; V, 24. *avia* (1 sing. imperf.): IV, 49. *avia* (3 sing. imperf.): II, 35. *aic* (1 sing. pret.): VIIIa, 3. *ac* (3 sing. pret.): Vida, 12. *aurai* (1 sing. fut.): IV, 22. *auretz* (2 pl. fut.): VIII, 33, 49. *auria* (3 sing. cond.): II, 43. *aya* (1 sing. pres. subj.): VII, 24. *ayas* (2 sing. pres. subj.): IV, 32. *aya* (3 sing. pres. subj.): II, 54. *agues* (3 sing. imperf. subj.): Vida, 8. (See also *aver en poder, aver tort, aver dreg, aver nom*.)
aver a (to have to): *ai a* (1 sing. pres.): II, 49.
aver (s.m., wealth, possessions): Vida, 10(4); VIII, 4; VIIIa, 15. *abers* (nom. sing.): VIIIa, 12.
avinenz (adj., m. nom. sing., pleasing, amiable): Vida, 1.

azirar (v. tr., to hate): *azir* (3 sing. pres. subj.): VIIIa, 36.
azirar, s' (reflex., to get angry, to become offended): *m'azir* (1 sing. pres. subj.): VII, 15.
avols (adj., m. nom. sing,. cowardly, wicked): IV, 10; VIIIa, 13. *avol* (m. nom. pl., used as a s.): V, 9.

bai (adj., m. sing., fair): VIII, 33.
baisar (v. tr., to kiss): *bais* (1 sing. pres.): IX, 5. *baises* (1 sing. imperf. subj.): IX, 29.
bas (adv., low): VIII, 18; VIIIa, 50.
baudor (s.f., joy, gaiety): IX, 24.
bautz (adj., m. nom. sing., gay, joyous): III, 17.
bel (adj., m. sing., handsome, beautiful): III, 25; IV, 11. *bels* (m. nom. sing.): Vida, 1. *belha* (f. sing.): VII, 38. *bels* (m. pl.): VIIIa, 45.
ben (s.m., good, goodness): III, 30; IV, 6, 37; VI, 8; VIII, 42; VIIIa, 40. *be*: V, 35. *bes* (nom. sing.): III, 54; V, 18; VI, 15; VII, 29. *bes* (pl.): Vida, 4.
ben (adv., well, certainly): Vida, 1; II, 14, 32, 36; III, 19; IV, 37, 39, 57; VI, 17, 51; VII, 17, 22; VIIIa, 26, 28, 47. *be*: II, 25; IV, 2, 15; VI, 7, 15. (See also *ben leu, si be.*)
beutat (s.f., beauty): *beutaz* (nom. sing.): VII, 40.
blasmamen (s.m., blame, censure): *blasmamens* (nom. sing.): VIIIa, 16.
blasmar (v. tr., to blame): *blasmada* (past. part., f. sing.): Vida, 8.
boca (s.f., mouth): VII, 11.
bon (adj., m. sing., good): Vida, 11 (three times); II, 53; IV, 53; VI, 1; VII, 4; VIII, 25; VIIIa, 49. *bon* (nom. sing.): VI, 12; VII, 34. *bos* (m. nom. sing.): I, 8; II, 38; III, 10; VI, 29, 58; VIIIa, 19. *bons* (m. nom. sing.): IX, 32. *bona* (f. sing.): I, 5; II, 64; VI, 33; VII, 13. *bons* (m. acc. pl., used as a s.): VIII, 42.
bontat (s.f., goodness): II, 63.
bordir (v. intr., to play, to frolic): IV, 19; VII, 3.
breu (adj., m. sing., short): *em breu* (soon): V, 45.

cabal (adj., f. sing., excellent, perfect): II, 33.
cal: see *qual*.
caler (v., imper., to matter, to be important): *cal* (3 sing. pres.): II, 42. *qual* (3 sing. pres.): III, 39. *no m'en cal(qal)* (3 sing. pres., it does not matter to me): V, 40; VI, 23.
calor (s.f., heat): IX, 18.
canorga (s.f., canonry): Vida, 2.
canorgue (s.m., canon): *canorgues* (nom. sing.): Vida, 1.
canso (s.f., song): *cansos* (acc. pl.): Vida, 5.

cantar, cantarai, cantava (see *chantar*).
cap: see *gap*.
capdelhar (v. tr., to govern, to direct): *capdelha* (3 sing. pres.): II, 5.
captenemen (s.m., behaviour, conduct): IV, 11. *chaptenemens* (acc. pl.): VIIIa, 10.
captener, se (v. reflex., to behave oneself): *vos captener* (inf.): VIII, 39.
car: see *quar*.
cargar (v. tr., to charge, to burden): *'s cargon* (reflex., 3 pl. pres.): I, 2. *cargatz* (past. part., m. nom. sing.): VIII, 24.
castagna (s.f., chestnut): IX, 17.
cauzir: see *chauzir*.
cazer (v. intr., to fall): VIII, 18. *chai* (3 sing. pres.): V, 13. *sui cazutz* (1 sing. perf.): VIIIa, 50.
ce: see *que*.
celat (s.m., silence, discretion): *a celat* (secretly): III, 36.
celatz (adj., m. nom. sing., discreet): III, 28.
cent (adj., a hundred): VI, 31.
chai: see *cazer*.
chan (s.m., poem, song): II, 2. *chans* (nom. sing.): IV, 3.
chantar (v. intr., to sing): VIIIa, 4. *chan* (1 sing. pres.): III, 2. *chant* (1 sing. pres.): III, 6. *cantava* (3 sing. imperf.): Vida, 1. *cantarai* (1 sing. fut.): VIIIa, 6. *chan* (1 sing. pres. subj.): VI, 2. *chant* (1 sing. pres. subj.): IV, 1; V, 2. *chant* (3 sing. pres. subj.): IV, 15.
chantar (inf. used as s.m., singing, song, poem): II, 4. *chantars* (nom. sing.): IV, 1.
cantar (nom. pl.): Vida, 2.
chaptenemens: see *captenemen*.
chauzir (v. intr. and tr., to choose): VI, 19; VII, 38. *cauzir*: IV, 41.
clamar (v. tr., to ask, to call, to cry for): *clam* (1 sing. pres.): IV, 23. *clama* (3 sing. pres.): II, 67. *clamava* (3 sing. imperf.): Vida, 7. *clama* (imp. sing.): VI, 46.
clars (adj., m. nom. sing., clear): VII, 41; IX, 34.
claure (v. tr., to close): *clau* (1 sing. pres.): VIIIa, 23.
color (s. f., complexion): IX, 30.
com (conj., as, according as): Vida, 10(6), 10(13); II, 61. *cum*: VIII, 12. *cum* (comp., as, than): VIII, 14. *cum si* (as if): III, 38, 44. *si cum* (as): Vida, 10; VIII, 27. (See also *cumsi*.)
cum (conj., how, why): III, 31; V, 20; VI, 44; VIII, 6 (twice); VIIIa, 29. *quo*: VI, 11. *cum que* (however): III, 26.
comandar (v. tr., to commend): *coman* (1 sing. pres.): IX, 11.
comenssar (v. tr., to begin): *comenssatz* (2 pl. pres.): VIII, 16.
cominal (adj., m. sing., similar): II, 15.
comjat (s.m., leave, dismissal): Vida, 9.
compagna (s.f., company, fellowship): IX, 14.

comtar (v. tr., to relate): Vida, 10(8); VIII, 14.
comte (s.m., count): Vida, 11.
conduit (s.m., feast): *conduitz* (pl.): VIII, 21.
confes (adj., m. nom. sing., indebted, beholden): VIIIa, 7.
confort (s.m., comfort, consolation): IV, 22.
conoisser (v. tr., to know): *conostra* (3 sing. fut.): IV, 29. *conogutz* (past. part., m. nom. sing.): VIIIa, 20.
conort (s.m., comfort, encouragement): Vida, 10(2); VII, 4; VIII, 2. *conortz* (nom. sing.): III, 10; IX, 32.
conortamen (s.m., comfort, consolation): *conortamens* (nom. sing.): VII, 44.
conquerre (v. tr., to conquer, to gain): *a conquis* (3 sing. perf.): VII, 19. *avia conques* (1 sing. pluperf.): VI, 31.
conseil (s.m., advice, plan): VIIIa, 52. *cosselh*: VI, 49.
consirar (v. intr. and tr., to consider, to think): *conssir* (1 sing. pres.): VIIIa, 25.; *cossir* (1 sing. pres.): VI, 9. *cossire* (1 sing. pres. subj.): II, 2.
consiros (adj., m. sing., anxious, thoughtful): Vida, 10.
contra (prep., against, towards, compared with): II, 26, 53; IV, 42; VII, 12.
cor (s.m., heart): II, 6, 51; IV, 46; V, 1, 31; VI, 38; VIIIa, 36. *cors* (nom. sing.): I, 41; II, 58; IV, 36; VI, 27; VIIIa, 9 (desire). *cor* (nom. pl.): VII, 33.
coral (adj., m. sing., sincere, faithful): II, 53.
cors (s.m., invar., body, person): VIII, 34; IX, 19. Used periphrastically as pers. pron. (her): *son cors*: V, 48; *lo cors de liey*: VI, 61.
cort (s.f., court): Vida, 3, 8. *cortz* (pl.): Vida, 2.
cortes (adj., m. sing., noble, courtly): VI, 6. *cortes* (m. pl. used as s.): V, 11.
cosselh: see *conseil*.
cossentir (v. tr., to grant, to permit): VIIIa, 43.
cossentir, se (reflex., to be in agreement, harmony): VII, 33.
cossi (adv., how): VI, 3, 24.
cossir, cossire: see *consirar*.
costar (v. tr., to cost): *costa* (3 sing. pres.): V, 34, 42.
coven (s.m., promise, agreement): *covens* (pl.): VII, 23; VIIIa, 2.
covenir (v. intr., to be suitable, fitting): *cove* (3 sing. pres.): II, 61. *coven* (3 sing. pres.): VIII, 40.
creire (v. tr., to believe): I, 8. *cre* (1 sing. pres.): II, 32; IV, 31; VI, 13; VIIIa, 34. *crey* (1 sing. pres.): III, 48. *cres* (2 sing. pres.): VI, 55. *creirai* (1 sing. fut.): VII, 21. *crei* (imp. sing.): VI, 52. *crezatz* (imp. pl.): II, 52. *creza* (3 sing. pres. subj.): I, 13. *crezut* (past. part.): Vida, 8. *cregutz* (past. part., nom. sing.): VIIIa, 47.
creysser (v. intr. and tr., to grow, to increase): *creys* (3 sing. pres.): I, 4; III, 9. *creguz* (past. part., m. nom. sing.): VIIIa, 48.
cubertz (adj., m. nom. sing., secret, discreet): III, 28.
cuende (adj., m. nom. pl., amiable): V, 12.

cugar (v. tr., to believe, to think, to intend): *cug* (1 sing. pres.): I, 42; IV, 31. *cuich* (1 sing. pres.): VIII, 48. *cuidiei* (1 sing. pret.): VIIIa, 4.
cum, cum que: see *com*.
cumsi (conj., according as): V, 48.
cura (s.f., care): I, 45 (see *prendre*).
cuy, cui (rel. pron., acc. and emphat., whom): see *que*.
cuy (rel. pron., dat., to whom, from whom): IV, 23.
cuy que (indef. pron., dat., to whomever): II, 30.

dan (s.m., damage, injury, loss): I, 43; IV, 5; V, 23; VI, 50. *dans* (nom. sing.): III, 54; IV, 55; V, 18.
dar (v. tr., to give): *dey* (1 sing. pret.): III, 37. *det* (3 sing. pret.): Vida, 9.
de (partit. art. (after negative), any): V, 17.
de (prep., of. Also used after the words indicated with the following meanings: by, of, on, with): Vida, 1 (three times), 3 (three times), 5 (*s'enamoret*), 8 (twice), 10(2), 12; I, 1, 2 (*cargon*), 15, 38, 44; II, 11 (*manenta*), 69; III, 23, 38; IV, 23; V, 15, 36 (*membra'm*), 48; VI, 16, 56 (*jauzir*), 61; VIII, 2, 24 (*cargatz*); VIIIa, 10 (*cors, talens*), 31; IX, 27 (*aisiz*), 28.
de (prep., from): Vida, 8, 9; III, 12, 14, 20, 54; IV, 20, 47, 49; VI, 8, 32, 37; VII, 31, 35; VIII, 52; VIIIa, 50.
de (prep., about, concerning): Vida, 1, 5, 10, 10(8); I, 10, 43; II, 2, 16, 23; IV, 2, 48; VI, 2, 9, 11, 23, 24, 26, 45 (twice), 48; VIII, 6, 14, 29, 43; IX, 7.
dechazer (v. intr., to decline, to worsen): *dechai* (3 sing. pres.): III, 7; V, 6.
definar (v. intr., to die): *definet* (3 sing. pret.): Vida, 12.
del (art., m. (contraction of *de lo*), of the): Vida, 9; III, 17 (after *bautz, letz*); VI, 19. (about, concerning the): II, 12; VIIIa, 49.
de la (art., f., of the): Vida, 9. (from the): IV, 44.
deman (adv., tomorrow): V, 32.
demandar (v. tr., to ask (for)): *deman* (1 sing. pres.): III, 13. *demandatz* (imp. pl.): V, 20. *deman* (3 sing. pres. subj.): V, 37.
denant (prep., before): II, 65, 68.
denhar (v. tr., to deign): *denha* (3 sing. pres.): II, 31. *denh* (3 sing. pres. subj.): II, 47; IV, 51.
den (s.f., tooth): *dens* (acc. pl.): VIIIa, 23.
departir (v. tr., to separate): *departen* (3 pl. pres.): IX, 6.
deport (s.m., pleasure, amusement): VII, 28.
deportar, se (v. reflex., to amuse oneself): *'s deport* (3 sing. pres. subj.): IV, 15.
descauzimen (s.m., injury, wrong): IV, 54.
dese (adv., at once): IV, 38.
deserenan (adv., henceforth): III, 3.
desmezura (s.f., injustice, outrage, insult): I, 24. *desmesura*: IX, 32.

despleyar (v. tr., to display, to show): *despley* (1 sing. pres. subj.): III, 4.
despolhar, se (v. reflex., to undress onseself): *'s despuelha* (3 sing. pres.): I, 49.
destrenher (v. intr., to decide): *destrenhetz* (imp. pl.): III, 50.
devenir (v. intr., to become): *devenon* (3 pl. pres.): I, 16.
dever (v. tr., to have to): *dei* (1 sing. pres.): VIIIa, 8, 39, 42. *dey* (1 sing. pres.): III, 14. *deu* (3 sing. pres.): I, 8; II, 51, 62; IV, 6, 11, 13, 57. *deuria* (3 sing. cond.): IV, 52. *degra* (3 sing. cond.): VIIIa, 47.
devire (v. tr., to share, divide, explain): II, 49. *an devis* (3 pl. perf.): VII, 1. *devis* (past. part., m. nom. sing.): V, 8.
dezacolhir (v. tr., to reject): *dezacuelha* (3 sing. pres. subj.): I, 14.
dezesperar, se (v. reflex., to despair): *'s dezesper* (3 sing. pres. subj.): IV, 7.
dezir (s.m., desire): *dezir* (nom. pl.): IV, 48.
dezirar (v. tr., to desire): *dezir* (1 sing. pres.): VI, 35. *dezire* (1 sing. pres.): II, 11.
dezirier (s.m., desire): VI, 10.
dezonor (s.m., dishonour): *dezonors* (pl.): I, 36.
dia (s.m., day): *dias* (nom. sing.): IX, 34. *dias* (pl.): II, 54.
dich: see *dit*.
Dieu (s.m., God): III, 15; IX, 11. *Dieus* (nom. sing.): VI, 61. *per Dieu* (in vain): IV, 24 (see note).
dig, digz: see *dit*.
dins (prep., in): II, 62.
dir (v. intr. and tr., to say, to speak): Vida, 10(8); IV, 17, 26; VI, 3; VII, 20; VIII, 5, 14; VIIIa, 11. *dire*: II, 20. *dic* (1 sing. pres.): III, 24; IV, 13; VI, 8, 20; VII, 18; VIIIa, 48. *ditz* (2 sing. pres.): IV, 19. *dis* (2 sing. pres.): IV, 33; VII, 12. *ditz* (3 sing. pres.): II, 25; IV, 10, 36; V, 29. *dis* (3 sing. pres.): I, 12. *dizon* (3 pl. pres.): VIII, 19. *dis* (1 sing. pret.): V, 36. *dis* (3 sing. pret.): Vida, 10; III, 34. *ai dig* (1 sing. perf.): VII, 11. *diray* (1 sing. fut.): V, 20. *dira* (3 sing. fut.): VII, 37. *diran* (3 pl. fut.): VI, 22. *di* (imp. sing.): III, 64. *diguatz* (imp. pl.): VI, 52. *digua* (3 sing. pres. subj.): II, 24. *diga* (3 sing. pres. subj.): VIII, 30. *digatz* (2 pl. pres. subj.): VIII, 43. *disses* (3 sing. imperf. subj.): III, 46. *digz* (past. part., m. nom. sing.): V, 39.
dit (s.m., word, opinion, promise): Vida, 9. *dich*: VIIIa, 19. *dig*: VII, 21. *digz* (pl.): VIIIa, 2, 45. *dich* (nom. pl.): VIIIa, 21.
doble (adj., m. sing., double): *a doble* (twice as much): VII, 28.
dolens (adj., m. nom. sing., grieving, painful): VIIIa, 3. *dolenz*: Vida, 10. *dolenta* (f. sing.): II, 3.
doler (v. intr., to hurt): *dolon* (3 pl. pres.): IX, 22. *duelha* (3 sing. pres. subj.): I, 21.
doler, se (reflex., to suffer): *m'en duelh* (1 sing. pres.): VII, 30.
dolor (s.f., pain, grief, sorrow): IX, 36. *dolors* (nom. sing.): I, 33; VI, 26.
domna (s.f., lady): Vida, 3; II, 27. *dompna*: I, 18, 25; II, 10, 33, 59; III, 50; VI, 33; VII, 7, 13. *dona*: I, 11; II, 50. *donna*: III, 57.

dompneyar (v. intr., to pay court): *dompney* (1 sing. pres.): III, 27.
don (s.m., gift): *dos* (pl.): VIII, 21.
don (rel. pron., whose): *dont*: III, 65. *don* (through whom): VI, 45. (on whom): V, 28. (through which, because of which): VII, 5; VIIIa, 49. (by which): I, 11. (from which): I, 41; VI, 27.
don (indef. emphat. pron., about what): IV, 1, 2.
don (conj., therefore, for this reason): Vida, 8. (whence, from where): IV, 22.
dona: see *domna*.
donar (v. tr., to give): *don* (1 sing. pres.): VIIIa, 52. *dona* (3 sing. pres.): V, 30. *donatz* (2 pl. pres.): III, 58. *don* (3 sing. pres. subj.): VIII, 27. *donar* (inf. used as s.m., giving): II, 12.
doncs (conj., then, therefore): III, 40. *donc*: III, 16. *doncx*: I, 5; IV, 17, 22, 25; V, 33, 38.
donna: see *domna*.
don (s.m., lord): *dons* (nom. sing.): IV, 54.
dont: see *don*.
dormir (v. intr., to sleep): used as s.m. (sleep, sleeping): VII, 2.
dos (adj., two): II, 44; VI, 5.
dous (adj., m. sing., sweet, gentle): VI, 29; IX, 31. *dousa* (f. sing.): IX, 1.
dreg: see *dreit*.
dreich: see *dreit*.
dreit (s.m., right, justice): *dreg*: V, 27. *dreitz* (nom. sing.): VIIIa, 35. *dregz* (nom. sing.): III, 55. *aver dreg* (v., to be right): *as dreg* (2 sing. pres.): IV, 37. *a dreich* (with good reason): VIII, 49.
dreitura (s.f., right): I, 17.
dreyt (adj., m. sing., straight): *a (de) dreyt huelh* (face to face): VII, 42, 45.
drut (s.m., (courtly) lover): III, 38, 49. *drutz* (nom. sing.): I, 8; II, 38; III, 27, 33; VIII, 44; VIIIa, 23, 26. *drutz* (pl.): III, 23. *drut* (nom. pl.): V, 12.
durar (v. intr., to last): *dura* (3 sing. pres.): I, 51. *agra durat* (3 sing. cond. perf.): V, 16.

e (conj., and): Vida, 1 (eight times), 2 (four times), 3 (twice), 4 (twice), 5 (three times), 6, 7, 8, 9 (twice), 10 (four times), 10 (2, 3, 7, 9, 10 (twice)), 11 (three times), 12; I, 3, 4, 14, 19, 20, 24, 45, 51; II, 5, 7 (three times), 15, 25, 32, 51, 52, 55, 61; III, 6, 9, 12, 13, 17, 20, 21, 28 (twice), 31, 42, 43 (twice), 45, 48, 50, 52, 53, 55, 58, 59, 62, 64, 65; IV, 1, 15, 17, 19, 21, 23, 28, 35, 38, 43, 44, 46, 47 (twice), 48, 50, 54, 57; V, 3, 4, 6 (twice), 7, 12 (twice), 18, 19, 23 (three times), 27, 30 (twice), 31, 33, 37, 45, 49; VI, 12, 15, 20, 22, 26, 34 (twice), 35, 36, 38, 42, 44, 53, 59, 61; VII, 1, 2, 3 (twice), 5, 6, 12, 17, 23, 24, 25, 26, 27, 40, 41, 44; VIII, 2, 3, 8, 9 (twice), 27 (twice), 28, 33, 34 (twice); VIIIa, 2, 5, 8, 11, 12, 17 (twice), 18, 21, 38, 46, 47, 51; IX, 3, 4, 5, 6, 9, 16, 20, 24, 25, 30, 32, 33, 34, 36. *et*: I, 30; II, 17; III, 27; IV, 3, 55, 56; V, 11, 29; VII, 20; VIII, 22, 38; IX, 3, 21.

GLOSSARY

eis (adv., even): III, 39. (See note.)

el (def. art., m. sing. See also *al* and *del*.): *l'*: Vida, 12; I, 7; V, 23; VIII, 41 (twice); VIIIa, 12; IX, 20. *'l*: Vida, 10, 10(2), 12; I, 3, 19, 20, 39, 51; II, 22, 56 (twice), 68; III, 10, 12; IV, 14; V, 15, 18 (twice), 23 (twice), 27; VI, 8, 19, 38; VII, 5, 22, 27, 29; VIII, 2, 34. *lo*: Vida, 10(2), 10(6), 10(12), 10(13), 11 (three times); I, 21; II, 65; III, 12, 23, 30, 64; IV, 40, 50, 52, 55; V, 8, 47, 48; VI, 25, 27, 38, 58, 61; VII, 29, 35, 43; VIII, 2, 11, 12, 43. *'ls* (pl.): VIIIa, 2. *los* (pl.): I, 15; V, 10, 11; VI, 17; VIII, 37, 39, 42 (twice); VIIIa, 2; IX, 21. *'l* (pl.): VII, 33. *il* (pl.): VIIIa, 21. *l'* (pl.): I, 2; V, 9. *li* (pl.): Vida, 2; IV, 48; V, 26.

el (pron., nom. sing., he, it): Vida, 8, 10 (twice), 12 (twice); II, 35; IV, 56; VI, 58.

el (prep., contracted form of *en lo*, in the): see *en*.

els (emphat. pron., m. pl., them): V, 14.

elha (pers. pron., nom. sing., she): I, 31, 34; II, 25; III, 35; VII, 20. *ela*: Vida, 8; IV, 38. *ella*: Vida, 4, 5 (twice), 6, 8 (twice).

em: see *en*.

en (prep., in, into. Abbreviated to *e'* and *'n*): Vida, 3, 8, 11; I, 6 (*em*), 19, 24; II, 6, 44 (twice), 50; IV, 35; V, 1, 27 (to), 34, 43; VI, 1, 54, 60; VII, 28; VIII, 16, 31; VIIIa, 19, 36; IX, 15, 28. *el* (in the): Vida, 10, 12; II, 22; VIIIa, 20.

en (pers. pron., some, of it, of her, of them. Abbreviated to *'n* and *n'*): Vida, 10(14); I, 14; II, 13, 14, 28, 35, 40; IV, 16 (for it), 26 (with it), 34 (after *jauzir*); V, 2, 33, 50; VI, 21, 31, 51; VII, 7, 8, 9, 30 (at it), 38; VIII, 7, 13; VIIIa, 11, 18; IX, 9 (after *far semblant*). (from it, from her, from them): II, 37, 43; III, 20, 42; IV, 32, 33, 37; V, 21, 24, 28; VI, 49; VII, 24, 34; VIIIa, 40, 41. (because of this, it, her): I, 16, 18; II, 29; III, 21, 45; IV, 18; V, 18 (twice), 19; VI, 43, 48; VII, 10, 11, 26, 30, 41; VIIIa, 6, 45; IX, 3, 22, 24.

en (pers. pron., roughly equivalent to 'concerning it, this'. It has no precise antecedent but relates to a general fact. Abbreviated to *'n* and *n'*.): Vida, 8; I, 26; IV, 40; VI, 49, 51.

En (s.m., (title), lord, my lord. Abbreviated to *'N* and *N'*): Vida, 10, 11 (three times); III, 64.

enamorar, s' (v. reflex., to fall in love): *s'enamoret* (3 sing. pret.): Vida, 5.

enan (adv., forward): V, 10; VI, 18 (see *traire*).

encontrada (s.f., region, district): Vida, 8.

engual (adj., m. sing., equal): *per engual* (equally): II, 60.

enoios (adj., m. sing., annoying, troublesome): used as s.: III, 32.

enquerre (v. tr., to demand, to seek after): *enqueron* (3 pl. pres.): I, 17. *enqeron* (3 pl. pres): Vida, 10(14). *enqeront* (3 pl. pres.): VIII, 7.

enseignamen (s.m., behaviour, breeding): *enseignamens* (nom. sing.): VIIIa, 17.

entendemen (s.m., opinion, intention): *entendemens* (nom. sing.): VIIIa, 38.

entenden (s.m., suitor, wooer): *entendens* (nom. sing.): VIIIa, 44.

entre (prep., among): Vida, 10(14); III, 11; VIII, 7. (between): VII, 1.

entremetre, s' (v. reflex., to trouble, concern oneself): *te'n entremetz* (2 sing. pres.): IV, 26.
enueg (s.m., grief, sorrow): IV, 47.
envilanir, s' (v. reflex., to dishonour, degrade oneself): IV, 56.
er: see *ara*.
era: see *ara*.
eras: see *ara*.
erba (s.f., grass): I, 4.
erebre (v. tr., to save): *ereb* (3 sing. pres.): VIIIa, 51.
ergolhar, s' (v. reflex., to be haughty, disdainful): *s'erguelha* (3 sing. pres.): I, 7.
erguelh (s.m., pride, haughtiness, arrogance): I, 23; II, 41, 45; V, 23; VII, 12.
ergulhos (adj., m. sing., proud, haughty): used as s.: III, 22.
esbaudeyar (v. tr., to cheer, to gladden): *esbaudey* (3 sing. pres. subj.): III, 5.
esbaudir, s' (v. reflex., to rejoice): *esbaudir* (after *far*): III, 1.
escarnir (v. tr., to mock, to insult, to deceive): IV, 12; VI, 17; VIIIa, 18. *escarnis* (3 sing. pres.): V, 29.
escazer (v. intr., to fall, to befall): *eschai* (3 sing. pres.): III, 18. *es escazegutz* (3 sing. perf.): VIIIa, 40.
escazer, s' (v. reflex., to be suitable, fitting): *s'eschai* (3 sing. pres.): VIII, 27.
escondire, s' (v. reflex., to justify, vindicate oneself): II, 31.
escut (s.m., shield, protection): *escutz* (nom. sing.): VIIIa, 12.
esdevenir (v. intr., to become): *esdeve* (3 sing. pres.): VII, 41.
esdevenir, s' (v. reflex., to happen): *s'esdeve* (3 sing. pres.): II, 23; IV, 16.
esgardar (v. tr., to look at): *esgarda* (3 sing. pres.): VII, 42. *esguardem* (1 pl. pres. subj.): VII, 45.
esjauzir, s' (v. reflex., to rejoice): IV, 6. *esgauzir* (after *far*): VIIIa, 46.
eslaisar, s' (v. reflex., to rush): *'m eslays* (1 sing. pres. subj.): IV, 45.
esmaiar (v. intr., to grieve, to lament?): *esmais* (1 sing. pres.): IX, 3 (see note).
esmaiar, s' (v. reflex., to grieve, to lament): *m'esmay* (1 sing. pres.): III, 51.
esmay (s.m., distress, trouble): *esmays* (nom. sing.): I, 46.
espaventar (v. tr., to alarm): *espaventa* (3 sing. pres.): II, 48.
esperit (s.m., spirit): *esperiz* (nom. sing.): IX, 20.
espirital (adj., m. sing., spiritual): IX, 12.
essenhatz (adj., m. nom. sing., educated, brought up): VI, 4.
esser (v. intr., to be): VIIIa, 47. *suy* (1 sing. pres.): I, 29, 38; II, 8; III, 13, 17, 23, 27, 33; VI, 39, 44, 45, 54; VII, 5, 7, 8, 17, 31. *sui* (1 sing. pres.): Vida, 10(10); VIII, 9; VIIIa, 13, 26, 27. *son* (1 sing. pres.): III, 43; VIIIa, 23. *yest* (2 sing. pres.): IV, 24. *es* (3 sing. pres.): Vida, 10(6), 10(13); I, 5, 33, 46; II, 10, 12, 38, 39, 40; III, 10, 44, 53, 54, 65; IV, 3, 8, 10, 16, 39, 55; V, 8, 9, 18 (twice), 39, 47; VI, 4, 7, 12, 15, 20, 22, 23, 24, 25, 29, 36, 58; VII, 17, 27, 34; VIII, 6, 12, 24, 30; VIIIa, 16, 19, 20, 32; IX, 31. *son* (3 pl. pres.): V, 12, 26. *era* (3 sing. imperf.): Vida, 3; VIIIa, 37.

GLOSSARY 139

fuy (1 sing. pret.): II, 13. *fo* (3 sing. pret.): Vida, 1 (three times), 8 (twice); VIIIa, 37. *foron* (3 pl. pret.): Vida, 2. *serai* (1 sing. fut.): IX, 26. *er* (3 sing. fut.): IV, 38; V, 39; VIII, 28, 35. *seretz* (2 pl. fut.): VIII, 45. *seria* (1 sing. cond.): V, 4. *fora* (1 sing. cond.): IX, 25. *fora* (3 sing. cond.): VIIIa, 35. *sias* (imp. sing.): VI, 53. *siatz* (imp. pl.): VIII, 37. *sia* (3 sing. pres. subj.): I, 26; III, 65; VI, 30, 59; VII, 44; VIIIa, 12. *fos* (1 sing. imperf. subj.): VI, 13; VIIIa, 44; IX, 27. *fos* (3 sing. imperf. subj.): III, 44; V, 15; VIIIa, 34, 48. *esser a* (to be necessary to): *er a* (3 sing. fut.): IV, 20, 55; VIIIa, 2. *d'aco no m'es* (that does not matter to me, I do not worry about that): VI, 23.

estar (v. intr., to be, to be situated, to suit): VIII, 23; VIIIa, 42. *estai* (3 sing. pres.): IV, 15; VIII, 19 (suits). *estet* (3 sing. pret.): Vida, 8, 11 (twice), 12. *ai estat* (1 sing. perf.): VIIIa, 6. *estara* (3 sing. fut.): IV, 39. *estera* (1 sing. cond.): VIIIa, 45. *estey* (3 sing. pres. subj.): III, 26. *estar, s'* (reflex., to be situated): *s'estai* (3 sing. pres.): V, 44. *m'estau* (1 sing. pres.): VI, 37.

estar (s.m., state, condition): *estars* (nom. sing.): IX, 31.

estiers de (prep., apart from): V, 14.

estorser (v. tr., to release): *a estort* (3 sing. perf.): IV, 43.

estragna (adj., f. sing., distant, foreign): IX, 15.

estros: *ad estros* (adv., immediately(?)): III, 59. (See Levy, *S.W.*, III, 351-3.)

et: see *e*.

eu: see *ieu*.

eyssamen (adv., in the same way): III, 42.

fag (s.m., deed, action): VII, 22. *faich*: VIIIa, 20. *fait*: III, 25. *faitz* (pl.): VIII, 10; VIIIa, 21, 46. *faiz* (pl.): Vida, 10(11).

fallir (v. intr., to fail, to go wrong): VI, 1.

far (v. intr. and tr., to do, to make, to say): III, 1; IV, 11; VI, 12, 14. *fas* (1 sing. pres.): VI, 16; IX, 17. *fatz* (1 sing. pres.): IV, 30; VI, 47. *fas* (2 sing. pres.): IV, 9, 31; VI, 48. *fa* (3 sing. pres.): VIIIa, 18. *fai* (3 sing. pres.): Vida, 10(6); II, 9, 25, 55, 59, 66; III, 30; V, 32; VI, 54; VII, 3, 15; VIII, 20; VIIIa, 32; IX, 23. *fay* (3 sing. pres.): I, 31; V, 5. *fan* (3 pl. pres.): V, 9, 24. *fetz* (3 sing. pret.): Vida, 4, 5, 10; V, 47; VIII, 20. *fey* (3 sing. pret.): III, 49. *a fag* (3 sing. perf.): IV, 54. *a fait* (3 sing. perf.): I, 12. *farai* (1 sing. fut.): VIIIa, 33. *faray* (1 sing. fut.): VI, 50. *faras* (2 sing. fut.): IV, 40. *fara* (3 sing. fut.): IV, 38. *feira* (3 sing. cond.): VIIIa, 46. *fera* (3 sing. cond.): I, 47. *agra fait* (3 sing. cond. perf.): III, 47. *fai* (imp. sing.): IV, 25 (say!), 27 (say!), 28. *far* (inf. used as imp.): VI, 50. *agues fait* (3 sing. pluperf. subj.): III, 38. *far a* (to bring it about that one . . . (see note)): *fai a* (3 sing. pres.): II, 27.

far, se (reflex., to make oneself, to become, to be suitable): *me fauc* (1 sing. pres.): III, 21. *'s fay* (3 sing. pres.): V, 48. *'s fan* (3 pl. pres.): III, 2. *fetz se* (3 sing. pret.): Vida, 2. *'us fassatz* (imp. pl.): VIII, 29.

fat (adj., m. sing., foolish, mad): *fatz* (nom. sing.): VII, 17. *fatz* (pl. used as s.): VIII, 37.
fe (s.f., faith, pledge): II, 64; III, 37. *per ma fe* (indeed! to be sure!): IV, 30. *per bona fe* (in good faith): II, 64.
femna (s.f., woman): IX, 8.
fenher, se (v. reflex., to occupy oneself): *s'en fenhon* (3 pl. pres.): II, 28.
fieu (s.m., fief): V, 27.
figa (s.f., fig): IX, 17.
fin (adj., m. sing., pure, true, faithful, perfect, certain): II, 6, 51. *fis* (nom. sing.): III, 23; V, 15; VII, 7.
flor (s.f., flower): *flors* (pl.): I, 1.
fol (adj., m. sing., mad, foolish): *fols* (nom. sing.): III, 13; VIII, 37. *folhs* (nom. sing.): IV, 24; VII, 17. Used as s.: I, 20. *fuelh* (nom. pl.): I, 16.
foldat (s.f., madness, folly): *foldatz* (nom. sing.): III, 55. *foudatz* (nom. sing.): VIII, 31.
forfaitura (s.f., wrong): I, 10.
fort (adv., much, well, cordially, very): Vida, 4; IV, 1, 15; VII, 40.
foudatz: see *foldat*.
fraitura (s.f., scarcity, want): IX, 33.
franc (adj., m. sing., noble, charitable, sincere): V, 31. *francs* (nom. sing.): VI, 53.
fre (s.m., bridle): IV, 44.
freia (adj., f. sing., cold): II, 3.
freidura (s.f., coldness): IX, 16.
fresquet (adj., m. sing., fresh): VIII, 34. *fresqetta* (f. sing.): IX, 30.
fronçir (v. tr., to knit (the brows)): *ai fronçitz* (1 sing. perf.): IX, 21.
fuelh (s.m., leaf): *fuelh* (pl.): I, 2.

gai (adj., m. sing., gay): VIII, 34. *guay* (nom. pl.): V, 12.
gap (s.m., humour, jest, praise): *guap*: III, 12. *gaps* (nom. sing.): VIII, 12. *caps* (nom. sing.): Vida, 10(6), 10(13).
gardar (v. intr. and tr., to look at, to take care, to protect): *aurai gardatz* (1 sing. fut. perf.): Vida, 10(11); VIII, 10. *gardatz* (imp. pl.): VIII, 15. *guart* (3 sing. pres. subj.): V, 48; VI, 61.
gauzens: see *jauzen*.
gelos (adj., m. pl., jealous): VI, 21.
gen (s.f., person, people): *gen*: Vida, 8, 9. *gens* (nom. sing.): V, 50.
gen (adj., sweet, gentle, kind): III, 25; IV, 5. *gens* (nom. sing.): VII, 41. *genta* (f. sing.): II, 21.
gen (adv., well, fittingly): VIII, 39.
gensar (v. intr., to become more beautiful): *gensa* (3 sing. pres.): I, 3.
genta: see *gen*.

GLOSSARY 141

gentils (adj., m. sing., noble (of noble character)): Vida, 1.
ges (adv., perhaps): IV, 17.
ges no (adv., not at all): I, 40; II, 15, 29, 48. *ges non*: VI, 1. *non ges*: V, 25.
giquir, se (v. reflex., to give up, to lose heart): IV, 13.
gran (adj., m. sing., great, large): Vida, 3, 12; I, 47; III, 14, 47; IV, 37; V, 3, 30; VI, 34; VIII, 24; IX, 4. *gran* (f. sing.): Vida, 3; I, 24, 31; II, 63, 67; VI, 26, 34. *grans* (m. nom. sing.): I, 46; IV, 18; V, 46; VIII, 35. *grans* (f. nom. sing.): I, 33. *grans* (m. pl.): Vida, 4.
grat (s.m., will, pleasure): *graz* (nom. sing.): VI, 36. *prendre en grat* (v.tr., to conceive a liking for): Vida, 6.
grazir (v. tr., to receive favourably, to praise, to thank): VIIIa, 8. *grasit* (past. part., m. nom. pl.): Vida, 2.
greu (adj., m. sing., difficult, hard, painful): *greus* (nom. sing.): IV, 3; VI, 25; VII, 27.
greu (adv., with difficulty, rarely): II, 37.
guaimentar, se (v. reflex., to grieve, to lament): *se guaimenta* (3 sing. pres.): II, 57.
guap: see *gap*.
guay: see *gai*.
guerir (v. intr. and tr., to cure, to be cured, saved): IV, 27; VI, 43. *gueritz* (past. part., m. nom. sing.): IX, 25.
guerra (s.f., war): V, 25.
guidar (v. tr., to guide, protect): *guida* (3 sing. pres.): II, 7.
guinh (s.m., glance): II, 56.
guirentir (v. tr., to guarantee, to assure): *guirenta* (3 sing. pres. subj.): II, 19.
guiza (s.f., manner): *a guiza de* (after the manner of): III, 22.

hi: see *i*.
hoc: see *oc*.
hom (s.m., man): Vida, 1; I, 38; III, 60; VII, 32, 37; VIII, 17.
hom (indef. pron., one): Vida, 10 (6), 10 (13); IV, 3, 6, 7, 10, 12, 13, 57; V, 14, 21; VII, 34; VIII, 12, 23. *om*: Vida, 10 (8); II, 24; III, 46; IV, 4, 11, 15; V, 5, 37; VI, 4; VII, 39, 43; VIII, 30, 40.
honor (s.f., honour, credit, reparation): Vida, 12; III, 47. *onor*: I, 37, 39. *honors* (nom. sing.): I, 26; VIII, 35. *onors* (nom. sing.): VI, 15.
hora (s.f., time, moment): VI, 2.
huelh (s.m., eye): II, 56. *oils* (pl.): IX, 29. *uls* (pl.): IX, 21. *huelh* (nom. pl.): I, 9. (See also *a (de) dreyt huelh*.)
huey (adv., today): V, 32.
humils (adj., m. nom. sing., humble): VI, 53.

i (adv., pron., roughly equivalent to the French *y*: there, in that, etc.): II, 46; VII, 39. *hi*: Vida, 12; IV, 41. *y*: VI, 47.

i a (imper. v., there is, there are): VIII, 13. *y a* (pres.): V, 17, 35. *i aura* (fut.): VI, 21.
ie: see *ieu*.
ieu (pers. pron., nom., I): I, 15, 29, 32, 38; II, 2, 8, 11, 17, 32; III, 2, 4, 13, 17, 20, 23, 33, 34, 37, 41, 46, 48, 51, 56, 57; IV, 9, 13, 18, 28, 30, 31, 34, 36, 42; V, 27, 36; VI, 2, 3, 8, 13 (twice), 20, 24, 31, 42, 44; VII, 6, 7, 24 (twice), 25; VIII, 47, 48; VIIIa, 13, 33, 39, 44. *eu*: Vida, 10(12); VIII, 11, 50; VIIIa, 3, 30, 34, 48; IX, 15, 25. *ie*: V, 20.
il (def. art., m. pl., the): see *el*.
ilh (pers. pron., nom., she): II, 16; III, 26, 29; V, 49. *ylh*: I, 28. *il*: II, 55. *'l*: I, 45.
il, ill (pers. pron., dat. sing., to him, her): see *li*.
ira (s.f., sorrow, sadness): V, 17; VII, 1, 2, 4; VIII, 41.
iraisser, s' (v. reflex., to become angry, annoyed): *'s irays* (3 sing. pres.): I, 18.
iratz (adj., m. nom. sing., sorrowful, afflicted): VI, 44. *irat* (nom. pl.): III, 2.

ja (adv., ever, formerly, certainly, indeed; used to reinforce an assertion): III, 32, 39, 60; IV, 20, 35; VI, 41; VII, 7, 18; VIIIa, 37.
ja no (adv., never, not (emphatic)): IV, 7; VIIIa, 12. *ja non*: V, 16; VII, 37.
ja no (conj., although . . . not): *ja mais no* (although . . . never): VIIIa, 41.
jai (s.m., joy): VIII, 41. *jay*: V, 34.
jauzen (adj., m. sing., joyful): IV, 46. *jauzens* (nom. sing.): VII, 5. *gauzens* (nom. sing.): VIIIa, 45.
jauzimen (s.m., joy, pleasure): IV, 32.
jauzir (v. intr., to enjoy (with *de*)): IV, 34.
jauzir, se (v. reflex., to enjoy (with *de*)): *me jauzir*: VII, 8. *te jauzir*: VI, 51, 56. *m'en jauzirai* (1 sing. fut.): VII, 9.
jauzire (s.m., nom., enjoyer): II, 13, 40.
jazer (v. intr., to rest, to sleep): VIII, 22.
joc (s.m., game, amusement): II, 15; VII, 25.
joglar (s.m., jongleur): *joglars* (nom. sing.): Vida, 2.
joi: see *joy*.
jorn (s.m., day): II, 44. *jorns* (nom. sing.): VII, 41. (See also *totz jorns*.)
jovent (s.m., youth): IX, 35.
joy (s.m., joy): II, 6, 69; III, 14, 20, 31, 42, 58; IV, 22, 23; V, 1, 49; VII, 1, 25. *joi*: Vida, 8. *joys* (nom. sing.): III, 9, 53; V, 3, 7, 13, 15; VI, 29; VII, 3. *jois*: IV, 18. *joy* (nom. sing.): VII, 5.
joyos (adj., m. sing., joyous, happy): III, 43.
jurar (v. tr., to swear): *jura* (3 sing. pres.): I, 13.
jutjar (v. intr., to judge, to decide): *vos jutgatz* (imp. pl.): III, 50.

la (def. art., the): Vida, 2, 3, 8; I, 3; IV, 8; IX, 30. *l'*: I, 4, 39, 44; VII, 4. *'l*: I, 40; VI, 26. *las* (pl.): I, 1; VIIIa, 23; IX, 22.

la (pron., acc. f. sing., her, it): Vida, 7; I, 42; II, 34; III, 16; V, 45; VII, 18, 37, 39.
 ·*l*: VI, 11. *l'*: I, 6, 28; III, 36, 39; VII, 42.
lai (adv., there): Vida, 10(14), 12; I, 49; III, 9; VI, 60; VII, 35; VIII, 7; IX, 19, 31.
 lay: III, 29, 62. (See also *sai e lai*.)
laidura (s.f., injury, wrong): I, 31.
laissar (v. tr., to leave, to let, allow): *lais* (1 sing. pres.): IX, 2. *laissa* (3 sing. pres.):
 I, 40. *'s laissa* (3 sing. reflex. pres.): VIII, 18. *laisset* (3 sing. pret.): Vida, 2.
 laissarai (1 sing. fut.): IV, 21. *laissa* (imp. sing.): IV, 27. *lays* (3 sing. pres. subj.):
 I, 39.
larcx (adj., m. nom. sing., generous, liberal): VI, 53.
lauzar (v. tr., to praise): VIIIa, 8. *lauza* (3 sing. pres.): II, 34. *lauzar* (inf. used as
 s.m., praise): *lauzars* (nom. sing.): VIIIa, 16.
lay: see *lai*.
leis: see *liey*.
lenta (adj., f. sing., slow): II, 12.
letras (s.f., pl., education): Vida, 1.
let (adj., m. sing., joyful, happy): *letz* (nom. sing.): III, 17.
leu (adv., easily): *ben leu* (perhaps): VI, 21; VII, 10.
leyal (adj., m. sing., loyal): II, 51.
li (def. art., m. pl., the): see *el*.
li (pers. pron., dat. m. sing., to him, to her): I, 51; II, 61. ·*l*: Vida, 9; I, 21. ·*lh*: III,
 65. *ill* : Vida, 4. *l'*: VIII, 19. ·*ls* (pl.): I, 19. *lor* (pl.): II, 56. *lur* (pl.): I, 26. *li* (f.
 sing.): I, 50; II, 67; III, 13, 37; IV, 52; VII, 31; VIIIa, 39, 42, 52; IX, 29. ·*l*: I, 27;
 III, 25; IV, 51; VI, 12, 14, 46; VII, 44. ·*lh*: II, 42; III, 34. *il*: VIIIa, 36. *l'*: II, 14;
 VI, 12; VII, 20.
liar, se (v. reflex., to adorn, to dress oneself): *se li* (3 sing. pres. subj.): II, 22.
liey (emphat. pron., f., her): VI, 8, 16, 24, 32, 48, 56, 61. *liei*: VIIIa, 33. *lieys*: I, 37
 acc.); II, 17, 26, 36, 42 (dat.); III, 9, 27, 31; IV, 23, 48; V, 48; VI, 5, 11, 14, 26, 45,
 57; VII, 25. *leis*: IX, 27.
lo, los (def. art., m., the): see *el*.
lo (pron., acc. m. sing., him, it): Vida, 10(6); I, 13; II, 42; IV, 26, 55, 57; V, 37.
 ·*l*: Vida, 9; I, 11; II, 66; III, 32, 60; IV, 12, 51; V, 14, 38. *l'*: Vida, 4; II, 49. *los*
 (pl.): Vida, 6; VIII, 40, 49. ·*ls* (pl.): I, 25; III, 5; VI, 32; VIII, 46.
lonc (prep., near, beside): II, 47.
lonc (adj., m. sing., long): *lonc* (nom. pl.): IV, 48. *lonc temps*: see *temps*.
longuas (adv., a long time): I, 51.
lor (pers. pron., dat. pl., to them): see *li*.
lor (poss. adj., f. sing., their): I, 25. *lur*: I, 17, 18.
luecx: see *luoc*.
luenh (adv., far): V, 44; VII, 31.
luenh de (prep., far from): VI, 37.

lui (emphat. pron., m., him, it): Vida, 10; II, 69. *luy*: V, 4.
luoc (s.m., place): VIII, 31. *luocs* (nom. sing.): VIII, 28. *luecx* (nom. sing.): IV, 16. *en luoc* (as the occasion demands): VIII, 37.
lur (pers. pron., dat. pl., to them): see *li*.
lur (poss. adj., f. sing., their): see *lor*.

ma: see *mon*.
mais (conj., except): see *mas*.
mais (adv., more): I, 36; II, 43; III, 6, 59; IV, 48; VII, 35; IX, 16. *mai*: Vida, 10(7); IV, 40, 53. *mai de* (more of): VIII, 13 (*en*). *mais que* (more than, rather than): VIII, 4. *mas que*: Vida, 10(4). *mai que mai* (above all): III, 56. *mais . . . no* (no other): V, 14; VI, 29. (See also *no·n poder mais*.)
mais no (adv., never): VIIIa, 41 (see *ja*). *anc . . . non mais* (may) (never): see *anc no*.
mal (s.m., evil, ill, injury, harm, suffering): I, 21; II, 37, 44; IV, 7; V, 23; VI, 54; VII, 29; VIII, 42. With *traire*: II, 17; III, 52; V, 19; VI, 48. *mals* (nom. sing.): I, 51; III, 54; V, 18, 28; VII, 27. *mal* (nom. pl.): V, 26.
mal (adj., m. sing., bad, ill, wicked): V, 31; VI, 3. *mals* (nom. sing.): VIIIa, 17. *mala* (f. sing.): I, 20. *mals* (m. pl. used as s.): VIII, 42. (See also *saber mal*.)
mal (adv., badly, wrongly): IV, 41; VI, 4; VIII, 19; IX, 23.
maldir (v. tr., to blame): IV, 12.
malmenar, se (v. reflex., to behave badly): ·*s malme* (3 sing. pres. subj.): II, 52.
maltrait (s.m., suffering): *maltraitz* (nom. sing.): VI, 25.
malvatz (adj., m. nom. sing., wicked): VIII, 23.
mandar (v. tr., to send, to send word, to let know, to order): *mant* (1 sing. pres.): VI, 57. *man* (1 sing. pres.): III, 24; V, 44; IX, 10. *manda* (3 sing. pres.): II, 58.
manenta (adj., f. sing., rich): II, 10.
manjar (v. intr., to eat): VIII, 22. *manjar* (inf. used as s.m., eating): VII, 2.
manta (adj., f. sing., many a): II, 59. *manz* (m. pl.): VI, 21.
mantener (v. tr., to maintain, to uphold, to countenance): IV, 53; VIII, 25. *mante* (3 sing. pres.): II, 41; V, 49.
manz: see *manta*.
marriment (s.m., sorrow, sadness): IX, 36.
marritz (adj., m. nom. sing., afflicted, grieved): Vida, 10; IX, 19.
mas (adv., more): see *mais*.
mas (conj., but): Vida, 12; I, 44; III, 9, 20, 36; IV, 2, 4, 8, 10, 25, 31, 39; V, 10, 17; VI, 37, 55; VII, 4, 10, 26; VIII, 24, 48, 51; VIIIa, 20, 28, 37.
mas (conj., except): III, 60; IV, 33; V, 7, 35; VI, 11. *mais*: VI, 14, 32; VIIIa, 49. *mas que* (except that): II, 24.
me (pers. pron., acc. sing., me. Abbreviated to *m'* and ·*m*): Vida, 10 (14); I, 34, 40; II, 5 (twice), 7 (three times), 9, 48; IV, 27, 33, 43, 45; V, 3, 46; VI, 39, 55; VII, 1, 13, 14, 16, 19, 20; VIII, 7; VIIIa, 28, 32, 36, 46, 51, 52. *mi*: I, 49; VI, 52; VII, 3.

GLOSSARY

me (pers. pron., dat. sing., to me, for me. Abbreviated to *m'* and *·m*): I, 31, 42; II, 4, 12, 15, 19, 20; III, 10, 18, 26, 30, 39, 47, 53, 54, 62, 64; IV, 1, 18, 36, 44, 47, 54, 55; V, 25, 37, 42; VI, 15, 23, 25, 27, 28, 29, 30, 46, 54; VII, 2, 4, 15, 18, 23, 27, 28, 34 (twice), 43; VIII, 43; VIIIa, 2, 12, 40, 41, 43, 47, 48; IX, 2, 4, 22, 31. *mi*: I, 37, 47; III, 58.

me (emphat. pron., me): II, 16; IV, 17; VIIIa, 22. *mi*: I, 45; II, 31, 49; VIIIa, 5. *mey*: III, 38.

me (pers. pron., eth. dat. Abbreviated to *m'* and *·m*): V, 40; VI, 24; VIIIa, 25.

meinz (adv., less): Vida, 10(7). *meins de* (less of): VIII, 13 *(en)*.

melhors (los) (superl. adj., m. pl., the best) used as s.: I, 15.

melhurar (v. tr., to improve the lot of): *melhura* (3 sing. pres.): I, 34.

membrar (imper. v., to remember): *membra·m de* (I remember): V, 36. *membre·lh* (3 sing. pres. subj., he may remember): III, 65.

membratz (adj., m. nom. sing., shrewd, clear-sighted): Vida, 10(10); VIII, 9.

mentir (v. intr., to lie): VII, 14; VIIIa, 15. *mens* (2 sing. pres.): VI, 22; VII, 11. *men* (3 sing. pres.): IV, 39. *menta* (3 sing. pres. subj.): II, 30.

mentir (s.m., lie): IV, 40.

meravillar, se (v. reflex., to be surprised, to marvel): *meravill me* (1 sing. pres.): VIIIa, 31.

merce (s.f., grace, mercy, pity): II, 43, 67; IV, 23; V, 21. *merces* (pl.): VI, 46.

mesorgua (s.f., lie): IV, 42.

metre (v. tr., to put): *a mes* (3 sing. perf.): IV, 44. *mezes* (3 sing. imperf. subj.): I, 49.

mey: see *me*.

mezeus: see *aqui*.

mi: see *me*.

midons (s.f., my lady): I, 44; III, 12, 24; V, 42 (dat.); VI, 2; VII, 12, 43 (dat.); VIIIa, 3. *midonz*: VIIIa, 28, 32.

mielhs(·l) (superl. adj., neut., the best) used as s.: VI, 19 (see note).

mieus (poss. pron., m. nom. sing., mine): IV, 55.

mirar, se (v. reflex., to look at oneself (in the mirror), to model oneself): *se mir* (3 sing. pres. subj.): VII, 39. *·s mire* (3 sing. pres. subj.): II, 22.

moillerat (s.m., husband): *moilleratz* (nom. sing.): VIII, 44.

molt: see *mout*.

mon (s.m., world): Vida, 12; II, 22; VI, 19. *totz lo mons* (nom. sing., everyone): IV, 52.

mon (poss. adj., m. sing., my): I, 43; II, 6; III, 6, 35, 63 (twice); IV, 21, 46, 49, 51; V, 1, 43; VI, 57, 60 (dat.); VIIIa, 22; IX, 7, 35. *mos* (nom. sing.): I, 41, 46; II, 58; IV, 36; VI, 36; VII, 17; VIIIa, 24; IX, 19. *ma* (f. sing.): Vida, 3; I, 33; II, 10; III, 57; IV, 30. *mos* (m. pl.): I, 43; III, 1; VII, 23; VIIIa, 10.

montagna (s.f., mountain): IX, 16.

morir (v. intr. and tr., to die, to kill): III, 59; VI, 41; VIIIa, 32. *murir*: IV, 20. *muer* (1 sing. pres.): III, 53; VI, 43. *muor* (1 sing. pres.): VIIIa, 33. *mors* (2 sing. pres.): VI, 43. *moretz* (2 pl. pres.): V, 41. *a mort* (3 sing. perf.): VII, 16 (has killed). *moris* (1 sing. imperf. subj.): III, 45. *fos mortz* (1 sing. pluperf. subj.): III, 46.
mort (s.f., death): IV, 8.
mortal (adj., m. sing., mortal): II, 17.
mostrar (v. tr., to show): *mostra* (3 sing. pres.): II, 42.
mot (s.m., word, remark): V, 36; VI, 5.
mout (adv., much, very): VI, 35, 52; VIIIa, 8; IX, 2. *molt*: I, 47; VII, 19.
mover (v. intr., to depend (in respect of a fief)): *mou* (1 sing. pres.): V, 28.
mudar (v. intr., to refrain from (followed by negative)): V, 2; IX, 13. *mudarai* (1 sing. fut.): III, 3.
murir: see *morir*.
mutz (adj., m. nom. sing., silent): VIIIa, 6.

nadal (s.f., Christmas): II, 65, 68.
naiser (v. intr., to be born): *nays* (3 sing. pres.): I, 4.
natura (s.f., nature): I, 38.
natural (adj., m. sing., natural, perfect, true): Vida, 1; II, 6; IV, 4.
negus (adj., m. nom. sing., no, any): III, 60. *neguna* (f. sing.): I, 10.
ni (conj., neither, nor, or): I, 9; II, 1, 9, 20, 22 (or), 23, 41, 58; III, 24, 25 (twice), 31, 32, 34, 35, 53 (or); IV, 7, 12, 25, 31; V, 39, 42; VI, 9, 10 (twice), 23, 29 (twice), 30; VIII, 21, 35; IX, 10.
ni (conj., and): Vida, 10 (8); I, 27, 40; II, 56; IV, 16; VI, 12; VIII, 6, 14; VIIIa, 9, 13; IX, 17, 18 (twice).
nien (pron., nothing): *per nien* (in vain): IV, 25.
noirir (v. tr., to sustain, to look after): *a noirit* (3 sing. perf.): V, 3.
noit (s.f., night): *noitz* (nom. sing.): IX, 34. *nuegz* (nom. sing.): VII, 41.
nom (s.m., name): VIIIa, 22. *aver nom* (to be called): *auretz nom* (2 pl. fut.): VIII, 44.
non (adv., not): Vida, 10 (4); I, 1, 7, 8, 41; II, 2, 8, 23, 33, 42, 52; III, 16, 35, 41, 44; IV, 1, 3, 22, 33, 35; V, 13, 27, 37, 38; VI, 4, 6, 13, 22, 36, 43; VII, 7, 32; VIII, 20, 21, 48; VIIIa, 7, 14, 19, 26, 27, 48; IX, 13. *no*: I, 39; II, 1, 4, 9, 19, 26, 41, 57; III, 2, 3, 4, 18, 39; IV, 6, 12, 13, 31, 34, 36, 45, 56; V, 2 (twice), 15, 22, 38, 39, 46; VI, 23, 27, 28, 29, 30, 36, 39, 44, 46, 47 (twice), 48, 50; VII, 8 (twice), 39 (twice); VIII, 29, 32, 35; VIIIa, 51; IX, 5 (twice), 9, 13, 24. (See also *anc non, ges non, re non, no . . . tan ni quan.*) *non* (equivalent to the French *ne* used in clauses preceded by the comparative *mais* or *plus*): VIII, 4. *no*: VII, 24, 30; IX, 17.
nonca (adv., never): I, 13.
nos (pers. pron., acc., us): ·*ns* : VII, 45; IX, 23.
nos (emphat. pron., us): Vida, 10 (14); III, 11; VIII, 7.

GLOSSARY

nostra (poss. adj., f. sing., our): IX, 6, 14.
novelh (adj., m. sing., new): III, 5.
nozer (v. intr., to harm (to kill)): *mi nogues* (1 sing. reflex. imperf. subj.): VIIIa, 35 (*mi* = reflex. pron., dat.).
nuegz: see *noit*.
nulh (indef. adj., m. sing., no): III, 49; IV, 32. *nulhs* (nom. sing.): VII, 32. *nulha* (f. sing.): VI, 2.

o (conj., or): Vida, 10(7) (twice); V, 41; VI, 5; VIII, 13 (twice), 44, 45, 46; VIIIa, 23 (either).
o (pron., acc. neut., it) II, 20; III, 19, 34; IV, 17, 38; V, 20, 24; VI, 20, 48; VII, 29; VIII, 48; VIIIa, 25; IX, 4, 10, 23.
o (adv., where): I, 49.
obezir (v. intr., to obey): IV, 52.
oc (adv., yes): III, 42; IV, 16; VI, 43, 52, 55; VII, 10, 20, 22. *hoc*: IV, 18, 34; VI, 42.
oils: see *huelh*.
om: see *hom*.
on (adv., where): VI, 39; VIII, 32. *on plus . . . plus* (the more . . . the more . . .): VIII, 17; VIIIa, 25.
onguan (adv., henceforth, this year): V, 38.
onor, onors: see *honor*.
ops (s.m., need, necessity): *ops l'es* (it is necessary for him): VIII, 26.
orde (s.m. and f., order (religious)): Vida, 12.
oscura (adj., f. sing., dark): IX, 34.
ostal (s.m., home): II, 62.

paiser (v. tr., to feed): *pais* (3 sing. pres.): II, 7.
pantais (s.m., torment, affliction): IX, 4.
paor (s.f., fear): *paors* (nom. sing.): I, 40.
parer (v. intr., to appear, seem): *par* (3 sing. pres.): IV, 4.
pareiser (v. intr., to appear): *pareyssen* (pres. part. used as s.m., appearance): I, 1.
parlar (v. intr., to speak): *parla* (3 sing. pres.): VI, 5.
partir (v. tr., to separate, to offer): IV, 33; VII, 32. *part* (3 sing. pres.): II, 15. *parti* (3 sing. pret.): Vida, 9. *a partiz* (3 sing. perf.): IX, 23.
partir, se (reflex., to separate oneself, to depart): *m'en partir*: VI, 49. *'m part* (1 sing. pres.): IV, 47. *se part* (3 sing. pres.): IX, 14. *m'en partrai* (1 sing. fut.): Vida, 10(5); VIII, 5. *'m parta* (1 sing. pres. subj.): VIII, 52.
partir (inf. used as s.m., departure): Vida, 10(12); VIII, 11.
parventa (s.f., appearance): *fai parventa* (3 sing. pres., pretends): II, 55.

passar (v. intr., to pass, to change): *passa* (3 sing. pres.): VII, 4. *passar pel ver* (to tell the truth): *passetz pel ver* (2 pl. pres. subj.): VIIIa, 14.
passar (inf. used as s.m., suffering): IV, 5 (see note).
patz (s.f., peace): I, 6, 24; VI, 54.
paubre (adj., m. sing., poor): III, 22.
pauc (adj., m. sing., small): V, 3. *paucs* (nom. sing.): I, 26.
pauc (adv., little, in a short time): I, 52; II, 14; V, 22 (with *de*); VI, 47; VII, 29.
per pauc (almost): VII, 16.
pauza (s.f., rest): V, 30.
pe (s.m., foot): *pes* (pl.): VIIIa, 42.
pejurar (v. intr., to grow worse): *pejura* (3 sing. pres.): IX, 35.
pel (s.m., hair): VIII, 33.
pel(s) = *per lo(s)*: see *per*.
pena (s.f., grief, sorrow): VI, 34. *a penas* (adv., scarcely): II, 18.
pendre (v. tr., to hang): *pendes* (3 sing. imperf. subj.): VIIIa, 52.
pensar (v. intr., to think): *pes* (1 sing. pres.): VI, 9. *pensa* (3 sing. pres.): II, 16.
pensius (adj., m. nom. sing., pensive): Vida, 10.
per (prep., as, because of, by, for, in order to, owing to, through): Vida, 2, 8, 9, 10(1), 10(4); I, 4, 29; II, 17, 34, 67; III, 1, 6, 31, 45, 53; IV, 6, 7, 17, 25, 43, 46; V, 13; VI, 13, 14, 16, 35; VII, 6, 15, 18, 25; VIII, 1, 4, 45; VIIIa, 2, 15, 22, 33, 52; IX, 10, 35. *pel* (=*per lo*): IV, 37; VIIIa, 40. *pelz* (= *per los*): VIIIa, 21. *per al* (for any other reason): II, 8. *per als*: IV, 33. *per so* (for this reason): II, 29, 57; IV, 21. *per so quar* (because): IV, 34. *per so car*: VIIIa, 27. (See also *per (mal')* *aventura*, *per Dieu*, *per engual*, *per ma fe*, *per bona fe*, *per nien*, *per pauc*, *passar pel ver*, *tener per*.)
percassar, se (v. reflex., to toil, to exert oneself): *'s percatz* (3 sing. pres. subj.): VIII, 26.
per que (conj., in order that, so that): II, 60. *per ce*: VIII, 30.
per que (for which reason, thus): III, 10; IV, 11; V, 2; VI, 7; VIIIa, 34. *per qe*: VIIIa, 39. *per que* (why): IV, 24; VII, 13; VIII, 20.
perdre (v. tr., to lose): *perdutz* (past. part., m. nom. sing.): VIIIa, 34. *perdut* (past part., nom. sing., useless, vain): V, 9 (see note).
perniz (s.f., partridge): IX, 28.
pero (conj., but): VI, 28.
pesar (v. intr., to be painful, annoying, important): *pesa* (3 sing. pres.): IX, 2. *pes* (3 sing. pres. subj.): V, 32; VI, 47.
pessamen (s.m., grief): *pessamens* (nom. sing.): VIIIa, 24.
petit (adv., little): II, 16.
plag (s.m., quarrel): *plagz* (nom. sing.): I, 26.
planher (v. intr. and tr., to bemoan, to lament): *planh* (1 sing. pres.): VII, 26. *plangz* (2 sing. pres.): VI, 41. *planh* (3 sing. pres.): II, 37.

planher, se (reflex., to complain, to lament): ·*s planh* (3 sing. pres.): I, 32. ·*m plagna* (1 sing. pres. subj.): IX, 13.

plazer (v. intr., to please): VIII, 36. *platz* (3 sing. pres.): IV, 47; V, 32; VI, 12, 28, 57; VIII, 52. *play* (3 sing. pres.): IV, 51. *plagra* (3 sing. cond.): IV, 1. *plassa* (3 sing. pres. subj.): II, 60. *plagues* (3 sing. imperf. subj.): VI, 14.

plazer (s.m., pleasure): I, 35; IV, 28.

plevir (v. tr., to promise, pledge): inf. used as s.m.: VII, 21.

plor (s.m., tear): *plors* (pl.): I, 19.

plorar (v. intr., to weep, lament): *plor* (1 sing. pres.): VII, 26.

ploure (v. intr., to rain): *plou* (3 sing. pres.): II, 1.

plus (adv., more): Vida, 10(7); III, 10, 13, 18; VII, 24, 30; VIII, 18. *de plus*: IV, 56. (See also *on plus*.)

plus (adv., most): II, 11; III, 23 (*lo p.*); V, 19.

poder (v. intr., to be able): *puesc* (1 sing. pres.): II, 18; IV, 47; V, 2; VI, 1, 17, 51; VII, 8; IX, 13, 24. *puosc* (1 sing. pres.): VIIIa, 29. *potz* (2 sing. pres.): VI, 43. *pot* (3 sing. pres.): VI, 27; VII, 32; VIII, 23. *podetz* (2 pl. pres.): VII, 14. *poc* (3 sing. pret.): IV, 56. *poiras* (2 sing. fut.): VI, 56. *poiria* (1 sing. cond.): VI, 3. *poiria* (3 sing. cond.): VIII, 32. *pogra* (3 sing. cond.): II, 36. *puesca* (3 sing. pres. subj.): IV, 12. *pogues* (1 sing. imperf. subj.): VI, 11. *pogues* (3 sing. imperf. subj.): VII, 38. *no·n poder mais* (to be utterly dejected): *no·n puesc mais* (1 sing. pres.): IX, 1.

poder (s.m., power): *aver en poder* (to be able, capable of): *ai en poder* (1 sing. pres.): IV, 35.

pois (conj., since): VIII, 20; VIIIa, 5.

pois (adv., then, after): VIII, 19. *pueis*: Vida, 12. *pueys*: I, 19; V, 35. *puois*: VI, 59; VIIIa, 20, 35.

pojar (v. intr., to rise, to climb): *poja* (3 sing. pres.): VIIIa, 24. *es pojatz* (3 sing. perf.): VIII, 17.

portar (v. tr., to carry, take): *porta* (imp. sing.): III, 62. *port* (3 sing. pres. subj.): VII, 43.

pregar (v. tr., to entreat): *prec* (1 sing. pres.): I, 43.

preizon (s.f., prison): IV, 44.

prendre (v. intr. and tr., to take, to receive; to arrive, arise (see note to IV, 18)): *pren* (3 sing. pres.): IV, 18; V, 22. *pres* (3 sing. pret.): Vida, 6. *pres* (past. part., m. nom. sing.): VI, 54. *prendre cura de* (to take care of): *prenda cura de* (3 sing. pres. subj.): I, 45. (See also *grat*.)

pres (adv., near): VII, 36.

pretz (s.m., merit, worth, virtue): Vida, 3; II, 50; III, 9, 20, 31, 42, 53, 58; IV, 53; V, 10, 49; VIII, 25; VIIIa, 19.

prezar (v. tr., to appraise, to esteem, to value): *pretz* (1 sing. pres.): IV, 42; VI, 32. *pres* (1 sing. pres.): VII, 29. *prezas* (2 sing. pres.): IV, 9.

prezentar, se (v. reflex., to present oneself, to be presented): *se prezenta* (3 sing. pres.): II, 46. *si prezen* (3 sing. pres. subj.): IV, 50.
prion, de (adv., profoundly): VIIIa, 25.
pro (adv., much): III, 16; VIII, 22.
pro (s.m., advantage, benefit, profit): I, 39; VI, 47. *pros* (nom. sing.): III, 54; V, 18; VIII, 35.
pros (adj., m. nom. sing., virtuous, noble, doughty): III, 65; VI, 53. *pros* (pl. used as s.m.): V, 10.
prometre (v. tr., to promise): *promes* (past. part., m. nom. sing.): VI, 30.
propdas (adj., m. nom. sing., neighbouring): VII, 31.
pueis, pueys, puois: see *pois*.

qan, etc.: see *quan*
qar: see *quar*.
qe, qez: see *que*.
qual: see *caler*.
qual (interrog. adj., m. sing., what): IV, 23.
qual (interrog. pron., m. sing., which one): V, 37; VI, 49. *cal*: VIII, 45. *quals* (nom. sing.): V, 39. *cals*: VIIIa, 23.
qual que (indef. pron., m. sing., whichever one): I, 35.
quan (adv., conj., when; since): I, 2; II, 34; IV, 5, 16, 47 (since); V, 26, 50; VII, 35. *quant*: Vida, 10(5), 10(11); I, 32; II, 38, 50; III, 44; IV, 3. *qan*: VIII, 5, 28. *qand*: VIII, 10. *qant*: IX, 26.
quan que (adv., conj., however much, long): VII, 9. (See also *tan de . . . quan, no . . . tan ni quan.*)
quant (indef. pron., that which, what): V, 9. (See also *tot quant.*)
quar (conj., for, because (occasionally equivalent to *que* (= that) as indicated)): I, 27, 31; III, 2, 7; IV, 6, 18, 33, 37; V, 21; VI, 36 (that); VII, 8, 18. *qar*: IV, 19, 53; IX, 2 (that), 5 (that), 14, 35. *car*: III, 16, 51; VIII, 17; VIIIa, 9 (that), 15. (See *per so quar.*)
quasqun (indef. pron., m. sing., each one): II, 61.
que (rel. pron., nom., who, which): Vida, 3; I, 4, 21, 23, 39; II, 40, 45, 66; III, 2, 5; IV, 37; V, 24, 47; VI, 22; VII, 27, 37. *qe*: VIIIa, 40. *qui*: I, 6, 16; IV, 14; VII 19, 42.
que (rel. pron., acc., whom, which): Vida, 10; I, 9, 12, 14; II, 11, 37, 47, 54; III, 30, 37; V, 5, 27, 36; VI, 8, 26; VII, 6. *qe*: VIII, 16, 47; VIIIa, 3. *cuy*: VI, 35.
que (rel. emphat. pron., whom, which): V, 13; VII, 15, 18. *cui*: IX, 10.
que (interrog. pron., acc., what): IV, 9 (how much), 26, 27, 40; V, 33, 34; VI, 41, 42, 51; VII, 11.
que (interrog. emphat. pron., what): IV, 3; VI, 45.

GLOSSARY 151

que (indef. pron., nom., that which, what): V, 32 (twice). (See also *segon*.)

que (indef. pron., nom. sing., he who): see *qui*.

que (conj., than): Vida, 10(8); II, 44; III, 11; IV, 41, 49, 53; VII, 24, 30, 36; VIII, 4. *qe*: I, 37; IV, 41. *ce*: VIIIa, 38.

que (conj., that): Vida, 8, 10(12); I, 11, 12, 42, 45; II, 2, 14, 18, 24, 35, 52, 56, 68; III, 4, 32, 39, 46, 48, 49, 58; IV, 4, 10, 13, 15 (twice), 16, 18, 19, 29 (when), 35, 36, 50, 51; V, 5, 9, 37, 45; VI, 2, 6, 7, 8, 13, 15, 19, 20, 30, 43, 58, 59; VII, 2, 24, 38, 39, 43, 44; VIII, 15, 28; VIIIa, 26, 34, 36. *ce*: VIII, 40, 49. *qe*: II, 21, 26, 33; VIII, 11, 19, 26, 43; VIIIa, 11, 35, 37, 44, 48, 52; IX, 8, 13, 22, 28. *qez*: VIIIa, 30.

que (conj., introducing final clause, so that, in order that): IV, 12, 45. *qe*: VIII, 5; VIIIa, 14.

que (conj., introducing consecutive clause, so that): II, 8; III, 46; V, 13; VII, 30. *qe*: I, 7.

que (conj., for, because): Vida, 10(5), 10(14); I, 15, 17, 22, 38, 42, 46, 52; II, 5, 13, 16, 25, 31, 32, 39, 43, 49, 50, 59; III, 19, 24, 29, 33, 42; IV, 42, 52; V, 3, 5, 14, 18, 20, 24, 25, 33, 34, 40, 49; VI, 4, 13, 15, 18, 24, 31, 48; VII, 15, 29, 32, 39; VIIIa, 4, 7. *qe*: VIII, 7, 21, 31; VIIIa, 19, 48. *ce*: VIII, 22, 40; VIIIa, 24.

quecx (indef. pron., nom. sing., each one, every one): II, 34.

querre (v. tr., to ask for, to look for, to seek): *quier* (1 sing. pres.): III, 25. *quers* (2 sing. pres.): VI, 50. *quiers* (2 sing. pres.): IV, 23. *quier* (3 sing. pres.): I, 50. *querra* (3 sing. fut.): I, 28. *queren* (pres. part.): I, 21.

quetz (adj., m. nom. sing., silent): III, 28.

qui (pron., nom. sing., he who, anyone who): I, 28 (him who); II, 19, 20; IV, 10; V, 19 (to him who), 22. *qi*: IX, 23. *que*: VIII, 25.

qui (equivalent to Latin *si quis* (see *Altprov. Elem.*, pp. 136–7) (if anyone)): II, 42; VIIIa, 15.

qui (rel. pron., nom., who): see *que*.

quo: see *com*.

quoras (adv., when): IV, 17, 38.

raïtz (s.f., nerves): IX, 22.

rancura (s.f., complaint, recrimination): I, 6.

raugolhar (v. intr., to have the death rattle): *rauguelha* (3 sing. pres.): I, 52. (See note.)

razo (s.f., right): *razos* (nom. sing.): III, 55.

re (s.f., thing, something, anything): II, 59; V, 24. *ren*: VI, 3. *res* (nom. sing., truth): III, 44; VI, 22. *no . . . re* (nothing, not at all): III, 24; V, 35, 42. *non re*: IV, 9; VII, 16. *non ren*: IV, 42. *non res*: V, 4. *re no*: II, 24; III, 39; VII, 15. *ren no*: VI, 9, 32. *de re no* (in no way, not at all): IV, 2.

recreire, se (v. reflex., to give up, to lose heart, to desist (from)): *se recre* (3 sing. pres.): IV, 10; V, 50. *recresutz* (past. part., m. nom. sing., cowardly, fainthearted): VIIIa, 13.
[*redoler, se* (v. reflex., to grieve, to suffer?): *redol m'en* (1 sing. pres.): IX, 3. (See note.)]
rei (s.m., king): Vida, 11 (twice).
remaner (v. intr., to remain): VIIIa, 7. *reman* (3 sing. pres.): IX, 20. *rema* (3 sing. pres.): VII, 5.
ren: see *re*.
rendre, se (v. reflex., to retire): *se rendet* (3 sing. pret.): Vida, 12.
res: see *re*.
rescos (adj., m. sing., hidden (past. part. of *rescondre*)): *a rescos* (in secret): III, 33.
respieich (s.m., hope, expectation): VIIIa, 49.
resplandir (v. intr., to shine, to glitter): *resplan* (3 sing. pres.): VII, 40.
respos (s.m., reply): VIII, 51.
retener (v. tr., to retain, to keep): VIII, 46. *rete* (3 sing. pres.): IV, 45; V, 46.
retraire (v. tr., to relate): *retrai* (3 sing. pres.): Vida, 10 (13); VIII, 12.
revenir (v. intr., to recover): VI, 27.
ribeira (s.f., plain, river): IX, 18.
ricautz (adj., m. nom. sing., proud): III, 21.
rir (v. intr., to laugh): IV, 19. *rire*: VII, 3. *rire* (inf. used as s.m., laughter): II, 4.
rir, se (de) (reflex., to rejoice (over)): *m'en ri* (1 sing. pres.): VII, 30.
ris (s.m., laugh, laughter): I, 19; III, 12; VII, 25.

sa: see *son*.
saber (v. intr. and tr., to know, to know how): Vida, 10 (5); VIIIa, 10. *sai* (1 sing. pres.): II, 14, 32; III, 48, 57; IV, 1; VI, 15, 20; VIII, 48. *say* (1 sing. pres.): III, 19; V, 41; VI, 24. *saps* (2 sing. pres.): IV, 26, 27, 35. *sabes* (2 sing. pres.): IV, 41. *sap* (3 sing. pres.): I, 11; III, 29; IV, 3, 5. *saupi* (1 sing. pret.): VI, 19. *saup* (3 sing. pret.): III, 35. *suy sauputz* (1 sing. perf.): VI, 18. *sabrai* (1 sing. fut.): Vida, 10 (12); VIII, 11. *sabretz* (2 pl. fut.): V, 39. *sapchas* (imp. sing.): IV, 18. *sapchatz* (imp. pl.): VI, 7; VIII, 38. *sapcha* (1 sing. pres. subj.): VIII, 5. *sapcha* (3 sing. pres. subj.): III, 32, 60; V, 45. *sapchatz* (2 pl. pres. subj.): VIII, 15; VIIIa, 11, 26. *sapchon* (3 pl. pres. subj.): I, 23. *saubes* (1 sing. imperf. subj.): IV, 2. *saubutz* (past. part., m. nom. sing.): VIIIa, 19. [*sabeos* (imp. pl.?): IX, 7 (see note).] *saber mal* (to displease): *sap mal* (3 sing. pres.): I, 27. *saber sal* (to please): *sap sal* (3 sing. pres.): II, 26.
saber (s.m., knowledge): Vida, 10 (9); VIII, 8.
sai (adv., here): Vida, 10 (3); III, 8, 11, 33; VIII, 3; VIIIa, 5. *çai*: IX, 20. *sai e lai* (here and there): VIII, 26. *e sai e lay*: V, 26.
sal (s.m., salt): see *saber*.

GLOSSARY

sals (adj., m. nom. sing., safe): IX, 25.
salut (s.m., salvation, greeting): *salutz* (nom. sing.): VIIIa, 41. *salutz* (pl.): V, 44.
salvar (v. tr., to save): *sal* (3 sing. pres. subj.): VI, 61.
sans (adj., m. nom. sing., sound, healthy): IX, 25.
saur (adj., m. sing., golden): VIII, 33.
savis (adj., m. nom. sing., wise): Vida, 1, 10 (10); VIII, 9. *savis* (m. pl., used as s.): VIII, 39.
saziontat (s.f., abundance): *saziontas* (nom. sing.): IX, 33.
sazo (s.f., time): *sazos* (nom. sing.): VIII, 28. *a sazos* (now and then): III, 21.
se (conj., if): see *si*.
se (reflex. pron. Abbreviated to *s'* and *'s*): see the verbs which it accompanies.
se (reflex. emphat. pron., himself, herself): Vida, 9; II, 34, 47.
se (reflex. pron., eth. dat. Abbreviated to *s'* and *'s*): I, 33, 35; II, 30 (twice); VI, 24. *si*: Vida, 1.
secors (s.m., help): I, 47, 50.
segle (s.m., world): IV, 14; VIII, 36. *segles* (nom. sing.): V, 8.
segon (prep., according to): *segon que* (according to what): VIII, 48.
seign'en (s.m., lord): VIII, 1, 50. *seingner*: Vida, 10 (1). *seinhor*: IX, 12. *senher*: V, 47. *senhor*: V, 28. *senhors* (pl.): I, 43.
sel (dem. pron., m. nom. sing., he, the person): II, 45; VIII, 25. *selieys* (f. acc. sing.): VII, 19. *seluy* (m. dat. sing.): II, 40. *selh* (m. emphat. sing.): VII, 42. *selhs* (m. nom. pl.): V, 24. *selhs* (m. emphat. pl.): I, 5.
semblan (s.m., appearance, look): III, 25. *semblant*: IX, 28. *far semblan* (to show, reveal): IX, 9.
semblar (v. intr., to seem): *sembla* (3 sing. pres.): V, 25.
sempre (adv., always): I, 16; VII, 10.
sen (s.m., (good) sense, intelligence, reason, reasoning, mind, view, feeling): Vida, 1, 10 (9); I, 29; IV, 4; VI, 38; VIII, 8, 29, 47. *sens* (nom. sing.): III, 55; VII, 17; VIII, 32, 35; VIIIa, 37.
senatz (adj., m. nom. sing., sensible, wise): VIII, 30.
senes: see *ses*.
senher, senhor: see *seign'en*.
sentir (v. tr., to feel, to experience): *senta* (3 sing. pres. subj.): II, 37. *se sentir* (reflex., to feel): *'m sent* (1 sing. pres.): IV, 2.
servir (v. intr. and tr., to serve): IV, 47; VI, 11; VIIIa, 39.
ses (prep., without): I, 6; II, 36; V, 4; VIIIa, 46. *senes*: Vida, 10 (7); VII, 21.
setz (ord., adj., m. nom. sing. (obj. = *sest*), sixth): III, 39 (see note).
sey: see *sieu*.
si (reflex. pron., eth. dat.): see *se*.
si (thus, so, so much): Vida, 8, 9; II, 30; IV, 30, 45; VI, 47, 50; VII, 1, 36. *si que* (so that): VI, 39.

si (conj., if): I, 13, 27, 37, 51; II, 28, 46; III, 52; IV, 2, 22, 39 (twice), 51, 54; V, 15, 46; VI, 5, 48, 54, 55; VII, 16, 33, 36; VIII, 18, 36, 52; VIIIa, 6, 31, 32, 34, 43, 51; IX, 27. *s'*: I, 31, 48; II, 35, 55, 63, 69; III, 13, 51; IV, 49; V, 28; VI, 31, 55, 57, 58; VIIIa, 13, 33. *se*: III, 45. (See also *cum si*.)

si (conj., whether): Vida, 10(6), 10(13); V, 41; VIII, 12, 13, 44, 46.

si be (conj., although): VI, 37.

si cum: see *com*.

sidons (s.f., his lady): II, 66.

sieu (lo) (poss. adj., m. sing., his, her): IV, 40. *'l sieus* (nom. sing.): III, 10. *sey* (nom. pl.): I, 9. *li sieu* (nom. pl.): Vida, 2.

sirventes (s.m., sirventes): Vida, 10.

si tot (conj., although): I, 25, 33; V, 44.

so (dem. pron., this, that): IV, 10; V, 41; VII, 18, 20. (See also *per so*.)

so que (dem. pron., nom., what): VI, 14. *so que* (acc.): I, 9, 12, 14 (*sso*); II, 11; III, 41; V, 7.

so(n) (s.m., poem, melody): III, 5.

soau (adv., pleasantly): VIII, 23.

sofrir (v. intr. and tr., to suffer, to endure, to tolerate, to be patient): IV, 55; VIIIa, 29. *sufrir*: I, 23; VI, 25; VII, 27. *suffrir*: IV, 5. *sofier* (1 sing. pres.): I, 34. *sofre* (imp. sing.): VI, 46. *sufre* (imp. sing.): VI, 54. *sofris* (3 sing. imperf. subj.): V, 22. *se soffrir(de)* (reflex., to abstain (from)): *'m soffrir de*: VIIIa, 4.

sufrire (s.m., nom., sufferer): II, 38.

sojorn (s.m., joy): *sojorns* (nom. sing.): V, 19.

sol (adv., only): III, 16; VIIIa, 43.

sol (conj., provided that): VIIIa, 28. *ab sol que* (provided that): VII, 22.

solamens (adv., solely, merely): VIIIa, 30.

solatz (s.m., gaiety, fellowship): Vida, 10 (2); VIII, 2.

soler (v. intr., to be accustomed): *suelh* (1 sing. pres.): VII, 24.

son (poss. adj., m. sing., his, her): II, 53, 62; III, 38; IV, 5, 29; VII, 21. *sos* (nom. sing.): III, 27, 33; VIIIa, 37, 38 (*ssos*), 44. *sos* (pl.): Vida, 5; IX, 29. *sa* (f. sing.): I, 11; III, 45; IV, 43 (twice), 44, 46; VII, 40; VIIIa, 51. *sas* (f. pl.): Vida, 5.

sonet (s.m., song, poem): III, 63.

sordeyar (v. intr., to grow worse): *sordeya* (3 sing. pres.): V, 6.

sorzer (v. tr., to exalt): *sors* (past. part., m. nom. sing.): I, 29 (see note).

sospirar (v. intr., to sigh): *sospir* (1 sing. pres.): VI, 33; VII, 26.

sostener (v. tr., to uphold, to sustain): *soste* (3 sing. pres.): II, 7; V, 7, 14.

sostraire (v. tr., to treat badly? See Levy, *S.W.*, VII, 846): *sostrays* (3 sing. pres.): I, 25.

soven (adv., often): VI, 33.

sovenir (imper. v., to remember): *l'en soven* (she remembers it): II, 14.

sufrir: see *sofrir*.

ta: see *tan*.
tal (indef. pron., m. sing., such): II, 18; VIII, 31. *tals* (m. nom. sing.): Vida, 10 (6), 10 (13); VIII, 12. *tal* (f. sing.): III, 49. *tal* (f. nom. sing.): II, 27. *tals* (m. pl.): I, 22.
talan (s.m., desire, longing, feeling, intention): III, 35; IV, 31; V, 31; VI, 10; IX, 7. *talens* (nom. sing.): VIIIa, 9.
tan (adv., so much, as much, so well): I, 17; II, 1; VI, 42; IX, 8. *tant*: V, 1; VIIIa, 43, 48; IX, 21, 27. *tan* (adv., before an adj. and adv., so, as): Vida, 10 (10); II, 21, 25, 33; III, 47; V, 15; VI, 26, 44; VII, 38, 40. *tant*: VIII, 9. *ta*: VI, 4. *tant de* (so much, as much): Vida, 10 (9); VIII, 8, 13. *tan com* (as long as): Vida, 12. *tan quan* (as long as): IV, 32. *tant cant*: VIII, 33. *tan de . . . quan* (as much . . . as): I, 30. *no . . . tan ni quan* (not at all): V, 17.
tanher, se (v. reflex., to be suitable, fitting): *'s tanh* (3 sing. pres.): III, 32.
te (pers. pron., acc. sing., you. Abbreviated to *t'*): IV, 34. *te* (dat. sing. Abbreviated to *t'* and *'t*): IV, 20, 30, 37, 39; VI, 47.
temer (v. tr., to fear, to be afraid of): VIII, 29. *tem* (1 sing. pres.): VI, 41.
temor (s.f., fear): Vida, 9.
temps (s.m., time, season): I, 3; IV, 16, 29. *lonc temps* (a long time): Vida, 8. *lonc tems*: Vida, 11. *totz temps* (always): VIIIa, 39, 42, 44.
tener (v. tr., to hold, to have, to keep): IV, 14. *te* (3 sing. pres.): II, 5. *ten* (3 sing. pres.): VIII, 21. *tener a* (to consider as): *teng a* (1 sing. pres.): IX, 4. *tener per* (to consider as): IV, 57.
tener, se (reflex., to remain): *vos tener* (inf.): VIII, 15. *'s te* (3 sing. pres.): V, 13. *ten se* (3 sing. pres.): V, 11.
terra (s.f., land): IX, 15.
tirar (v. intr., to delay, to drag on): *tir* (3 sing. pres. subj.): VII, 9.
tolre (v. tr., to take (away)): *tuelh* (1 sing. pres.): VII, 18. *tolh* (3 sing. pres.): II, 4; VII, 2. *tuelh* (3 sing. pres.): I, 37. *tuelha* (3 sing. pres. subj.): I, 42. *toilla* (3 sing. pres. subj.): VIII, 27.
tolre, se de (v. reflex., to desist from, to renounce): *tol te* (imp. sing.): IV, 20.
ton (poss. adj., m. sing., your): IV, 28, 31; VI, 50.
tornar (v. intr., to change, to become): *torna* (3 sing. pres.): I, 19; V, 34; VII, 28. *torn* (3 sing. pres. subj.): VI, 6.
tort (s.m., wrong, injustice): IV, 29; V, 23. *tortz* (nom. sing.): III, 55; VIIIa, 17, 32. *aver tort* (to be in the wrong): *a tort* (3 sing. pres.): VII, 10, 11.
tos (s.m., young man): III, 64.
tost (adv., soon, quickly): Vida, 10 (3); I, 28; IV, 20, 29; V, 13; VIII, 3.
tot (adj., m. sing., all): IV, 28, 46, 49; VI, 8. *totz* (nom. sing.): III, 54; IV, 52. *tota* (f. sing.): V, 50. *totz* (m. pl.): I, 15; II, 60 (used as s.); III, 23; VII, 23. *tuich* (nom. m. pl. used as s.): VIII, 19. *tot l'als* (everything else): V, 5. *totz jorns* (always): IV, 19. *totz temps* (always): VIIIa, 39, 42, 44.

tot (adv., all, completely): IV, 11, 27; VII, 9, 16; VIIIa, 27. *totz* (m. nom. sing. form of adj.; see *Altprov. Elem.*, p. 123): III, 28; VI, 6; VIIIa, 3.
tot (indef. pron., everything): IV, 53; V, 34. *del tot* (completely): IV, 14. (See also *si tot.*)
tot quant (indef. pron., all that): IV, 8; V, 47; VI, 12; VII, 34. *tot quan*: III, 8, 11; IV, 9; VI, 16.
traïr (v. tr., to betray): *trays* (3 sing. pres.): I, 11.
traire (v. tr., to suffer): *trac* (1 sing. pres.): II, 17; VI, 34. *tray* (1 sing. pres.): III, 52. *tras* (2 sing. pres.): VI, 48. *tray* (3 sing. pres.): V, 19. *traïr' enan, se* (v. reflex., to advance): *me traïr' enan*: VI, 18 (see *enan*).
trametre (v. tr., to send, to convey): *tramet* (1 sing. pres.): IV, 50. *tramet* (3 sing. pres.): II, 65. *ai trames* (1 sing. perf.): VI, 38. *trames* (past. part., m. nom. sing.): VI, 59.
trassaillir (v. tr., to break, to violate): VIIIa, 1.
trebalhar, se (v. reflex., to take trouble, pains): *trebalhas te* (2 sing. pres.): IV, 24.
trenta (adj., thirty): I, 36; II, 28.
tro que (conj., until): I, 18, 34; VII, 45.
trobar (v. intr. and tr., to find, to write poetry): *trob* (1 sing. pres.): IX, 10. *trop* (1 sing. pres.): II, 19. *trobava* (3 sing. imperf.): Vida, 1.
trop (adv., much, too much, too, very): I, 46; III, 7; IV, 6, 7; V, 46; VI, 42; VIII, 29, 30.
tu (pers. pron., nom., you): III, 61; IV, 9, 26, 27, 35, 40; VI, 39, 55; VII, 11.
tuich: see *tot*.

uls: see *huelh*
un (indef. art., m. sing., one, a): I, 35; II, 44; III, 5; V, 36; VI, 5. *us* (nom. sing.): IV, 18. *una* (f. sing.): I, 37, 48; II, 21, 35; VII, 6; IX, 28. *un* (used as s.m., one): VIII, 41. *uns* (nom. sing.): II, 46. *us* (nom. sing.): I, 7; II, 33. *una* (f. sing.): II, 26.
.us: see *vos*.

valenta (adj., f. sing., useful, helpful): II, 39.
valer (v. intr., to be worth, to be useful, helpful): VIII, 32. *val* (3 sing. pres.): II, 24; VI, 46. *valon* (3 pl. pres.): IV, 48. *valra* (3 sing. fut.): VIII, 31.
valor (s.f., worth, merit): Vida, 3.
vas (prep., to, towards): IV, 8, 45. *ves*: I, 7.
vejaire (s.m., opinion, view): *vejaire m'es* (it seems to me): VIII, 47.
venir (v. intr., to come, to arrive): *ve* (3 sing. pres.): II, 50; IV, 37; V, 28. *ven* (3 sing. pres.): VIII, 18; VIIIa, 36. *veno* (3 pl. pres.): VIIIa, 21. *venc* (3 sing. pret.): VIIIa, 9. *soi vengutz* (1 sing. perf.): VIII, 3, 4 (*vengutz* understood). *son vengutz* (1 sing. perf.): Vida, 10(3). *sui vengutz* (1 sing. perf.): Vida, 10(4) (*vengutz* understood). *etz vengutz* (2 pl. perf.): VIIIa, 5. *venra* (3 sing. fut.): IV, 29. *vengues* (3 sing. imperf. subj.): VIIIa, 41. *s'en venir* (reflex., to come, to arrive): *s'en venc* (3 sing. pret.): Vida, 3.
vne (s.m., wind): *vens* (nom. sing.): VII, 35. *vens* (pl., thin air): VIIIa, 31 (see note).

GLOSSARY

venser (v. tr., to conquer): *vens* (3 sing. pres.): VII, 29.
ventar (v. intr., to blow, to be windy): *venta* (3 sing. pres.): II, 1.
ver (s.m., truth): Vida, 10(12); IV, 42; V, 29; VIII, 11, 43; VIIIa, 14 (see *passar*).
veray (adj., m. sing., true): V, 49.
verdura (s.f., verdure): I, 3.
vers (adj., m. nom. sing., true): III, 44; IV, 39; VI, 7.
vers (s.m., poem): II, 65, 68; IV, 50; VI, 1, 58; VII, 43. *vers* (pl.): Vida, 5.
vertat (s.f., truth): IV, 41. *vertatz* (nom. sing.): VI, 20.
vertut (s.f., virtue, power, miracle): *vertutz* (nom. sing.): VIIIa, 51. *vertutz* (pl.): VIIIa, 33.
ves: see *vas*.
vetz (s.f., time, occasion): I, 48.
vezer (v. tr., to see): Vida, 10(1); VIII, 1. *vey* (1 sing. pres.): I, 15; III, 8, 11, 16; IV, 34; V, 5; VI, 36. *ves* (2 sing. pres.): VI, 39. *ve* (3 sing. pres.): VII, 39. *vi* (3 sing. pret.): I, 14. *veyray* (1 sing. fut.): V, 45. *veira* (3 sing. fut.): VIII, 28. *veiran* (3 pl. fut.): I, 9. *vis* (3 sing. imperf. subj.): VII, 37. *vezer* (inf. used as s.m., seeing): III, 17.
vezi (s.m., neighbour): *vezis* (nom. sing.): VII, 31. *vezis* (pl.): III, 1.
viatz (adv., quickly, promptly): Vida, 10(3); VIII, 3.
vilan (adj., m. sing., low, mean): IV, 57. *vilas* (nom. sing.): VI, 6.
virar (v. tr., to turn): *vire* (3 sing. pres. subj.): II, 56.
vivre (v. intr., to live): II, 9, 18, 27, 36, 45, 54, 63, 66, 69. *viv* (1 sing. pres.): III, 45; IV, 43; VIIIa, 31. *vivetz* (2 pl. pres): V, 41. *vivray* (1 sing. fut.): V, 40. *vivras* (2 sing. fut.): IV, 32. *vivra* (3 sing. fut.): I, 52. *visques* (1 sing. imperf. subj.): VIIIa, 49.
voler (v. tr., to wish, want): *vuelh* (1 sing. pres.): I, 30, 36, 39, 44; III, 59; IV, 50; V, 37; VI, 30, 49; VII, 6, 43. *vol* (1 sing. pres.): VI, 59. *voill* (1 sing. pres.): Vida, 10(5). *vuoill* (1 sing. pres.): VIII, 43; VIIIa, 7, 11, 26. *vols* (2 sing. pres.): IV, 17, 19, 33; VI, 51, 55. *vol* (3 sing. pres.): I, 22; II, 30, 41, 45, 63, 69; IV, 14, 53; VIII, 25; VIIIa, 15. *voletz* (2 pl. pres.): VIII, 36; VIIIa, 22. *volon* (3 pl. pres.): VII, 33. *volretz* (2 pl. fut.): VIII, 46. *vuelha* (3 sing. pres. subj.): I, 35. *volgues* (3 sing. imperf. subj.): VIIIa, 43. *volgutz* (past. part., m. nom. sing.): VIIIa, 27.
voler (s.m., desire): IV, 49.
voltitz (adj., m. pl., large, round): IX, 29.
voluntiers (adv., willingly): IV, 28.
vos (pers. pron., nom. pl., you): III, 50, 58. *vos* (acc.): VIIIa, 8; IX, 2, 11. *·us* (acc.): VI, 36; IX, 5 (twice). *vos* (dat.): VI, 38; VIII, 6, 31; VIIIa, 9; IX, 10. *·us* (dat.): V, 20, 39; VIII, 32, 35, 52; IX, 9. *vos* (emphat.): Vida, 10(2), 10(8); III, 53, 54, 60; VI, 35, 37; VIII, 2, 6, 14, 52; VIIIa, 2. *·us* (eth. dat.): V, 41 (twice).
vostre (poss. adj., m. sing., your): Vida, 10(4); VIII, 4, 51. *vostres* (m. pl.): Vida, 10(11); VIII, 10.

For all words in *y* see *i*.

Index of Proper Names

Aimeric lo tos (Aimeric de Lara, nephew of Ermengarda): III, 64.
Alverne (the Auvergne): Vida, 1.
Anfos d'Arago (King Alfonso II of Aragon): Vida, 11.
Anfos de Castela (King Alfonso VIII of Castille): Vida, 11.
Bastart (probably a *joglar*): III, 61.
Bon Respieich (*senhal* for Raimbaut d'Orange's lady): VIIIa, 50.
Clarmon (Clermont): Vida, 1.
Dieu: see Glossary.
Dreit-n'avetz (*senhal* for an unidentified lady): VI, 60.
Ermengarda (the Viscountess Ermengarda of Narbonne): Vida, 3.
Espanha (Spain): Vida, 11.
Granmon (Grandmont): Vida, 12.
Joy-aver (description employed for the poet's lady): IV, 21.
Narbona (Narbonne): Vida, 3.
Narbones (the Narbonne area): V, 43.
Peire (the poet's first name): Vida, 1; VIIIa, 1, 29. *Peir*: I, 50; II, 64.
Rambaut d'Aurenga (the troubadour Raimbaut d'Orange): Vida, 10. *Raimbaut*: Vida, 10(1), 11. *Rambaut*: VIII, 50. *Raymbaut*: VIII, 1.
Raimon de Toloza (Count Raimond V of Toulouse): Vida, 11.
Rogier (the poet's surname): I, 50; II, 64. *Rogiers*: Vida, 1. *Rotgier*: VIIIa, 1, 29.
Santz (possibly Sancho, brother of Alfonso II of Aragon; see note): IV, 54.
Saves (Savès was formerly a district in the present-day Department of Gers): VI, 60.
Tort-n'avetz (*senhal* for Peire Rogier's lady): III, 6, 63; IV, 51; V, 43; VI, 57. *Tort-n'avez*: Vida, 7.

Appendices

APPENDIX I

Extract from *Les Vies des plus célèbres et anciens Poëtes provensaux, qui ont floury du Temps des Comtes de Provence*, Jehan de Nostre Dame, Lyons, 1575, pp. 202–4. (Chabaneau-Anglade edition, pp. 122–3.)

De Peyre Roger

Pierre Rogier fut chanoyne de Clermont. Sainct Cezari, et le Monge des Isles d'Or (lesquels de leur seule auctorité et renom vaincroyent tous les autres qui ont escript de nos poëtes Provensaux, ores qu'il n'amenassent aucune rayson), dyent qu'il estoit chanoyne d'Arles, et de Nynmes: ayant quicté le canonicat, se voyant jeune, beau et de bonne qualité, estant asseuré qu'il feroit plus de proffict au monde, qu'en religion ou il ne voyait que toutes abominations, envies, et debatz entre les Religieus, sortant de son cloistre s'addonna a la poësie en nostre langue vulguere Provensalle, et se feist Comique, et inventa de belles et ingenieuses Comedies, qu'il jouoit par les cours des Princes et grands seigneurs avec grand appareil. Tout ce qu'il faisoit et inventoit estoit trouvé bon et plaisant: arriva a la cour de dame Esmengarde de Narbonne femme de Roger Bernard Comte de Foix, dame de grand valleur, belle et bien aprise aux lettres, de laquelle Pierre Roger receut beaucoup de biens et de faveurs, et devint amoureux de l'une des damoyselles de la Comtesse nommee Huguette des Baulx, surnommee Baussette, fille de Hugues des Baux qui fut depuis mariee à Blacaz de Beaudinar sieur d'Aulps en Provence, pour laquelle il chanta plusieurs bonnes chansons. Sainct Cezari dict, qu'il receut d'elle de grandes faveurs, et les derniers effects d'amour: laquelle chose ne fault croyre, car par une chanson qu'elle luy envoya il appert, qu'elle ne se soucioit et ne avoit agreable rien qu'il feist qui se commence,

> Lo non m'en kal de tas rymas grossieras
> Ny mays d'y estre (ont que sia) mentauguda,
> Sabes qu'y ha, fay qu'yeu en sia moguda,
> Car non las hay ren en grat volontieras.

Toutesfois le Monge des Isles d'Or dict qu'elle ne luy envoya ceste chanson a autres fins, que pour couvrir l'amour, et l'affection qu'elle luy portoit, et que Roger luy adressa un traicté *Contra la dama de mala merce*. Sainct Cezari poursuyvant la vie de ce Roger dict qu'il fleurissoit du temps du roy Robert de Sicille Comte de Provence, et testifie neantmoins le dict Roger avoir esté present en la Cité de Grasse en Provence, lors que Pierre de Corbaria antipape surnommé Nicolas 5. du nom, en un presche qu'il feist dans l'eglise, se desdict publiquement des erreurs qu'il avoit tenus, que fut environ 1330, duquel temps ce pauvre Roger fut mys traistrusement a mort par les parans de dame Huguette par faux rapport.

APPENDIX II

Ermengarda, Viscountess of Narbonne, and her relations with other troubadours

Ermengarda's court is described in the *Histoire générale de Languedoc* (VI, p. 151) as one of the most flourishing in the Midi at that time. This description and Ermengarda's general renown are borne out by the number of troubadours who, apart from Peire Rogier, appear to have been acquainted with her.

Bernart de Ventadour sends his poem *La dousa votz ai auzida* to *midons a Narbona* (l. 58) (Appel, *B. von Vent.*, 23, pp. 134–7). The close relationship between the lines which refer to *midons a Narbona* and the earlier lines 53–6 which concern the poet's beloved lady suggests to Appel that it is a question of the same lady in each case (*op. cit.*, p. 139). He follows for l. 58 the MS which offers *a Narbona* in preference to the other MS which gives *de Narbona*, and suggests that Bernart may be alluding to his lady *in* Narbonne and not to Ermengarda, the lady *of* Narbonne. Diez (*Leben und Werke*, p. 30) and Jeanroy (*AdM.*, XVIII, 1906, 249) also express doubts about the identification of Ermengarda with *midons*.

On the other hand, the brief description of the lady in question would certainly seem to match the reputation which Ermengarda had acquired.

> que tuih sei faih son enter,
> c'om no·n pot dire folatge. (ll. 59–60)

Bergert (*Damen*, pp. 9–10) is confident that Ermengarda is the lady concerned. He refers to the possible similarity in content between this poem and other poems, addressed to *Conort* and *Tristan*, in which Bernart complains about his lady's conduct in paying heed to the *lauzengers*. Bergert's view, however, is that, far from being identified in the poem with the object of the troubadour's complaints, Ermengarda is intended to form a striking contrast with her, as the generous description cited above would suggest. It is therefore in her capacity as a renowned patron of the troubadours and their poetry that, according to Bergert, the viscountess is named here. Appel (*op. cit.*, p. lii) observes, in fact, that *midons* can have merely a titular meaning ('lady') and is not always used to denote the poet's beloved lady. He gives as an example ll. 27 and 29 of Bertran de Born's *Domna, pois de me no'us chal* (Appel, *B. von Born*, 5, p. 12), in which the two meanings of *midons* are used side by side.

The same *joglar* (*Corona*) who is charged with the poem discussed above is asked to deliver to *midons* the poem *Per melhs cobrir lo mal pes e'l cossire* (Appel, *B. von Vent.*, 35, pp. 199–202). Bergert (*op. cit.*, p. 10) considers that *midons* is clearly the lady of Narbonne, whereas Appel (*op. cit.*, p. lii) is more cautious and leaves the question open. Anglade (*RLR*, LVIII, 1915, p. 221, 'Onomastique des troubadours') indicates that a reference to Ermengarda may perhaps also be found in *Lancan vei la folha* (Appel, *op. cit.*, 25, pp. 145–9), but there appears to be no evidence to support this suggestion.

Although we cannot be certain that Bernart ever sang of Ermengarda in his love poems, it would not be unreasonable to assume that he visited the court of Narbonne, particularly as the similarity between his poetry and Peire Rogier's may suggest that the two troubadours knew each other. (*Cf.* p. 9 above and Appel, *op. cit.*, p. lii.)

Peire d'Alvernhe's poem *Ab fina joia comensa* (Del Monte, *P. d'Alvernha*, III, pp. 34–8) is sent to Narbonne as well as to the Counts in Provence:

> Als comtes mand en Proenssa
> lo vers e sai a Narbona
> lai on pren joi mantenenssa
> segond aqels per cui reigna. (ll. 49–52)

Zenker (*P. von Auvergne*, p. 30) identifies the counts as Raimon Bérenguer IV of Barcelona and his nephew, Raimon Bérenguer III of Provence, and, with Diez (*op. cit.*, p. 62), sees in the next line a reference to Ermengarda. The viscountess was, as we have noted above, a close ally of Raimon Bérenguer IV and supported him with her troops against the Sarracens at the siege of Tortosa in 1148 (see *Hist. gen. Lang.*, III, p. 737). The following two lines of the *tornada* would confirm the reputation which Ermengarda had gained. The words *sai a Narbona* imply that Peire d'Alvernhe was not far from Narbonne at the time. (*Cf.* Zenker, *loc. cit.*; Bergert, *op. cit.*, p. 9.) Anglade goes as far as assuming that the poem was actually composed at Narbonne, and sees in subsequent lines a further reference to Ermengarda in the person of the *dompna* who retains the troubadour described as her *amaire*. Both Zenker (*loc. cit.*) and Bergert (*loc. cit.*), however, reject this view and believe that it is a question of a different lady altogether from the viscountess. Jeanroy (*loc. cit.*), on the other hand, accepts that one lady only is involved but hesitates to identify her with Ermengarda.

Azalaïs de Porcairagues, who was born of a noble family, probably about the middle of the twelfth century, and became one of the earliest *trobairitz* (*cf.* M. G.

Charvet, *Les Troubadours d'Alaïs aux XIIIe et XIIe siècles*, p. 131), sends her one extant poem, *Ar em al freg temps vengut*, to Narbonne to *lei cui jois e jovens guida*. (Riquer, *Lírica*, pp. 392–4; see ll. 49–52.) It is generally assumed that Ermengarda is the lady in question. (*Cf.* Riquer, *op. cit.*, p. 391; G. Azaïs, *Les Troubadours de Béziers*, p. 146; M. G. Charvet, *op. cit.*, p. 135.)

According to the *Vida*, Sail d'Escola stayed with 'N'Ainermada de Nerbona' and when she died returned to Bragairac (Bergerac, Dordogne), his place of birth. (See Boutière and Schutz, *Biographies*, p. 64, No. X.) Boutière and Schutz (*loc. cit.*, note 3) consider that the lady concerned is probably Ermengarda, whose name may well have been corrupted in copying. The brief mention in the *Histoire générale de Languedoc* (VI, p. 151) of Sail d'Escola's relations with Ermengarda is no doubt based entirely on the reference in the *Vida*.

Appel (*P. Rogier*, p. 6, note) seeks confirmation of the troubadour's acquaintance with the viscountess in the Monk of Montaudon's *Pois Peire d'Alverne a chantat*, the eleventh stanza of which is devoted to Sail and contains a reference to *Narbones*:

> E quant a vendutz sos conres
> El s'en vai pois en Narbones
> Ab u fals cantar per presen (ll. 64–6)

(O. Klein, *Die Dichtungen des Mönchs von Montaudon*, Marburg, 1885, I, pp. 22–30). However, a comparison between the stanza as a whole and the *Vida* reveals very little difference in the information contained in them. It is therefore quite possible that the stanza, rather than confirming the details found in the *Vida*, was itself the source from which the biographer obtained his material. (*Cf.* Jeanroy, *Poésie Lyrique*, I, p. 166, note 3.) If this were the case it would be difficult to establish with certainty Sail d'Escola's relationship with Ermengarda, as the stanza refers only to *Narbones* and does not mention the viscountess by name. It should also be noted that the only poem attributed to Sail d'Escola (*Gran esfortz fai qui chanta ni's deporta* (Riquer, *op. cit.*, pp. 308–9)) makes no reference to Ermengarda or to Narbonne.*

In his poem *La flors del verjan* Giraut de Bornelh suggests consulting *Midons de Narbona* about a particular matter of love. The question is whether a lover, by being impetuous and gaining a certain amount of immediate enjoyment from love, does not lose, in the process, the promise of a thousand times more enjoyment (Kolsen, *G. de Born.*, 26, ll. 99–105). Kolsen (*op. cit.*, II, p. 57) considers that Giraut may be alluding here to the fate of Peire Rogier, whom he had perhaps met at Raimbaut d'Orange's court or whose misfortune he may have heard about there. (*Cf.* pp. 24–5 on the relationship between Giraut and Raimbaut.) It would not be unreasonable to suppose, however, that Giraut's reason for referring

---

* These observations on the eleventh stanza of the satire were suggested to me by Dr. Michael Routledge during his work on a critical edition of the satire. (See *RLR*, LXXVIII (1969), 102–37.)

to Ermengarda was her reputation for resolving general questions of this kind relating to the theory of love. (*Cf.* G. Paris, 'Les cours d'amour . . .; étude d'histoire littéraire', *Journal des Savants*, 1888, second article, p. 732.) Chabaneau (*RLR*, xxv, 1884, p. 102, note 1) has suggested that Andreas Capellanus may even have known this poem of Giraut's at the time he wrote the second book of *De Amore*, in which he attributes to Ermengarda five of the twenty judgements listed. (*Trattato d'amore—Andreae Capellani Regii Francorum 'De amore' Libri Tres*, Latin text and translation by S. Battaglia, Rome, 1947, pp. 320–30 (Nos. VIII, IX, X, XI, XV).) We have noted earlier Ermengarda's role as arbiter in disputes of a general nature between eminent lords and princes.

Anglade is of the view that *velha rica*, mentioned in Peire Vidal's poem *Car' amiga dols'e franca*, may possibly be an allusion either to Ermengarda or to Eleanor of Aquitaine. (*Cf. Les Póesies de Peire Vidal*, Paris, 1913, p. 184 (reference to VI, l. 41) and *Onomastique*.) The suggestion is refuted by Avalle, who gives the poem a date later than that of Ermengarda's death and considers that the reference has no historical basis but relates to a literary type. (*Cf. Peire Vidal: poesie*, Milan, 1960, I, p. 138, note to XV, l. 41.) We discuss earlier a possible reference by Peire Vidal to a close relative of Ermengarda (see note on VIII, l. 36).

According to Anglade (*Mélanges Chabaneau*, p. 743), the following allusion to *Narbones* in the *tornada* of one of the two *cansos* attributed to Pons d'Ortafas enables us only to speculate about the possibility of a connection between the troubadour and Ermengarda's court:

> En *Narbones* es gent plantatz
> L'arbres que'm fai aman morir,
> Et a Cabestanh gent cazatz,
> En mout ric loc senes mentir.
>
> (Mahn, *Gedichte*, 13: *Aissi cum la naus en mar* (text of C))

Anglade (*loc. cit.*) suggests that Cabestanh denotes the village of that name in the Eastern Pyrenees, where Ortaffa itself is situated (canton of Perpignan),* and that the lord Bérenger mentioned earlier in the poem is probably Pons's lord, Raimon Bérenguer IV of Barcelona, whose friendship with Ermengarda we have already noted above. However, the later period in which Jeanroy (*op. cit.*, I, p. 414) tentatively places Pons would rule out the possibility of a connection with the viscountess: he suggests that Pons is perhaps to be identified with Pons I, lord of Ortaffa, who is named in a document of 1217 and whose will is dated 1240.

Ermengarda may possibly have been on unfriendly terms with the troubadour Bérenguier de Poizrenger, of whose work only one *cobla* is extant. (Pillet and

---

* Anglade (*loc. cit.*) observes that Barbieri (MS χ) offers a different reading, mentioning Monpeslier instead of Cabestanh and attributing the poem to Miquel de la Tor (see Pillet and Carstens, 300a).

Carstens, 48, 1; *cf.* Bergert, *op. cit.*, p. 10.) The *Histoire générale de Languedoc* (III, p. 844) reports the dispute of 1164, which was referred to King Louis le Jeune, between the viscountess and one of her vassals, Béranger, lord of Puiserguier. We cannot be certain, however, that this is a reference to the troubadour, as his birthplace may have been the Puyrenier in the commune of Mareuil, *arrondissement* of Nontron (Dordogne), rather than this Puiserguier situated in the *arrondissement* of Béziers. (*Cf.* Jeanroy, *op. cit.*, I, p. 342.)

It has been suggested that Ermengarda's reputation had also reached the ears of the Vikings of the Orkneys (*cf.* Appel, *B. von Vent.*, p. lii). The *Orkneyinga Saga* (G. Vigfusson, *Orkneyinga Saga*, 1887; trans. G. W. Dasent, *The Orkneyingers' Saga*, London, 1894, pp. 163–8) recounts that in 1151 a fleet of ships, led by Earl Rognvald, set sail for Galicia in Spain, and that on the way south they stayed for a time at a 'sea town' named Nerbon where they were received with lavish hospitality by the head of the town, Ermingerda. We are told that Ermingerda's father, the former head, had died and that she was governing his lands with the counsel of the most noble of her kinsfolk. Rognvald and one or two of his followers sang songs of love in her honour both during their stay in Nerbon and later as they continued their voyage to Galicia.

In view of the difficulties raised by the geographical position of the Nerbon in question as well as by the identity of Ermingerda's father, whom the saga names as Germanus, we cannot conclude with any certainty that the lady concerned is Ermengarda.*

---

* Arguments for and against identification with Narbonne and Ermengarda are found in the following works: Vigfusson, *op. cit.*, p. 163, note 2; R. Dozy, *Recherches sur l'histoire et la littérature de l'Espagne pendant le moyen-âge*, Paris and Leyden, 1881; J. S. Clouston, *A History of Orkney*, Kirkwall, 1932; A. B. Taylor, *Proceedings of the Orkney Antiquarian Society* (Kirkwall), XI (1933), and *The Orkneyinga Saga*, Edinburgh and London, 1938 (in which reference is made to earlier articles by the following scholars: H. Gering, 'Die Episode von Rognvaldr und Ermingerðr', *Zeitschrift für deutsche Philologie*, XLIII (1911), 428–34, and XLVI (1914), 1–17; F. Jónsson, 'Rognvald jarls Jorsalfaerd,' in the Danish *Historisk Tidsskrift*, 8, R. IV (1912), 151–65; R. Meissner, 'Ermengarde und Rognvaldr', *Arkiv for nordisk Filologi*, XLI (1925), 140–91).

Bibliography

(Abbreviations used in the text and notes are shown in parentheses)

(a) *General works, studies, texts*

Ajalbert, J., 'Les troubadours d'Auvergne' in *Mercure de France*, CXXXVII (Jan.–Feb. 1920), 50–83.
Almqvist, K., *Les Poésies du troubadour Guilhem Adémar*, Uppsala, 1951. (*G. Adémar*)
Andraud, P., *La Vie et l'oeuvre du troubadour Raimon de Miraval*, Paris, 1902.
Anglade, J., *Las Leys d'Amors*, four vols., Toulouse and Paris, 1919–20.
— *Les Poésies de Peire Vidal*, Paris, 1913.
— 'Les troubadours à Narbonne' in *Mélanges Chabaneau*, Erlangen, 1907.
— 'Onomastique des troubadours' in *RLR*, LVIII (1915). (*Onomastique*)
Appel, C., *Bernart von Ventadorn, Lieder*, Halle, 1915. (*B. von Vent.*)
— *Das Leben und die Lieder des Trobadors Peire Rogier*, Berlin, 1882. (*P. Rogier*)
— *Die Lieder Bertrans von Born*, Halle, 1932. (*B. von Born*)
— *Provenzalische Chrestomathie*, second edition, Leipzig, 1902. (*Prov. Chr.*)
— *Raïmbaut von Orange*, Berlin, 1928. (*R. von Orange*)
Avalle, d'Arco S., *Peire Vidal: poesie*, two vols., Milan, 1960.
Azaïs, G., *Les Troubadours de Béziers*, second edition, Béziers, 1869.
Balaguer, V., *Los trovadores*, Madrid, 1883.
Bartsch, K., *Denkmäler der provenzalischen Literatur*, Stuttgart, 1856. (*Denkmäler*)
— Review of Appel's edition of Peire Rogier in *Literaturblatt*, IV, 66 ff.
— *Provenzalisches Lesebuch*, Elberfeld, 1855. (*Lesebuch*)
— and Koschwitz, E., *Chrestomathie Provençale*, Marburg, 1904. (*Chrest.*)
Battaglia, S., *Trattato d'amore—Andreae Capellani Regii Francorum 'De Amore' Libri Tres*, Rome, 1947.
Bergert, F., *Die von den Trobadors genannten oder gefeierten Damen*, Halle, 1913. (*Damen*)
Bertoni, G., *Il canzoniere provenzale della Biblioteca Ambrosiana R71* (*Gesellschaft für romanische Literatur*, XXVIII), Dresden, 1912.
— *Il canzoniere provenzale di Bernart Amoros (Complemento Càmpori)*, Friburg, 1911.
— *I trovatori d'Italia*, Modena, 1915.
Bohs, W., ' "Abrils issi'e mays intrava," Lehrgedicht von Raimon Vidal von Bezaudun' in *Romanische Forschungen*, XV (1904).

Boutière, J., 'Quelques observations sur le texte des vidas et des razos dans les chansonniers provençaux AB et IK' in *French and Provençal Lexicography* (U. T. Holmes and K. R. Scholberg), Ohio, 1964.

— and Schutz, A. H., *Les Biographies des troubadours*, Paris, 1964. (*Biographies*)

Buhler, C. F., 'The Phillips manuscript of Provençal poetry now MS 819 of the Pierpont Morgan Library' in *Speculum*, XXII (1947), 68–74.

Chabaneau, C., *Les Biographies des troubadours en langue provençale*, Toulouse, 1885 (in vol. X of *Hist. gen. Lang.*). (*Biographies*)

— Review of Appel's edition of Peire Rogier in *RLR*, XXV (1884), 102–4.

— and Anglade, J., *Jehan de Nostredame, Les vies des plus célèbres et anciens poètes provençaux*, Paris, 1913.

Charvet, M. G., 'Les troubadours d'Alaïs aux XIIIe et XIIe siècles' in *Mémoires et comptes-rendus de la Société scientifique et littéraire d'Alaïs*, XII, 129 ff.

Chaytor, H. J., *Savaric de Mauléon, Baron and Troubadour*, Cambridge, 1939.

Cluzel, I., 'Princes et troubadours de la maison royale de Barcelone–Aragon' in *Boletín de la Real Academia de Buenas Letras de Barcelona*, XXVII (1957–58).

Cocito, L., 'Sul canzoniere di Peire Rogier' in *Romania—scritti offerti a F. Piccolo nel suo LXX compleanno*, Naples, 1962, pp. 217–39.

Crescini, V., 'Le caricature trobadoriche di Pietro d'Alvernia' in *Atti del Reale Istituto Veneto di scienza, lettere ed arti*, vol. 83, pp. 781–95; vol. 86, pp. 203–26 and pp. 1203–56, Venice, 1923–24 and 1926–27.

Debenedetti, S., 'Flamenca' in *Opusculi di filologia romanza*, Turin, 1921.

De Lollis, C., *Il canzoniere provenzale O* (*Atti della R. Accademia dei Lincei, serie quarta, classe di scienze morali, storiche e filologiche*, II, part 1^a, pp. 1 ff), Rome, 1886.

— 'Su e giù per le biografie provenzali' in *Mélanges Chabaneau*, Rome, 1907.

— 'Un frammento di canzoniere provenzale' in *Studi medievali*, I, 561–79.

Del Monte, A., *Peire d'Alvernha: liriche*, Turin, 1955. (*P. d'Alvernha*)

Diez, F., *Leben und Werke der Troubadours*, Leipzig, 1882. (*Leben u. Werke*)

Ermengaud, M., *Le Breviari d'Amor*, ed. G. Azaïs, two vols., Société archéologique, scientifique et littéraire de Béziers, 1862–81. (*Breviari*)

Favati, G., *Appunti per un'edizione critica delle biografie trovadoriche*, Bologna, 1953. (*Appunti*)

— *Le biografie trovadoriche*, Bologna, 1961. (*Biografie*)

Gentile, A., *Antichi testi provenzali*, Genoa, 1947. (*Ant. testi*)

Gröber, G., 'Die Liedersammlungen der Troubadours' in *Romanische Studien herausgeg. von E. Boehmer*, Strasbourg, 1877.

Grützmacher, *Die provenzalische Liederhandschrift Plut. XLI cod. 43 der Laurenzianischen Bibliothek in Florenz* (*Archiv.*, XXXV, 363 ff), Brunswick, 1864.

Histoire littéraire de la France, Paris, 1733– .

Hoepffner, E., *Le Troubadour Peire Vidal*, Paris, 1961.

— *Les Troubadours dans leur vie et dans leurs oeuvres*, Paris, 1955.

Jeanroy, A., 'Les troubadours en Espagne' in *Annales du Midi*, XXVII–XXVIII (1915–16), 141–75.
— *La Poésie lyrique des troubadours*, two vols., Paris and Toulouse, 1934. (*Poésie lyrique*)
Klein, O., *Die Dichtungen des Mönchs von Montaudon*, Marburg, 1885.
Kolsen, A., *Sämtliche Lieder des Trobadors Giraut de Bornelh*, two vols., Halle, 1910 and Halle/Saale, 1935. (*G. de Born.*)
La Salle de Rochemaure, duc de, and Lavaud, R., *Les Troubadours cantaliens*, two vols., Aurillac, 1910. (*Troub. Cant.*)
Lejeune, R., 'La galerie littéraire du troubadour Peire d'Alvernhe' in *Actes et mémoires du IIIe Congrès international de langue et littérature d'oc*, Bordeaux, 1964, II, pp. 35–54.
Linskill, J., *The Poems of the Troubadour Raimbaut de Vaqueiras*, The Hague, 1964.
Mahn, C. A. F., *Die Biographien der Troubadours in provenzalischer Sprache*, Berlin, 1878. (*Biogr.*)
— *Die Werke der Troubadours*, four vols., Berlin, 1846–53. (*M.W.*)
— *Gedichte der Troubadours in provenzalischer Sprache*, four vols., Berlin, 1856–73. (*Gedichte*)
Menéndez Pidal, R., *Poesía juglaresca y juglares*, Madrid, 1924.
Meyer, P., *Le Roman de Flamenca*, Paris, 1865.
Milá y Fontanals, M., *De los trovadores en España*, Barcelona, 1889.
Millot, C. F. X., *Histoire littéraire des troubadours*, three vols., Paris, 1774.
Mouzat, J., *Les Poèmes de Gaucelm Faidit*, Paris, 1965.
Nelli, R., *L'érotique des troubadours*, Toulouse, 1963.
— and Lavaud, R., *Les Troubadours*, two vols., Bruges, 1960, 1966.
Nostre-Dame, Jehan de, *Les Vies des plus célèbres et anciens Poètes provensaux, qui ont floury du Temps des Comtes de Provence*, Lyons, 1575.
Pakscher, A., and De Lollis, C., 'Il canzoniere provenzale A' (*Studi di filologia romanza*, III, 1891).
Panvini, B., 'Appunti per una classificazione dei manoscritti che contengono le biografie provenzali' in *Studi in onore di Salvatore Santangelo Siculorum Gymnasium*, Catania, 1955, pp. 98–121. (*Appunti*).
— *Le biografie provenzali: valore e attendibilità*, Florence, 1952. (*Biografie*)
Paris, G., 'Les cours d'amour du moyen-âge; étude d'histoire littéraire' in *Journal des Savants*, 1888, second article (727–36).
Pattison, W. T., 'The background of Peire d'Alvernhe's *Chantarai d'aquest trobadors*' in *Modern Philology*, XXXI, 19–34.
— 'The troubadours of Peire d'Alvernhe's satire in Spain' in *PMLA*, I, 14–24.
— *Life and Works of the Troubadour Raimbaut d'Orange*, Minneapolis, 1952. (*R. d'Orange*)
Pelaez, M., 'Il canzoniere provenzale c' in *Studi di filologia romanza*, VII, 244 ff.

Philippson, E., *Der Mönch von Montaudon*, Halle, 1873.
Piccolo, F., *Primavera e fiore della lirica provenzale*, Città di Castello, 1948. (*Primavera*)
Pillet, A., 'Die apr. Liederhandschrift N²' in *Archiv*, 101, pp. 365 ff, and 102, pp. 179 ff.
Rajna, P., 'Il più antico trovatore italiano' in *Romania*, XLIX (1923), 77–97.
Raynouard, F. J. M., *Choix des poésies originales des troubadours*, six vols., Paris, 1816–21. (*Choix*)
Ricketts, P. T., *Les Poésies de Guilhem de Montanhagol*, Toronto, 1964. (*G. de Montanhagol*)
Riquer, M. de, *La lírica de los trovadores*, vol. 1 (*Poetas del siglo XII*), Barcelona, 1948. (*Lírica*)
— 'Los problemas del "Roman" provenzal de *Jaufré*' in *Recueil de travaux offert à M. Clovis Brunel*, Paris, 1955, pp. 444–7.
— *Resumen de literatura provenzal trovadoresca*, Barcelona, 1948.
Rochegude, H. P. de, *Le Parnasse occitanien ou choix de poésies originales des troubadours, tirées des manuscrits nationaux*, Toulouse, 1819. (*Parn. Occ.*)
Selbach, L., *Das Streitgedicht in der altprovenzalischen Lyrik und sein Verhältnis zu ähnlichen Dichtungen anderer Litteraturen*, Marburg, 1886.
Shepard, W. P., *The Oxford Provençal Chansonnier*, Princeton and Paris, 1927.
— and Chambers, F. M., 'Lanqan chanton li auzeil en primier' in *Romance Philology*, II (1948), 84–90.
— *The Poems of Aimeric de Peguilhan*, Evanston (Illinois), 1950.
Stengel, E., *Die apr. Liedersammlung c der Laurenziana in Florenz nach einer in seinem Besitz befindlichen alten Abschrift*, Leipzig, 1899.
Storost, J., *Ursprung und Entwicklung des altprovenzalischen sirventes bis auf Bertran de Born*, Halle, 1931.
Stronski, S., *Le Troubadour Folquet de Marseille*, Cracow, 1910. (*Folq. de Mars.*)
Suchier, H., review of Appel's edition of Peire Rogier in *Goettingenische gelehrte Anzeigen*, 1883, 1339–44. (*Goett. gel. Anzeigen*)
Taylor, A. B., *The Orkneyinga Saga*, Edinburgh and London, 1938.
— Article on the Orkneyinga Saga in *Proceedings of the Orkney Antiquarian Society* (Kirkwall), XI (1933).
Teulié, H., and Rossi, G., *L'Anthologie provençale de maître Ferrari de Ferrare* (*Annales du Midi*, XIII, 60 ff, 199 ff, 371 ff, and XIV, 197 ff, 523 ff, 1901–2).
Topsfield, L. T., *Les Poésies du troubadour Raimon de Miraval*, Paris, 1971.
Witthoeft, F., *Sirventes joglaresc*, Marburg, 1891.
Zenker, R., *Die Lieder Peires von Auvergne*, Erlangen, 1900. (*P. von Auvergne*)
Zingarelli, N., 'Ricerche sulla vita e le rime di B. de Ventadorn' in *Studi medievali*, I, 309–93.

(b) *History*

Annuaire du département du Cantal, Aurillac, 1830.

Audigier, P., *Histoire de la ville de Clermont*, Clermont-Ferrand, 1887, vol. I.

Beaunier, Dom, *Recueil historique, chronologique et topographique des archevêchez, evêchez, abbayes et prieurez de France* . . ., two vols., Paris, 1726.

— *Recueil historique des archevêchés, évêchés, abbayes et prieurés de France* (*Abbayes et prieurés de l'ancienne France*) . . ., new edition, revised and completed by the Benedictine monks of Ligugé (Ligugé-Chevetogne), Introduction, 1906.

Becquet, Dom J., *Les Institutions de l'Ordre de Grandmont au moyen-âge*, Mabillon, 1952.

Belperron, P., *La Croisade contre les Albigeois, et l'union du Languedoc à la France, 1209-49*, Paris, 1948.

Bouillet, J. B., *Nobiliaire d'Auvergne*, Clermont-Ferrand, 1852, vol. V.

Chevalier, C. U. J., *Répertoire des sources historiques du moyen-âge. Topobibliographie*, two vols., Montbéliard, 1903.

Clouston, J. S., *A History of Orkney*, Kirkwall, 1932.

Couderc, C., *Les Manuscrits de l'abbaye de Grandmont* (*Bibliothèque de l'Ecole des Chartes*, vol. 62), Nogent-le-Rotrou, 1901.

Darras, E., *Le Prieuré Grandmontain de Notre-Dame des bonshommes du Meyrel-lez-Maffliers 1169-1791*, Pontoise-L'Isle-Adam, 1928.

Devic, C., and Vaissete, J., *Histoire générale de Languedoc*, sixteen vols., Toulouse, 1872-1905. (*Hist. gen. Lang.*)

Dozy, R., *Recherches sur l'histoire et la littérature de l'Espagne pendant le moyen-âge*, two vols., Paris and Leyden, 1881.

Farcy, Canon, *Une Page de l'histoire de Rouen. Le Prieuré de Grandmont des origines jusqu'à nos jours*, Rouen, 1934.

Farnier, R., *La Condition juridique des personnes et des biens de l'Ordre de Grandmont des origines au XVIIIe siècle*, Limoges, 1913.

Guibert, L., *Les Manuscrits du séminaire de Limoges* (*Bulletin de la Société archéologique et historique du Limousin*), Limoges, 1892.

Imberdis, A., *Histoire générale de l'Auvergne depuis l'ère gallique jusqu' au XVIIIe siècle*, Clermont-Ferrand, 1868, vol. I.

Laîné, M., *Archives généalogiques et historiques de la Noblesse de France*, Paris, 1834, vol. IV.

Lecler, A., *Histoire de l'abbaye de Grandmont* (*Bulletin de la Société archéologique et historique du Limousin*, vols. 57-60), Limoges, 1907-10.

Levesque, J., *Annales ordinis grandimontis*, Troyes, 1662.

Prou, M., *Additions et corrections au Gallia Christiana* (*Mélanges d'archéologie et d'histoire de l'Ecole française de Rome*, Rome, V, 1885).

Renaud, F., *Histoire de la commune de Clermont-Ferrand*, Clermont-Ferrand, 1873.

Sainte-Marthe, D. de, *Gallia Christiana*, Paris, 1720, vol. II.
Salazar y Castro, L. de, *Historia genealogica de la casa de Lara*, four vols., Madrid, 1694–97.
Tardieu, A., *Histoire de la ville de Clermont-Ferrand*, Moulins, 1870–71, vol. I.
Vigfusson, G., *The Orkneyingers' Saga*, vol. III of Icelandic Sagas and other historical documents relating to the settlements and descents of the Northmen on the British Isles, ed. G. Vigfusson and trans. Sir G. W. Dasent, four vols., London, 1887–94.

c) *Grammars, dictionaries, works of reference, etc.*

Augé, C., *Larousse du XXe siècle*, six vols., Paris, 1928–33. (*Larousse*)
— *Nouveau Larousse Illustré*, eight vols., Paris, 1898–1907. (*NLI*)
Anglade, J., *Grammaire de l'ancien provençal, ou ancienne langue d'oc*, Paris, 1921. (*Anglade*)
Bédier, J., *Le Lai de l'Ombre*, Paris, 1913.
— 'La tradition manuscrite du Lai de l'Ombre' in *Romania*, LIV (1928), 161–96 and 321–56.
Brunel, C., *Bibliographie des manuscrits littéraires en ancien provençal*, Paris, 1935.
Frank, I., *Répertoire métrique de la poésie des troubadours*, two vols., Paris, 1953 and 1957. (Vol. 1: *Frank*)
Grandgent, C. H., *An Outline of the Phonology and Morphology of Old Provençal*, Boston, 1905. (*Grandgent*)
Jeanroy, A., *Bibliographie sommaire des chansonniers provençaux*, Paris, 1916.
Joanne, P., *Dictionnaire géographique et administratif de la France*, Paris, 1902.
Levy, E., *Provenzalisches Supplement-Wörterbuch*, eight vols., Leipzig, 1894–1924. (*S.W.*)
— *Petit dictionnaire provençal–français*, Heidelberg, 1961. (*Pet. Dict.*)
Mistral, F., *Lou tresor doú felibrige ou dictionnaire provençal—français*, ed. V. Tuby, Paris, 1932.
Pillet, A., and Carstens, H., *Bibliographie der Troubadours*, Halle, 1933.
Raynouard, F. J. M., *Lexique romane, ou dictionnaire de la langue des troubadours*, six vols., Paris, 1838–44. (*Lex. rom.*)
Roncaglia, A., *La lingua dei trovatori*, Rome, 1965. (*Roncaglia*)
Schultz-Gora, O., *Altprovenzalisches Elementarbuch*, Heidelberg, 1936. (*Altprov. Elem.*)
Stengel, E., *Die beiden ältesten provenzalischen Grammatiken 'Lo donatz proensals' und 'Las rasos de trobar'*, Marburg, 1878.

(d) *Periodicals*

Annales du Midi, Toulouse, Paris, 1889– . (*AdM*.)
Archiv für das Studium der neueren Sprachen und Literaturen, Braunschweig, 1846– . (*Archiv*.)

Archivum Romanicum, twenty-five vols., Geneva and Florence, 1917–41.
Goettingenische gelehrte Anzeigen, Göttingen, 1753– . (*Goett. gel. Anzeigen*)
Journal des Savants, Paris, 1816– .
Literaturblatt für germanische und romanische Philologie, Heilbronn, Leipzig, 1880– . (*Literaturblatt*)
Mercure de France (série moderne), Paris, 1890– .
Modern Language Notes, Baltimore, 1886– .
Modern Philology, Chicago, 1903– . (*Mod. Phil.*)
Publications of the Modern Language Association of America, Baltimore, 1886– . (*PMLA*)
Revue des langues romanes, Montpellier, 1870– . (*RLR*)
Romance Philology, Berkeley and Los Angeles, 1947– .
Romania, Paris, 1872– .
Romanische Forschungen, Erlangen, 1883– .
Speculum, a Journal of Mediaeval Studies, Cambridge, Mass., 1926– .
Studi di filologia romanza, Rome, 1885–1903.
Studi medievali, four vols., Turin, 1904–13.